Contents

Teacher's Guide ii

Syllable Guide iii

Reading Instructional Guide Template iv

Reading Assessment Answer Document vi

Unit 1: Ready or Not 1

Unit 2: Batman vs. Iron Man 24

Unit 3: Image: Unattainable 48

Unit 4: Circle of Friends 72

Unit 5: Riding Dubs 96

Unit 6: The Right to Support Them 120

Unit 7: A Moment to Lose 143

Unit 8: Journey of the Tiger 166

Unit 9: Above the Influence 189

Unit 10: Blood In, Blood Out 212

Rubrics 236

Notes 239

Lexile Measures 244

Principle Woods, Inc.
One San Jose Place, Suite 11
Jacksonville, Florida 32257
www.pwimpact.com

Text copyright © 2008 by Principle Woods, Inc.
All rights reserved. No part of this book may be used or reproduced in any manner without the prior written permission of Principle Woods, Inc.

Printed in the United States of America
ISBN 978-0-9796954-2-1

Writers: Jon Kern, Tori Friedrich, Tiffany Clark, Deborah Hansen, Julie Piccirilli
Editor: Laura Jacqmein
Project Manager: Susan Anderson
Graphic Designer: Rebecca Russo, Principle Design Group

Answer Key — Answer Key — Answer Key

Teacher's Guide

Step One
Teacher leads students through the Before Reading activities in the High-Interest Article Reading Instructional Guide.

Step Two
Students individually read the article. Teacher leads students through the During Reading activities in the High-Interest Article Reading Instructional Guide.

Step Three
Teacher leads students in a class discussion using the Discussion Starter Questions in the After Reading Section of the Reading Instructional Guide.

Step Four
Teacher discusses the Reading Strategy sheet. Students work together in groups to complete the strategy sheet and then participate in a class discussion about the answers.

Step Five
Students work in groups to discuss the Reading Comprehension multiple-choice questions and come to a group consensus on the answers. Students participate in a class discussion about the answers.

Step Six
Teacher discusses the Interpreting the Data section and gives mini-lessons on each section. Students work individually or in pairs/groups to complete each section.

Step Seven
Students use rubrics found in the back of the book to participate in a class discussion about their short and extended written responses to Interpreting the Data questions. Teacher uses rubrics to grade responses and monitor student progress.

Step Eight
Students complete Reflect and Respond section. Teacher uses rubric to grade responses. Students participate in a class discussion using the Reflect and Respond section as the prompt.

Step Nine
Teacher and students repeat Steps One, Two, and Three using the Technical Extension and all sections of the Technical Extension Reading Instructional Guide.

Step Ten
Students individually complete Reading Comprehension multiple-choice questions to test comprehension and critical thinking skills. Students participate in a class discussion about the answers.

Step Eleven
Students individually complete the Technical Writing Prompt. Teacher uses rubric to grade responses and monitor student progress.

Step Twelve
Students individually read Vocational Extension and answer Looking Forward and Ethical Dilemma questions.

Step Thirteen
Students participate in a class discussion about the Looking Forward and Ethical Dilemma questions. Teacher uses rubrics to grade writing responses.

Step Fourteen
Students individually complete the Unit Vocabulary Assessment. Teacher grades the assessment and reviews correct answers with the class.

Step Fifteen
Students complete the Authentic Assessment individually or in groups. Teacher uses rubric to grade responses.

©2008 PRINCIPLE WOODS, INC. Removal of copyright notice and copying are violations of Federal Law.

Answer Key — Answer Key — Answer Key

Syllable Guide

The Syllable Guide is an instructional tool designed to help students learn to break unfamiliar words into manageable parts.

Guide to Breaking Words Into Syllables	Guide to the Detailed Rules of Breaking Words Into Syllables	Quick Reference Guide
1. Count the vowel sounds in the word. 2. Subtract any silent vowels (like *e*). 3. The final number should be the number of syllables. 4. Break the word into that many chunks. 5. The chunks should be small parts you can say.	1. Count the vowel sounds in the word. 2. Subtract any silent vowels (like *e*). 3. The final number should be the number of syllables. 4. Slash between parts of compound words. 5. Slash after beginning parts. 6. Slash before end parts. 7. Slash between two middle consonants (except for two different consonants that make one sound, like *ph, th, ch, wh*). 8. Sometimes slash before a single middle consonant (except for short vowel sounds, like *cabin: cab-in*). 9. Slash before a consonant-*le* (like -*ble, -cle, -tle*). 10. Try to say the words using these small "chunks."	1. Circle vowel sounds (don't count silent vowels). 2. / compound parts (*cup/cake*) 3. prefixes/ & /suffixes (*con/fine/ment*) 4. C/C (*inves/tigative*) (not *ph, th, ch*, etc.) 5. Sometimes /C (*trau/ma*) 6. /Cle (like -*ble, -cle, -tle*, etc.) 7. Say the word using these "chunks."

Basic Vowel Sounds

ai (raid) *au* (taught) *ay* (may) *ea* (bread, seat) *ee* (sleep) *oa* (road) *oi* (coin) *oo* (soon, look) *ou* (proud)	*ow* (cow, flow) *oy* (toy) *ar* (harm) *er* (perm) *ir* (sir) *or* (horn) *ur* (burn) *a*(c)*e* (date) *e*(c)*e* (eve)	*i*(c)*e* (slide) *o*(c)*e* (note) *u*(c)*e* (accuse) *a* (hat, carry, father) *e* (let, merry) *i* (tin) *o* (go, to, mop) *u* (up) *y* (sky)

Basic Beginning Parts (Prefixes) and Their Meanings

ab-: from *ad-*: to, at, toward *an-*: not *be-*: to make, about, by *co-, col-, con-, com-*: together/with *de-*: from, down, away, off *dis-*: apart, not, opposite	*en-*: in, into, make *ex-*: out *fore-*: in front, before *in-, im-, il-, ir-*: in, into, without, not *mis-*: wrongly, incorrect *post-*: after *pre-*: before	*pro-*: moving forward, in front of, defending *re-*: back, again *sub-*: under *trans-*: across, through, beyond *un-*: not *uni-*: one

Basic End Parts (Suffixes) and Their Meanings

-al: relating to, process (adj.) *-ance*: action, state of (n.) *-ar, -er, -or*: one who/that/which (n.) *-ate*: make, cause (v.) *-cide*: kill (n.) *-dom*: quality (n.) *-en*: make (v.), made of (adj.) *-ful*: full of (adj.)	*-fy*: make (v.) *-ice*: condition (n.) *-ion, -sion, -tion*: state of (n.) *-ish*: a characteristic of (adj.) *-ism*: system, condition (n.) *-ive*: related to, tending (adj.) *-ize*: to cause or make (v.) *-less*: without (adj.) *-like*: resembling (adj.) *-ly*: manner of (adv.)	*-ment*: process, result of, act of (n.) *-ness*: state of (n.) *-ous*: having (adj.) *-ology, -alogy*: study of (n.) *-tude*: condition of (n.) *-ward*: in a particular direction (adj.) (adv.) *-y*: having (adj.)

©2008 PRINCIPLE WOODS, INC. Removal of copyright notice and copying are violations of Federal Law.

Answer Key — Answer Key — Answer Key

Reading Instructional Guide Template

BEFORE READING

Front-Loading Background Knowledge through Read Aloud/Think Aloud

Search the Internet for recent articles and use them to model the effective habits of readers through a Read Aloud/Think Aloud.

Check out articles at the following websites to determine if they would be appropriate for your RATA:
- *(Websites are provided for each unit.)*

(Please keep in mind that it is the responsibility of the teacher to determine if articles from suggested sites are appropriate. The sites may have changed content since this publication. The publisher takes no responsibility for the current content of the site.)

Looking at the Words

Determining How the Word Sounds (Phonics)
Using the Syllable Guide found in the beginning of the book, follow one of the sets of steps to help students learn how to break a word into manageable parts. The goal is to break the word into syllables that the students can say. Then they can put those parts together to "sound the word out." However, remember that the rules for syllabification do not always work because our language is so diverse. The rules can also become rather complex for low readers, so keep in mind that their overall objective is just to figure out how the word sounds. They may not be able to break the word into syllables perfectly, but they should at least be able to figure out how to say the word based on their attempt at following one of these sets of steps. Lesson One is a more basic set, while Lesson Two attempts to give the students the more specific rules without becoming too complicated. Take your time when teaching either set, and understand that many of the lower readers are not going to understand right away. It will take time, practice, and repeated application before many of them are able to use these strategies on their own.

Determining What the Word Means (Vocabulary)
After students have spent time breaking the words apart to figure out how they sound, use the lists of prefixes and suffixes and their meanings found in the Syllable Guide to have students try to add whatever meaning they can to the words before looking at the definitions. After giving the students the definitions, have them try to figure out which words apply the meaning of any of the prefixes or suffixes.

(Words are provided for the high-interest and technical articles.)

Words to Study	Breaking into Syllables	Short Definition

Activating Background Knowledge

Anticipation Guide
Have students mark each of the following statements True or False:
(Five True/False Statements are provided.)

Answer Key — Answer Key — Answer Key

Starter Questions
After completing the Anticipation Guide, have a group or class discussion with the students using the following questions:
(Five Starter Questions are provided.)

Make a prediction about what you think the article will be about.

DURING READING

- Have the students skim the article for 45–60 seconds. Have them circle any words they don't know or can't read fluently.
- When the students are finished, decode and determine the meaning of unknown words.
- Have the students skim the questions for 30–45 seconds.
- Have the students read the article. They should question, summarize, clarify, and predict as they read, making notes in the margins of the article. Encourage students to construct mental images of the content as they read.
- Remind students to constantly ask themselves if they understand each paragraph as they finish it. If they don't, they must reread the paragraph for clarification and identify problem sentences, concepts, or words. This is called monitoring for understanding.
- When the students finish reading the article, they are ready to answer the questions.

The Strategy Sheet

You may choose to have students complete the strategy sheet for each section before they answer the multiple-choice questions. Or you could have them complete the questions, work on the strategy sheet with a partner, and then go back over the questions to see if the use of the strategy sheet helped them more easily find the answers to any of the questions.

AFTER READING

Discussion Starter Questions

(Five Discussion Starter Questions are provided.)

Teacher Reflection

When you are finished with the article, strategies, and questions, ask yourself the following:

1. Did I get the students to THINK about what they have read?

2. Did I teach them (even a little bit) about how to read more effectively?

If you answered yes to both questions, you can feel good about the day.

©2008 PRINCIPLE WOODS, INC. Removal of copyright notice and copying are violations of Federal Law.

Answer Key — Answer Key — Answer Key

Reading Assessment Answer Document

Student Name: _____ Grade: _____

Directions: Using capital letters, write the answer to each multiple-choice question in the boxes below. Note that each question has a benchmark or concept that is being reviewed.

	Ready or Not? Date: Score:	Batman vs. Iron Man Date: Score:	Image: Unattainable Date: Score:	Circle of Friends Date: Score:	Riding Dubs Date: Score:	Concepts/Benchmarks
HIGH-INTEREST ARTICLES					
WORDS AND PHRASES					
1.	D	A	D	B	D	Analyze Words/Text
2.	G	I	F	H	H	Analyze Words/Text
3.	B	B	C	A	C	Conclusions/Inferences
MAIN IDEA/AUTHOR'S PURPOSE					
4.	H	G	H	G	I	Details/Facts
5.	C	D	D	C	B	Author's Point of View
6.	G	F	G	I	H	Patterns of Organization
7.	D	B	C	D	A	Author's Purpose
8.	F	G	I	G	F	Main Idea/Essential Message
9.	C	C	A	B	B	Char. Dev./Desc. Lang./Tone/ Conflict & Resolution/Plot Dev.
COMPARE & CONTRAST/CAUSE & EFFECT					
10.	F	H	I	G	F	Cause and Effect
11.	D	A	C	D	C	Comparison
REFERENCE & RESEARCH					
12.	G	H	F	G	H	Validity & Accuracy of Information/ Validity & Reliability/ Locate, Organize, Interpret Information/ Synthesize Information
13.	D	B	D	A	A	
14.	H	I	G	G	I	

©2008 PRINCIPLE WOODS, INC. Removal of copyright notice and copying are violations of Federal Law.

Answer Key — Answer Key — Answer Key

Reading Assessment Answer Document

Student Name: _____ Grade: _____

Directions: Using capital letters, write the answer to each multiple-choice question in the boxes below. Note that each question has a benchmark or concept that is being reviewed.

	HIGH-INTEREST ARTICLES					
	The Right to Support Them Date: Score:	A Lifetime to Build, a Moment to Lose Date: Score:	Journey of the Tiger Date: Score:	Above the Influence Date: Score:	Blood In, Blood Out Date: Score:	Concepts/Benchmarks
	WORDS AND PHRASES					
1.	B	C	D	B	B	Analyze Words/Text
2.	I	I	G	F	F	Analyze Words/Text
3.	C	B	D	D	A	Conclusions/Inferences
	MAIN IDEA/AUTHOR'S PURPOSE					
4.	I	G	G	F	I	Details/Facts
5.	A	C	B	D	C	Author's Point of View
6.	G	I	G	G	H	Patterns of Organization
7.	D	A	D	D	D	Author's Purpose
8.	H	I	H	H	F	Main Idea/Essential Message
9.	C	D	B	C	B	Char. Dev./Desc. Lang./Tone/ Conflict & Resolution/Plot Dev.
	COMPARE & CONTRAST/CAUSE & EFFECT					
10.	F	F	H	F	F	Cause and Effect
11.	C	B	C	C	D	Comparison
	REFERENCE & RESEARCH					
12.	F	F	H	F	I	Validity & Accuracy of Information/ Validity & Reliability/ Locate, Organize, Interpret Information/ Synthesize Information
13.	C	A	A	C	A	
14.	F	I	G	I	I	

©2008 PRINCIPLE WOODS, INC. Removal of copyright notice and copying are violations of Federal Law.

Answer Key — Answer Key — Answer Key

Reading Assessment Answer Document

Student Name: _____ Grade: _____

Directions: Using capital letters, write the answer to each multiple-choice question in the boxes below. Note that each question has a benchmark or concept that is being reviewed.

	TECHNICAL ARTICLES					
	The Election of an American President Date: Score:	The Case for Comics Date: Score:	Whose Body Is It? Date: Score:	Integrity On and Off the Field Date: Score:	Car Buying 101 Date: Score:	Concepts/Benchmarks
	WORDS AND PHRASES					
1.	D	B	B	A	C	Analyze Words/Text
2.	F	G	H	F	G	Analyze Words/Text
3.	C	B	B	C	A	Conclusions/Inferences
	MAIN IDEA/DETAILS					
4.	I	I	F	H	F	Details/Facts
5.	B	C	D	C	D	Patterns of Organization
6.	H	F	H	I	H	Main Idea/Essential Message
	COMPARE & CONTRAST/CAUSE & EFFECT					
7.	C	A	B	A	C	Cause and Effect
8.	I	G	F	G	I	Comparison
	REFERENCE & RESEARCH					
9.	A	A	B	B	D	Validity/Accuracy of Information
10.	G	I	F	I	G	Locate, Organize, Interpret Information
11.	C	C	D	D	D	Synthesize Information

©2008 PRINCIPLE WOODS, INC. Removal of copyright notice and copying are violations of Federal Law.

Answer Key — Answer Key — Answer Key

Reading Assessment Answer Document

Student Name: _____ Grade: _____

Directions: Using capital letters, write the answer to each multiple-choice question in the boxes below. Note that each question has a benchmark or concept that is being reviewed.

	TECHNICAL ARTICLES					
	The Information Highway Date: Score:	Big Brother and the Right to Privacy Date: Score:	Training to Perfection Date: Score:	Underage Drinking: No Minimal Problem Date: Score:	The Writing on the Wall Date: Score:	Concepts/Benchmarks
WORDS AND PHRASES						
1.	D	B	C	D	D	Analyze Words/Text
2.	G	I	H	G	G	Analyze Words/Text
3.	B	D	B	C	D	Conclusions/Inferences
MAIN IDEA/DETAILS						
4.	G	G	F	F	H	Details/Facts
5.	C	C	B	B	B	Patterns of Organization
6.	I	H	I	I	H	Main Idea/Essential Message
COMPARE & CONTRAST/CAUSE & EFFECT						
7.	C	A	C	D	D	Cause and Effect
8.	I	I	F	F	G	Comparison
REFERENCE & RESEARCH						
9.	A	B	D	D	A	Validity/Accuracy of Information
10.	G	F	F	H	H	Locate, Organize, Interpret Information
11.	C	A	D	C	A	Synthesize Information

©2008 PRINCIPLE WOODS, INC. Removal of copyright notice and copying are violations of Federal Law.

— Unit 1 —
READY★OR★NOT

Reading Instructional Guide for High-Interest Article

BEFORE READING

Front-Loading Background Knowledge through Read Aloud/Think Aloud

Search the Internet for recent articles on the 2008 presidential election and use them to model the effective habits of readers through a Read Aloud/Think Aloud.

Check out articles at the following websites to determine if they would be appropriate for your RATA:

- "Top of the Ticket: New Poll: U.S. More Ready for Black Prez than Female One." *Los Angeles Times* Blogs. http://latimesblogs.latimes.com/washington/2008/01/blacks.html.
- Nagourney, Adam. "The Pattern May Change, if…." *New York Times*. December 10, 2006. http://www.nytimes.com/2006/12/10/weekinreview/10nagourney.html.

(Please keep in mind that it is the responsibility of the teacher to determine if articles from suggested sites are appropriate. The sites may have changed content since this publication. The publisher takes no responsibility for the current content of the site.)

Looking at the Words

Determining How the Word Sounds (Phonics)
Using the Syllable Guide and the Reading Instructional Guide Template found in the beginning of the book, follow the steps to help students learn how to break a word into manageable parts.

Determining What the Word Means (Vocabulary)

Words to Study	Breaking into Syllables	Short Definition
candidacy	can-di-da-cy	(n.) the campaign of a person who seeks an office
Caucasian	Cau-ca-sian	(adj.) relating to the white race of humans
democracy	de-moc-ra-cy	(n.) government by the people
minority	mi-nor-i-ty	(n.) a member of a smaller group that is part of a larger group
platform	plat-form	(n.) a political candidate's written statement of principles and plans
perceive	per-ceive	(v.) to become aware of or recognize
unique	u-nique	(adj.) unusual

Activating Background Knowledge

Anticipation Guide
Have students mark each of the following statements True or False:

1. ____ A president is elected/re-elected every four years.

2. ____ The process of electing a president changes with every election.

Unit 1

Answer Key — Answer Key — Answer Key

3. ____ The 2008 election marks the first time a woman attempted to run for president.

4. ____ Barack Obama and Hillary Clinton both served as United States senators prior to running in the 2008 presidential election.

5. ____ During the Democratic contest, election, both Barack Obama and Hillary Clinton received criticism relating to the race and gender factor.

Starter Questions

After completing the Anticipation Guide, have a group or class discussion with the students using the following questions:

1. Who are some famous United States presidents from the past?

2. What was significant about the 2008 contest for the Democratic nomination?

3. Who were the Democratic contenders in the 2008 presidential election?

4. Who was Victoria Woodhull?

5. Who was Frederick Douglass?

Make a prediction about what you think the article will be about.

DURING READING

Use the Reading Instructional Guide Template found in the front of the book.

AFTER READING

Discussion Starter Questions

1. Do you think our society is now ready to vote in presidential elections based strictly on the issues and the qualifications of the candidates?

2. How do you think people would view Frederick Douglass and Victoria Woodhull if they were running for president today?

3. Do you think is it right for the media to mention a politician's race and/or gender in the presidential election? Why or why not?

4. Would you vote for a candidate based solely on race or gender? Why or why not?

5. What other firsts for minorities do you think we will see in our lifetime?

Teacher Reflection

Use the Reading Instructional Guide Template found in the front of the book.

Ready or Not?
The Changing Face of American Leadership

When you think of a president, what comes to mind? Is it the person who led the country in the aftermath of September 11, 2001? Is it a smooth-talking man who was known for economic expansion?

Chances are, Bill Clinton and George W. Bush are the first two presidents you can remember in your lifetime. But they were the 42nd and 43rd presidents to lead our country. Many have come before. Perhaps you can remember a few from your history books. Does the honesty of George Washington come to mind? Or maybe the courage of Abraham Lincoln? Maybe it's the popularity of John F. Kennedy that you think of. Each president has been unique, with his own mission for the country. But in a way the face of the president has remained the same. All of the United States presidents have been Caucasian males, most living in the middle to upper class of society.

Every four years Americans head to the polls to elect a president. The process of electing a president is a tradition set by the Constitution of the United States. It is part of what sets America apart as a democracy. While each and every election is significant, no election has drawn more attention to the changing face of American leadership than the 2008 election. Two candidates who tried to win the Democratic nomination stand out. One is an African American, and one is a woman. Never before has America elected a female or a minority to the presidency. But the 2008 Democratic contest was a new step for America.

Barack Obama was raised in the Pacific Islands. Hillary Rodham Clinton has spent her life achieving firsts for women in her field. Their backgrounds and lives may be very different, but together they stand for something big. They show that America may finally be ready to associate the presidency with a new kind of face. The Democratic nomination was a very close race between a minority and a woman. And for the first time in American history, an African American is the presidential nominee for a major political party.

It might surprise you to know that minorities and women have been running for president for a long time. Female candidates have the longest history, dating all the way back to 1872. Victoria Woodhull, a women's rights advocate, ran for president in that year. Her party also nominated Frederick Douglass, a former slave, for the vice presidency. Woodhull's name didn't actually appear on the ballot, and she didn't receive any electoral votes. She ran at a time when women weren't even considered citizens. This is one reason her candidacy failed—the president must be a citizen. Since then, almost 30 women have been nominated by a party to run for president or have made the ballot as an independent. Even more have been nominated to run as a vice-presidential running mate. However, Hillary Clinton stands apart from previous female candidates in that she was a front-runner in a close Democratic primary. Never before has a woman made such an impact upon an election.

The Vocabulary of the Presidency

Ballot. The list of candidates to be voted on.

Caucus. A meeting of party leaders to select candidates for the presidential election.

Electoral vote. Votes cast by elected representatives of each state in a presidential election, generally representing the popular vote in that state.

Party. An organization with common political opinions.

Popular vote. Votes cast by all eligible voters in an election.

Primary. A preliminary election in which voters of each party nominate candidates for office.

Similarly, never before has an African American been so close to the presidency. Barack Obama has built his political platform on the premise of making a difference through change. His becoming president would represent a major change not only for the United States, but for the world. Obama is not the first African-American candidate. Civil rights leader Jesse Jackson made several runs for the presidency, winning the primaries in several states in 1988. However, Jackson's bids were unsuccessful. Some political analysts have described Obama's campaign as successful because he has presented himself as a "candidate who happens to be black, rather than a black candidate." He took the focus off race.

Clinton's and Obama's candidacies have opened questions in politics about race and gender. Clinton's campaign noted examples of sexism in comments made about her. Some television and radio figures were accused of making these remarks. Radio host Rush Limbaugh asked whether Americans really wanted to "watch a woman get older before their eyes on a daily basis." Obama's team detected prejudice in misinformed comments about his Muslim middle name (Hussein) and remarks about his drug use in his youth. Even former president Bill Clinton's reference to Obama's campaign as a "fairy tale" was perceived by some as an attempt to make race a political issue. However, the democratic contest came down to a tight race between a woman and an African American.

Today most Americans polled say that they would support an African-American presidential candidate. One survey showed that 94% of men and 95% of women would vote for such a candidate. Fifty years ago less than half those surveyed felt the same way. Another recent poll resulted in 85% of surveyed registered voters saying they would vote for a qualified female candidate and 92% saying they would vote for a qualified black candidate.

Recent history suggests that Americans will now vote for president based on the issues and the qualifications. This will eventually break the cycle of electing only Caucasian male presidents. Only time will tell what the face of America's leadership will be in the future. There is no one "face" of America. Part of what makes our country unique is the ability to find unity in diversity. Is America ready for a minority president? No matter the outcome of the general election, America is now in a reality that just a few years ago was only a dream. The face of America is changing, and the 21st century will mark political firsts for many minority groups. What firsts do you think we'll see in our lifetime?

Answer Key — Answer Key — Answer Key   READY★OR★NOT

Reading Comprehension

After reading "Ready or Not?" choose the options that best answer questions 1–14.

1. Read this sentence.
   Two candidates who tried to win the Democratic nomination stand out.

   What is the meaning of the word *nomination* as it is used in the sentence?
   A. initiation
   B. demotion
   C. disapproval
   D. recommendation

2. Read this sentence.
   Never before has a woman made such an impact upon an election.

   What is the meaning of the word *impact* as it is used in the sentence?
   F. crash
   G. effect
   H. struggle
   I. controversy

3. From this article, the reader can tell that
   A. both 2008 Democratic candidates have had strenuous campaign schedules.
   B. all of the presidents in the past have fallen into a specific demographic group.
   C. Clinton is a sincere individual who listens to voters with the aspiration of acquiring more votes.
   D. both candidates attended Ivy League universities and are well prepared for office.

4. A significant contribution of Obama's and Clinton's participation in the 2008 presidential election was
   F. changing the process for electing a president.
   G. creating a governmental plan to unite everyone regardless of race or gender.
   H. encouraging voters to change the existing stereotype of the American president.
   I. using education as the main platform and persuading high school students to do well in school.

5. In the author's opinion,
   A. Frederick Douglass should have been elected president.
   B. either Obama or Clinton would have done a great job as president.
   C. Americans are more willing to support a minority president than in the past.
   D. our society is not ready to elect an African American or a woman for president.

6. The author organizes the article by
   F. comparing the beliefs and platforms of each candidate.
   G. discussing the significance of the 2008 election with historical flashbacks.
   H. providing questions and answers from a recent Democratic presidential debate.
   I. describing the political process of electing a president with past election stories.

©2008 PRINCIPLE WOODS, INC. Removal of copyright notice and copying are violations of Federal Law.

Unit 1

Answer Key — Answer Key — Answer Key

7. Why does the author mention Victoria Woodhull?
   A. to explain that she was a supporter of Hillary Clinton
   B. to question why our society has not yet elected a woman as president
   C. to encourage the reader to break stereotypical beliefs and vote for a minority
   D. to show the reader that a woman had run for president prior to the 2008 election

8. Which title best fits the article?
   F. Winds of Change
   G. Democrats in Charge
   H. The Special Gift of Time
   I. The Best Presidential Election

9. Which sentence best expresses Obama's perspective on being a minority candidate?
   A. He believes that he should be awarded extra delegates because of his race.
   B. He thinks that Americans should vote for him just because he is an African American.
   C. He believes that he is a political contender for president who happens to be an African American.
   D. Our society is long overdue for an African-American president, and it is up to Obama to change the way we view politics.

10. Why was the Democratic contest difficult for Hillary Clinton and Barack Obama?
    F. Both of their campaigns endured criticism regarding race or gender.
    G. Both candidates wished to change political parties but missed the deadline.
    H. The rigorous schedule made it difficult for them to spend time with their family.
    I. The stress of the election damaged the friendship they had when they worked together.

11. What is true of both Barack Obama and Jesse Jackson?
    A. They are brothers.
    B. They were both Christian ministers.
    C. They were both senators prior to running in the presidential election.
    D. They are both African-American men who have desired to be president of the United States.

12. How does the author organize the first two paragraphs of the article?
    F. by providing information on each candidate
    G. by presenting famous presidents from the past
    H. by illustrating the results of Democratic candidate polls
    I. by describing the backgrounds of Frederick Douglass and Victoria Woodhull

13. People who read the text box will learn
    A. how to vote for a president.
    B. why voting is an important right we have as Americans.
    C. the necessary steps to become a registered voter in our country.
    D. essential vocabulary to help with understanding the presidential election.

14. Based on the information about BOTH Clinton and Obama, which of these conclusions is accurate?
    F. Only Clinton made history in the 2008 Democratic nomination contest.
    G. Only Obama made history in the 2008 Democratic nomination contest.
    H. Each hoped to win out over the other for the nomination, but both Clinton and Obama made history.
    I. Obama and Clinton will continue campaigning after the 2008 election with the goal of winning the 2012 presidential election.

Answer Key — Answer Key — Answer Key

Reading Strategy

Directions: Use information from the article to write facts about Hillary Clinton and Barack Obama in the chart below. Feel free to add background knowledge that you have about the two Democratic candidates in addition to facts from the article.

What: The presidential election process
When: Every four years
Why: Established by the Constitution as a part of the democratic process
Who: The candidates for the Democratic nomination in the 2008 presidential election

Hillary Clinton ★ Barack Obama

Hillary Clinton
- First woman to be a leading candidate
- Spent her life achieving firsts for women
- Reached the status of front-runner

Both
- Both faced questions regarding race/gender
- Both ran for Democratic nomination in 2008 election
- Both achieved firsts in coming so far

Barack Obama
- First African American to be a leading candidate
- Raised in Pacific Islands
- Built his platform on "making a difference through change"

Unit 1 — *Answer Key — Answer Key — Answer Key*

Interpreting the Data

PART I

How have politicians in television and movies led the way for female and minority presidential candidates?

Refer to Table 1 to answer questions 15–17.

Table 1. Female and minority presidents portrayed in film and television

Actor	Political office	Film/TV program	Race/gender	Year
James Earl Jones	President	*The Man*	African-American	1972
Patty Duke	President	*Hail to the Chief*	Female	1985
Tommy Lister	President	*The Fifth Element*	African-American	1997
Morgan Freeman	President	*Deep Impact*	African-American	1998
Dennis Haysbert	President	*24*	African-American	2002
Chris Rock	President	*Head of State*	African-American	2003
Jimmy Smits	President	*The West Wing*	Hispanic	2004–2006
Mary McDonnell	President	*Battlestar Galactica*	Female	2004
Geena Davis	President	*Commander in Chief*	Female	2005
Cherry Jones	President	*24*	Female	2009

15. According to the information in Table 1, what minority race has been most represented as president in film and television?

African-American

16. What percentage of presidents in Table 1 are female?

40%

17. What percentage of presidents in Table 1 were portrayed in this decade (2000–2009)?

60%

©2008 PRINCIPLE WOODS, INC. Removal of copyright notice and copying are violations of Federal Law.

Answer Key — Answer Key — Answer Key   READY★OR★NOT

18. Most minority and female presidents in film and television have been in movies or programs that were released recently. Why do you think this is? What do you think this might mean for real-life politics today?

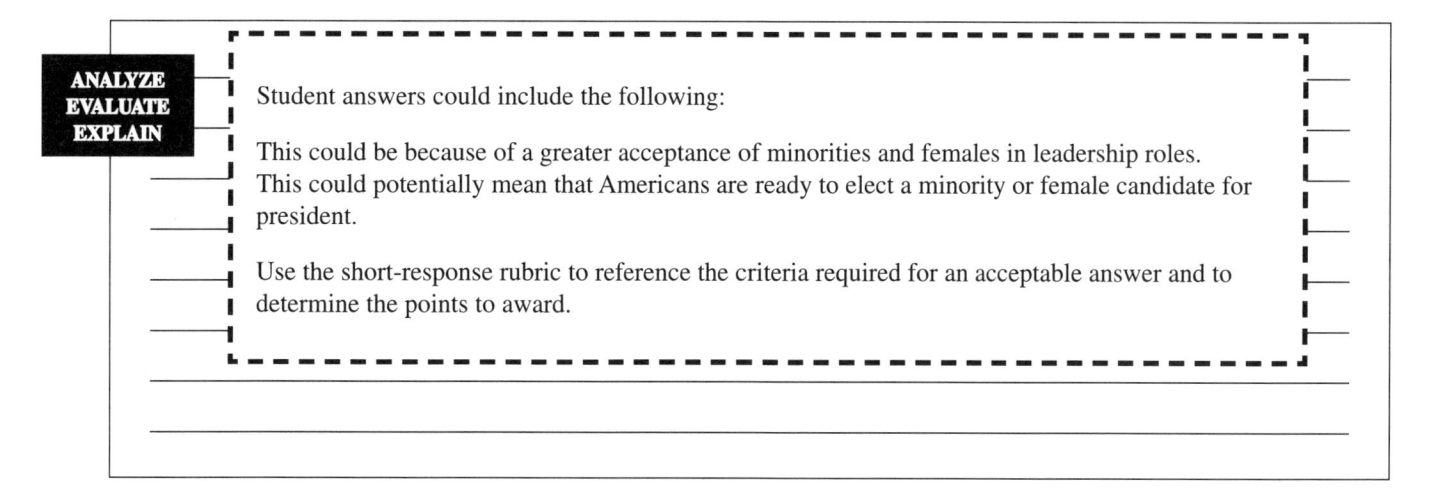

ANALYZE EVALUATE EXPLAIN

Student answers could include the following:

This could be because of a greater acceptance of minorities and females in leadership roles. This could potentially mean that Americans are ready to elect a minority or female candidate for president.

Use the short-response rubric to reference the criteria required for an acceptable answer and to determine the points to award.

PART II

How have minority and female presidents in television and movies compared to real-life leaders in American government?

(Students may complete this section individually or in groups.)

19. Choose a political position to study. Examples may include congressional representative, senator, governor, etc. Use periodicals and the Internet to research this position to determine how many minority and/or female members have been elected to this position since 1970. Represent this information in a table similar to Table 1.

Answer Key — Answer Key — Answer Key

Unit 1

20. How many minority politicians have held the position you researched? How many female politicians have held the position you researched? Design a table or graph that compares the data you collected to the data in Table 1.

21. In real life, why do you think there have been minority and female non-presidential politicians but no minority or female presidents?

THINK EVALUATE EXPLAIN

Student answers could include the following:

Student answers may vary but should be supported by student research and/or the data in Table 1.

Use the short-response rubric to reference the criteria required for an acceptable answer and to determine the points to award.

Answer Key — Answer Key — Answer Key

READY★OR★NOT

Reflect and Respond

22. What qualities do you think are important for a president? Explain how a president on television or in a movie might have different qualities than one in real life. Use specific examples from real life and the article to support your answer.

> Answers may vary, but students should address each part of the question. The question is meant to elicit strong classroom conversation about character. Students should be able to demonstrate an ability to discern what qualities make good leaders.
>
> Use the character education rubric to reference the criteria and number of points to award.

©2008 PRINCIPLE WOODS, INC. Removal of copyright notice and copying are violations of Federal Law.

Answer Key — Answer Key — Answer Key

Unit 1

Reading Instructional Guide for Technical Extension

BEFORE READING

Looking at the Words

Determining How the Word Sounds (Phonics)
Technical texts often necessitate the use of multisyllabic words that are unfamiliar to students. Use the Syllable Guide to help students decode any words they might have trouble reading.

Determining What the Word Means (Vocabulary)

Words to Study	Breaking into Syllables	Short Definition
advertisement	ad-ver-tise-ment	(n.) a public broadcast to promote something
appealing	ap-peal-ing	(adj.) attracting interest; pleasing
ballot	bal-lot	(n.) a paper on which a voter marks a vote
convention	con-ven-tion	(n.) a formal meeting
disagreement	dis-a-gree-ment	(n.) a difference of opinion
officially	of-fi-cial-ly	(adv.) formally
primary	pri-mar-y	(n.) an early election in which voters of each party nominate candidates

Activating Background Knowledge

Graphic Organizer
Either individually or in groups, students may brainstorm about the Electoral College, recalling anything previously learned and any prior experience with the subject. Next, encourage students to see the relationships between their ideas by having them complete a concept map to demonstrate what they already know about the Electoral College and its participants.

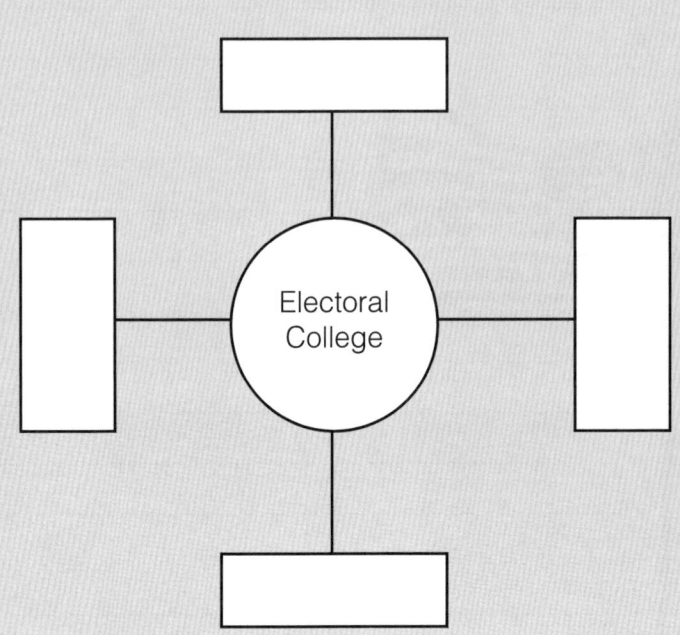

©2008 PRINCIPLE WOODS, INC. Removal of copyright notice and copying are violations of Federal Law.

Answer Key — Answer Key — Answer Key   READY OR NOT

Starter Questions
After completing the Graphic Organizer, generate a group or class discussion to come up with questions about the subject, a prediction about the article, and at least one learning goal. The first question has been provided for you.

Question: How is the president of the United States selected?

Question: _____

Prediction: _____

Goal: _____

DURING READING
Use the Reading Instructional Guide Template found in the front of the book.

AFTER READING
After reading, you may teach reading strategy use by giving students opportunities to do the following:
- Review, paraphrase, and summarize
- Participate in main-idea discussions by describing the information in their own words
- Reflect on concept maps and generate additional discussion starter questions based on the mappings
- Participate in small-group discussions using discussion starter questions

Discussion Starter Questions

The first question has been provided for you.

1. Do you think the United States Constitution should be amended to alter the way the president of the United States is elected? Why or why not?

2. _____

3. _____

©2008 PRINCIPLE WOODS, INC. Removal of copyright notice and copying are violations of Federal Law.

Unit 1

Answer Key — Answer Key — Answer Key

Technical Extension

★ THE ELECTION OF AN AMERICAN PRESIDENT ★

Americans are being flooded with television advertisements about the upcoming presidential election. The candidates are also making sure they are included in every evening's news programs. The race for the top elected position in our country holds everyone's attention for at least a year. Election Day is once every four years on the second Tuesday in November.

Most young people are not very interested in exactly how a president is elected. But there have been cases of disagreement, even as recently as 2000. So, let's look at the process and find out what happened!

Citizens in our country decide which of the two major political parties best matches their own ideas. The Republican and Democratic parties both have long histories filled with famous names like Abraham Lincoln, Franklin D. Roosevelt, and John F. Kennedy.

The first step for Americans is to register to vote. This can be done at many public places like libraries and driver's license offices. On primary election days, these registered voters show up at their local polling place. They mark their ballots for the candidate they believe can best lead the country. At the end, we know which two candidates will probably be on the final ballot in November.

The two major parties then have huge conventions over the summer. They officially decide who their candidates will be. They also decide on the issues that they will support during the campaign season. Before leaving the convention, they choose their vice-presidential candidates. They try to make the team of presidential and vice-presidential nominees as appealing as they can. After all, they want to win!

When presidential Election Day finally rolls around in November, the candidates have done all they can do. Americans go to the polls again to vote. The results are usually known before dawn the next morning. Does that mean the person who received the most votes wins? You would think so, wouldn't you?

Most of the time that is exactly what happens. However, occasionally a part of our government that most people do not understand comes into the picture to make the final choice, especially if the popular vote is very close.

> **The Electoral College is part of our Constitution,**
> specifically Article II, Section 1, Clause 3.
> Here are the highlights:
>
> - The electors shall meet in their respective states and vote by ballot.
> - The results are then sealed and transmitted to the president of the Senate.
> - The president of the Senate opens all the certificates, and the votes are then counted.
> - The person having the greatest number of votes shall be the president of the United States.
>
> The Article then goes on to outline what happens if no one gets a majority of the votes of all the electors, and that's when it has gotten interesting several times in our country's history!

The Electoral College is in our U.S. Constitution as one of the "checks and balances" in our government. It's not really a college. The electors, or people who cast the votes, never even meet in one place at the same time. But the process still has to happen to meet the terms of the Constitution. Each state gets two votes (or electors) plus the same number of votes that equals its number of representatives in the House of Representatives at that particular time.

©2008 PRINCIPLE WOODS, INC. Removal of copyright notice and copying are violations of Federal Law.

Answer Key — Answer Key — Answer Key

READY·OR·NOT

It has been said that the men who wrote the Constitution were not sure that ordinary citizens would make the best choices when they voted. Many people in the 1700s and 1800s were people who could not read or write, and they didn't get much information about the candidates or the issues. The electors are chosen as those who are informed about those things and will hopefully make the best selection for the country.

Most of the time, the electoral votes are cast for the candidate who received the most popular votes in their state. However, there have been just a few times when the person who received less popular votes ended up being the president. In the 2000 election, Al Gore received 50,996,582 votes, but the Electoral College chose George W. Bush even though he received 50,456,062 votes. How did that happen?

The system gives more power to larger states. Each state's number of electors depends on its population. So candidates have to campaign harder in certain states than in others to put together the right combination of votes. The formula is that they must end up with 270 electoral votes out of a possible 538.

In the disputed 2000 election between Gore and Bush, Florida's electoral votes were finally awarded to George Bush. It took over a month to go through the process. When the dust settled, President Bush had received 271 electoral votes to Gore's 266.

Simple? Not really. In fact, several times in our history there have been calls to change this part of our Constitution. However, the system remains. So keep your eyes on the candidates to determine why they spend so much more time in some states than in others. The system may not be perfect, but it was created to be as fair as possible.

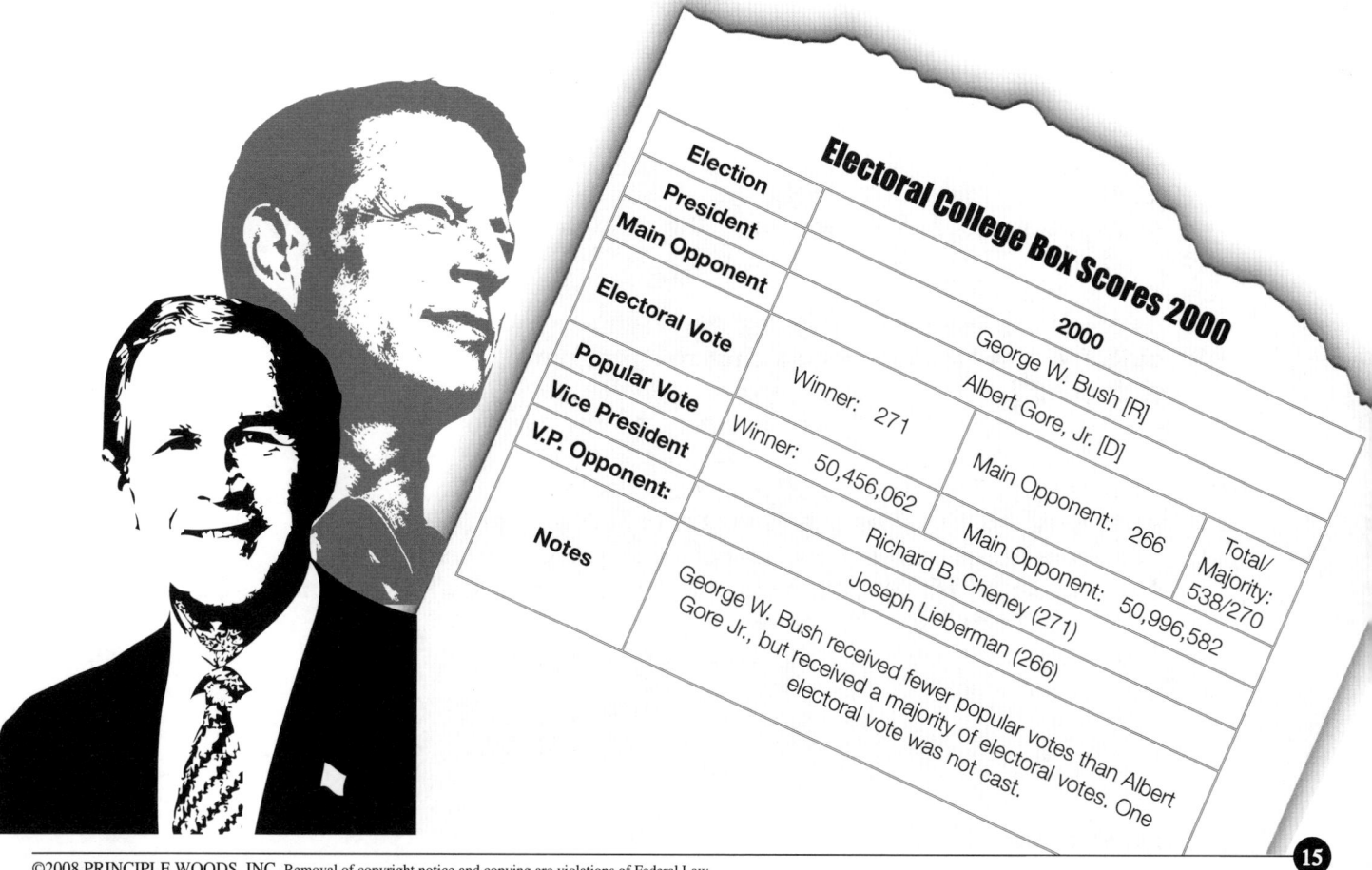

Electoral College Box Scores 2000

	2000
Election	
President	George W. Bush [R]
Main Opponent	Albert Gore, Jr. [D]
Electoral Vote	Winner: 271 Main Opponent: 266 Total/Majority: 538/270
Popular Vote	Winner: 50,456,062 Main Opponent: 50,996,582
Vice President	Richard B. Cheney (271)
V.P. Opponent:	Joseph Lieberman (266)
Notes	George W. Bush received fewer popular votes than Albert Gore Jr., but received a majority of electoral votes. One electoral vote was not cast.

©2008 PRINCIPLE WOODS, INC. Removal of copyright notice and copying are violations of Federal Law.

Unit 1 — Answer Key — Answer Key — Answer Key

Reading Comprehension

After reading "The Election of an American President," choose the options that best answer questions 1–11.

1. Read this sentence.
   They try to make the team of presidential and vice-presidential nominees as appealing as they can.

   What is the meaning of the word *nominees* as it is used in this sentence?
   A. the winners of a competition
   B. those who choose the electors
   C. the runners-up in an election at the national level
   D. the candidates chosen by a particular group for election to office

2. Read this sentence.
   When the dust settled, President Bush had received 271 electoral votes to Gore's 266.

   What is the meaning of the phrase *when the dust settled* as it is used in this sentence?
   F. when all the ballots were counted
   G. the night of voting was very dusty
   H. when the candidates settled in to sleep
   I. when people had time to decide on a candidate

3. According to the article, the two main political parties in the United States
   A. are changed each year.
   B. have always been the same.
   C. are the Democratic and the Republican parties.
   D. are not determined until after the conventions each summer.

4. The article explains that the purpose of the Electoral College is
   F. to take power away from the larger states.
   G. to hold the conventions during election years.
   H. to educate people about voting in the United States.
   I. to elect a president who represents the majority of the people in our country.

5. The author organizes the article by
   A. discussing several past presidential elections.
   B. outlining how American voters choose a president.
   C. discussing designated polling places and processes.
   D. comparing the Electoral College to other countries' election processes.

6. Which statement BEST expresses the main idea of this article?
   F. Abraham Lincoln was one of the creators of the Electoral College.
   G. Americans must become part of one of the two major political parties.
   H. The process by which Americans choose a president can be complicated, but it was created to be as fair as possible.
   I. The Electoral College is an outdated system that will be changed in the near future as long as we all write letters to our senators.

©2008 PRINCIPLE WOODS, INC. Removal of copyright notice and copying are violations of Federal Law.

Answer Key — Answer Key — Answer Key

7. Why do those running for president spend more time campaigning in some states than in others?
    A. Their budgets are limited by law.
    B. Most states don't have any electoral votes.
    C. Some states award more electoral votes than others.
    D. States have different rules for campaigning within their borders.

8. Why do larger states get more electoral votes?
    F. The electoral votes become easier to count.
    G. The smaller states become more important.
    H. The larger states get more votes because they offset the smaller states.
    I. The larger states get more electoral votes because they have larger populations.

9. Which statement about the 2000 presidential election is the LEAST accurate?
    A. George Bush received more popular votes than Gore.
    B. Gore finally received the larger number of electoral votes.
    C. Florida's electoral votes were finally awarded to Al Gore.
    D. George Bush received more popular votes and more electoral votes than Gore.

10. People who read this article will understand
    F. how electors are chosen.
    G. how the Electoral College can affect a presidential election.
    H. the United States Constitution and its impact on the Electoral College.
    I. that the Electoral College is not an important part of the United States Constitution.

11. According to information provided in the article and the text box titled "Electoral Box Scores, 2000,"
    A. Al Gore received 50,456,062 votes.
    B. only 4 candidates can run for President.
    C. George W. Bush and Richard Cheney were elected in 2000.
    D. Joseph Lieberman became vice president of the United States.

Unit 1 — **Answer Key — Answer Key — Answer Key**

Technical Writing Prompt

12. Imagine that you are a voter who believes that our current law which allows the Electoral College to overpower the popular vote is unfair. Write a proposal to your state senator explaining why the law should be changed. Write clearly and use specific examples from the text as well as your own experience to answer the prompt.

> Student answers may vary.
>
> The student should address the question to the best of his/her ability using the article and personal experience. The question is meant to prepare students to be active citizens who can accurately and effectively use written communication skills.
>
> Use the technical writing rubric to reference the criteria and determine the number of points to award.

Vocational Extension

HELP WANTED: Do you like to be in the middle of the action? The local office of a major political party is searching for an administrative assistant. Applicant must be organized, computer literate, and able to deal with office staff and the public. College degree or business administration courses preferred, but determined high school graduate will also be considered. Send recent resume to George Jones at jonesg@democraticparty.org.

An administrative assistant's job in any organization is fast-paced, but it's even more so in a political candidate's office. The candidate has long days with many appointments throughout the weeks. He or she also has to organize the calendar and keep the candidate on schedule. The assistant manages the information that flows through the office, including e-mail, telephone calls, and mail.

Another important part of the assistant's job is to deal with campaign volunteers. These people are not paid, so the assistant must make sure they are treated with respect. However, they must still get the tasks done. The administrative assistant must also interact with the public when the candidate is out on the campaign trail. Paid office staff must be trained and scheduled, and the assistant often handles that responsibility too.

The assistant may be asked to prepare reports and presentations that reflect the candidate's political position. Therefore, typing and effective writing are skills that an assistant must have in order to be successful.

Administrative assistants hold positions of responsibility in hundreds of other types of businesses as well. Their job duties depend on the business itself. Assistants must understand how their companies work. They must identify the proper channels to follow to get things done professionally and on time. It's also important to be able to complete work without much direction. Bosses depend on their assistants to run the office smoothly without having to ask what to do next.

Pay for administrative assistants ranges between $11 and $16 per hour, depending on experience. Salaries are higher in large cities like Los Angeles and New York. Companies with more employees, including the federal government, pay at the highest end of the scale. Both men and women fill positions as administrative assistants; however, most are women. An interesting fact is that assistants with a college degree make an average of only 48¢ more per hour than high school graduates.

A career as an administrative assistant could be a perfect fit if you are a responsible, organized person who enjoys working in an environment that has new challenges every day. But be prepared to carry a lot of responsibility! Many people will be looking to you for all the answers.

Unit 1 — *Answer Key — Answer Key — Answer Key*

Looking Forward

13. If you were to interview for an administrative assistant position, you might be asked to tell about your professional experience. Think about a time (real or imagined) when you organized an event or assisted in planning an event. Using both personal experience and information from the article, write about the role you played. What lessons did you learn, and what would you change the next time you help with an event?

> Student answers may vary.
>
> The student should address the question to the best of his/her ability using the article and personal experience. The question is meant to encourage students to explore areas of interest for their future and begin to determine how they will prepare for a future career.
>
> Use the extended-response rubric to reference the criteria and determine the number of points to award.

Ethical Dilemma

14. As the administrative assistant for a local politician's campaign for state representative, it's your responsibility to coordinate weekly receptions for important donors, including ordering the food for those attending. Several volunteers are assigned to help you set up the room and make sure fact sheets are ready to distribute to attendees. On the evening of this week's reception, you realize that in the rush you forgot to order the food. The candidate arrives and begins to raise her voice at one of the volunteers, apparently believing it was the volunteer's responsibility to order the food. Will you let the volunteer take the blame? What will you do about the food?

> Student answers may vary.
>
> The student should address the question to the best of his/her ability using background knowledge from the article as well as personal opinion and experience. The question is meant to encourage students to contemplate scenarios and make ethical decisions.
>
> Use the character education rubric to reference the criteria and number of points to award.

Answer Key — Answer Key — Answer Key

Unit Vocabulary Assessment

Matching
Match each word in Column I to its definition in Column II.

Column I
- __B__ 1. ballot
- __A__ 2. Caucasian
- __E__ 3. minority
- __C__ 4. democracy
- __D__ 5. convention

Column II
- a. relating to the white race of humans
- b. a paper on which a voter marks a vote
- c. government by the people
- d. a formal meeting
- e. a member of a smaller group

Multiple Choice
Choose the word that MOST NEARLY replaces the underlined word in each sentence.

6. On January 2, he officially became president of the United States.
   - A. finally
   - B. secretly
   - **C. formally**
   - D. hopefully

7. The dress was unique; he had never seen anything like it before.
   - A. ugly
   - **B. unusual**
   - C. concerning
   - D. understood

8. I could tell by their loud voices that the sisters were having a disagreement.
   - A. party
   - **B. conflict**
   - C. meeting
   - D. harmony

9. Although the offer sounded appealing, we decided not to pursue it.
   - A. distant
   - B. similar
   - C. different
   - **D. interesting**

Word Bank
- advertisement
- candidacy
- perceive
- platform
- primary

Fill in the Blank
Choose a word from the word bank to fill in the blank in the sentence below.

10. The **advertisement** for medical research stirred public interest in the subject.

11. I am a success if people **perceive** me as a dedicated person, recognizing my hard work.

12. He ran on a **platform** of principles that focused on healthcare for the poor.

13. Barack Obama's **candidacy** to become the first minority president is seen as historic.

14. Hillary Clinton ran in the Democratic **primary**.

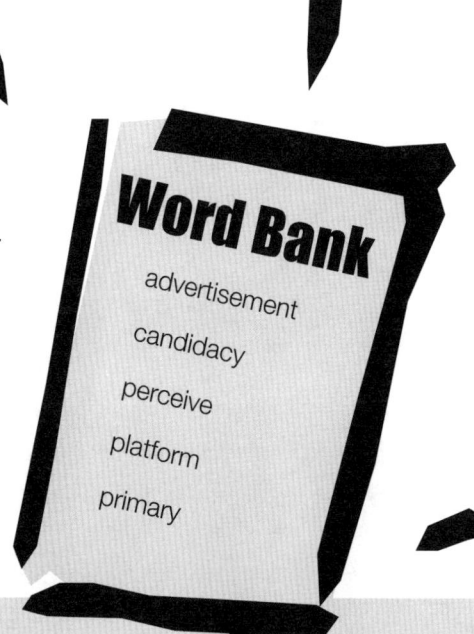

Unit 1 — Answer Key — Answer Key — Answer Key

Authentic Assessment

Students will participate in a mock election based on the unit "Ready or Not." This activity combines the authentic components of research and writing linked to the comprehension of a written text. Participating in this activity will allow students to identify various roles and participate in different parts of the election process.

Instructions for a Mock Election

1. **Brainstorming.** Have students spend time brainstorming to recall the process of a U.S. presidential election. They should come up with a list of people involved in this process and what each person does. They are going to fill these roles, so here is a sample list.

   Voter registration official: Signs people up to vote

   Candidates: May be "real" or fictitious

   Vice-presidential candidates: Run with the presidential candidates

   Debate moderator: Directs candidate debates

   Pollster: Takes polls about issues and candidates

   Campaign advisors: Help the candidates know what the people want

   Advertisers: Design and run ads for the candidates

   Voting supervisor: Runs the booth on Election Day

   Vote tabulator: Counts votes

   Electoral College members: Vote to represent their "states" (as many as you need)

2. **Research.** This assessment can be as complex or as simple as you design it to be. Each student should choose or be assigned a role in the mock election. The student should research this role and write several paragraphs about the jobs involved in the role and the importance of the role in the overall election.

Answer Key — Answer Key — Answer Key　　READY★OR★NOT

3. **Mock election.** Next, you will run a mock election in the classroom. You may have students research to determine the identity and platform of the candidates, or you may simply assign them. You may set up a debate among presidential candidates and/or vice-presidential candidates. You may also have students work in teams of "parties" to design advertising campaigns for the election platforms. Finally, students will go to the polls and place their votes, culminating in the voting of the Electoral College.

4. **Assessment.** Assess the mock election using the following rubric.

Mock Election Rubric

31–40 points	The student thoughtfully and accurately identifies and fulfills his or her election role. The student's written response to his or her role is complete and well put-together. Additional information provided by the student is related to the assigned task and acts as a support for his/her role.
21–30 points	The student accurately identifies and fulfills his or her election role. The student's written response to his or her role is complete. Additional information provided by the student is related to the assigned task and acts as a support for his/her role.
11–20 points	The student generally identifies and fulfills his or her election role. The student's written response to his or her role is mostly complete. The student is missing specific details and support research that would prove his/her full understanding of the assigned task.
0–10 points	The student shows very little understanding of what is being asked in the assigned task and does not correctly identify or fulfill his or her election role.

©2008 PRINCIPLE WOODS, INC. Removal of copyright notice and copying are violations of Federal Law.

Unit 2

Batman vs. Iron Man

Reading Instructional Guide for High-Interest Article

BEFORE READING

Front-Loading Background Knowledge through Read Aloud/Think Aloud

Search the Internet for recent articles on young heroes and use them to model the effective habits of readers through a Read Aloud/Think Aloud.

Check out articles at the following websites to determine if they would be appropriate for your RATA:
- Morse, Ben. "Take 10: Teen Heroes." *Marvel News*. February 27, 2008. http://www.marvel.com/news/comicstories.2722.
- "You Can Be a Hero Too." ThinkQuest Library. Oracle Education Foundation. http://library.thinkquest.org/CR0212302/hero2.html.

Please keep in mind that it is the responsibility of the teacher to determine if articles from suggested sites are appropriate. The sites may have changed content since this publication. The publisher takes no responsibility for the current content of the site.)

Looking at the Words

Determining How the Word Sounds (Phonics)
Using the Syllable Guide and the Reading Instructional Guide Template found in the beginning of the book, follow the steps to help students learn how to break a word into manageable parts.

Determining What the Word Means (Vocabulary)

Words to Study	Breaking into Syllables	Short Definition
avenger	a-veng-er	(n.) one who inflicts punishment as an act of justice
emblem	em-blem	(n.) a symbol or design
frightful	fright-ful	(adj.) causing shock or scare
inherit	in-her-it	(v.) to receive a possession after someone has died
miscellaneous	mis-cel-la-ne-ous	(adj.) consisting of different kinds; assorted
shrapnel	shrap-nel	(n.) a shell containing lead pellets that can explode
vengeance	venge-ance	(n.) revenge

Activating Background Knowledge

Anticipation Guide
Have students mark each of the following statements True or False:

1. ____ Bruce Wayne's secret identity is Batman.

2. ____ Bruce Wayne's parents were killed in a car accident.

Answer Key — Answer Key — Answer Key   **Batman vs. Iron Man**

3. ____ Batman's costume has remained the same over the years.
4. ____ Tony Stark's nickname is Iron Man.
5. ____ Iron Man's costume is gray and blue.

Starter Questions
After completing the Anticipation Guide, have a group or class discussion with the students using the following questions:

1. What type of protective gear did Iron Man design?
2. How did Tony Stark inherit his father's business?
3. How does Iron Man's protective suit help him in battle?
4. What training did Batman receive for fighting crime in Gotham City?
5. What gadgets does Batman use in battle?

Make a prediction about what you think the article will be about.

DURING READING
Use the Reading Instructional Guide Template found in the front of the book.

AFTER READING

Discussion Starter Questions

1. How might Bruce Wayne's life have been different if a bat had not flown into his window?
2. Why do you think the latest Batman is more violent than the earlier Batman?
3. What similarities and differences do you see between Batman and Iron Man?
4. How do you think today's society would be different if Iron Man really existed?
5. What can Batman and Iron Man teach us about values and character?

Teacher Reflection
Use the Reading Instructional Guide Template found in the front of the book.

©2008 PRINCIPLE WOODS, INC. Removal of copyright notice and copying are violations of Federal Law.

Batman

Secret Identity

Bruce Wayne is Batman. He is a rich businessman who mixes with high society. He gives money to charity organizations. Sometimes he acts scatterbrained to hide his identity as Batman.

Costume

Batman wears a hood with pointed, bat-like ears. The hood covers half of his face and hides his true identity. He wears a cape that looks like bat wings. His costume is gray and blue, with a bat emblem on the chest. There have been several different authors of Batman comics. Each has interpreted Batman differently, and the costume has changed looks slightly over the years.

DC Comics

DC, originally standing for Detective Comics, publishes Batman comics. Batman first graced its pages in 1939. DC also features other world-famous heroes, including Superman and Wonder Woman. After over 60 years of comic publishing, the company boasts nearly 1,000 comic book titles each year.

Background/Creation

When Bruce was a child, a petty thief shot and killed his parents as they were walking through Gotham City after a movie. Following his parents' death, Bruce vowed to work against crime. He trained in martial arts, acrobatics, science, and detective skills. He wanted to increase his ability to solve and put an end to crime in Gotham. One night a bat flew through his window. Taken by its frightful sight and connection with the dark, he decided to become a bat-like creature. Then he could strike fear in the hearts of criminals. He would become a creature and true avenger of the night.

Weapons/Gadgets

Batman wears a utility belt that holds gadgets and weapons. Some are batarangs, sharp metal throwing devices shaped like bats. Also included on the belt are a grappling hook, small explosive devices to create diversions, and other miscellaneous tools. These tools help him do detective work and fight criminals. He is also famous for his transportation, including the Batmobile.

Miscellaneous

In later years, Batman teams up with other superheroes to fight crime throughout the world. He sometimes runs into conflicts with other superheroes. He battles Superman from time to time over differences about how the world should be saved. Because of his dark personality, sometimes it is hard for Batman to separate his desire to do good from his wanting to take vengeance on those who do wrong to others.

Villains and Enemies

The Batman story has introduced famous villains such as the Joker, the Penguin, and the Riddler. In the early years of the comics, Batman captured the criminals but refrained from actually killing them. In a later comic series, however, Batman has a more violent role and punishes some criminals with death.

Answer Key — Answer Key — Answer Key

Batman vs. Iron Man

Iron Man

Secret Identity

Tony Stark is Iron Man. He was born with high intelligence and rich parents. He lived the high life until his parents were killed in a tragic car accident. Following their deaths, he inherited his father's business, Stark Enterprises. This gave him money and technological capabilities. His brains and education allowed him to put the two together.

Weapons/Gadgets

Tony always creates new suits, each more technologically advanced than the last. This allows him to have more advantages over his foes. He can even store the inner layers of the Iron Man suit in his bones. The suit has become an extension of him, speeding up his reaction time. The armor includes rocket-propelled boots that allow him to fly. He has the ability to withstand bullets and can even be hit by rockets and suffer only minor damage. He can fire rays from his hands with a ton of force.

Costume

Iron Man's armor is red and yellow, and it covers his body. There are tiny slits for his eyes.

Marvel Comics

Marvel Comics has laid claim to over 5,000 characters during its 60-plus years of publishing history. They have some of the world's most popular superheroes such as Iron Man, Spider-Man, Ghost Rider, the X-Men, the Hulk, and Captain America. Iron Man first appeared in Marvel comics in 1963. The company has been one of the top-selling magazine distributors in the nation over the past few years.

Background/Creation

While Stark was visiting the U.S. military in a war zone, an evil warlord captured him. He tried to force Stark to create weapons for the enemy army. During his capture, Tony was hit in the chest by exploding metal. This metal worked its way toward his heart. He designed an iron suit that kept the shrapnel in his chest from killing him. With the armor, he could protect himself and attack others. Stark escaped his captor by wearing the Iron Man suit for the first time. Once he returned home, he began his life as a superhero.

Miscellaneous

Regardless of the millions of dollars he sinks into his suit, weapons, and armor, Tony Stark knows that being a superhero does not make one's life perfect. That is a lesson that all real-life heroes can relate to: they are all still human, and humans aren't perfect.

Villains and Enemies

Some of Iron Man's enemies have been Black Widow, Iron Monger, Mandarin, and Hawkeye. And despite his powers, Tony Stark is still human and therefore must also battle his personal demons. Throughout his life, he has found it difficult to deal with alcohol. Part of his story is that he is an alcoholic and struggles to keep that side of his life under control. Also, he can never escape the grasp of politics. He's even had to face off against other superheroes such as Captain America and the Hulk.

©2008 PRINCIPLE WOODS, INC. Removal of copyright notice and copying are violations of Federal Law.

Unit 2 — Answer Key — Answer Key — Answer Key

Reading Comprehension

After reading "Batman vs. Iron Man," choose the options that best answer questions 1–14.

1. Read this sentence.
   Because of his dark personality, sometimes it is difficult for Batman to separate his desire to do good from his wanting to take vengeance on those who do wrong to others.

   Based on these lines, what does the author mean by the phrase *dark personality?*
   A. bad side
   B. strong work ethic
   C. dark-colored costume
   D. inability to make friends

2. Read this sentence.
   The armor includes rocket-propelled boots that allow him to fly.

   What is the meaning of the word *armor* as it is used in the sentence?
   F. mansion
   G. weapons
   H. automobile
   I. protective covering

3. From the article, the reader can tell that
   A. Iron Man enjoyed spending time in the war zone.
   B. reading comic books is a hobby enjoyed by many people.
   C. Batman devotes a lot of time helping charities in Gotham City.
   D. Batman's personality allows him to make and keep many friends.

4. According to the article, which of these is likely to occur?
   F. Iron Man will continue to create protective garments.
   G. DC Comics will continue to publish many comic books.
   H. Marvel Comics will sell more copies of comic books than DC Comics.
   I. Batman's costume will likely be altered to keep up with a changing society.

5. With which statement would the author of the passage MOST likely agree?
   A. Batman was more popular than Iron Man.
   B. Iron Man was a better crime fighter than Batman.
   C. The writers of Iron Man need to create an automobile for him like the Batmobile.
   D. Money and power cannot make one's life perfect—even that of a fictitious character.

6. The author organizes the article by
   F. comparing and contrasting two superheroes.
   G. using an essay format to present the information.
   H. starting with a description of Iron Man, followed by Batman.
   I. listing the reasons why Batman is a better character than Iron Man.

Answer Key — Answer Key — Answer Key   **Batman** vs. **Iron Man**

7. Why does the author mention Iron Man's alcoholism?
   A. to encourage the reader to feel sorry for Iron Man
   B. to show that even superheroes have to overcome obstacles
   C. to introduce the reader to the devastating effects of alcoholism
   D. to illustrate how to help someone who has difficulty with alcohol consumption

8. Which title BEST fits the article?
   F. The Disastrous Duo
   G. Splendid Superheroes
   H. Batman's Background
   I. Investigating Iron Man

9. What would Batman most likely do if he witnessed present-day crime?
   A. encourage others to fight crime
   B. encourage Iron Man to work with him to fight crime
   C. continue to battle those individuals who commit crimes
   D. transfer the role and responsibilities to another character so he can rest

10. Why did Iron Man create his iron suit?
    F. to earn extra money
    G. to make more friends
    H. to prevent shrapnel from killing him
    I. to change his career path to government and politics

11. Batman and Iron Man are alike in that they
    A. are both superheroes.
    B. have the same uniform.
    C. battle the same villains.
    D. use the same protective weapons.

12. Which statement about Batman is LEAST accurate?
    F. Batman got his identity from a bat.
    G. Batman's costume has changed over time.
    H. Bruce Wayne's parents encouraged him to become Batman.
    I. Batman has battled many villains to decrease crime throughout the world.

13. According to the information provided about Batman and Iron Man,
    A. Iron Man is stronger than Batman.
    B. Batman was created before Iron Man.
    C. Both Batman and Iron Man live in Gotham City.
    D. Neither Batman nor Iron Man has a secret identity.

14. Based on the information about BOTH Batman and Iron Man, which of these conclusions is accurate?
    F. Both Batman and Iron Man have battled Superman.
    G. Both Batman and Iron Man fight crime during the day.
    H. Both Batman and Iron Man received their identity from an animal.
    I. Batman and Iron Man had personal experiences that have influenced their superhero lives.

©2008 PRINCIPLE WOODS, INC. Removal of copyright notice and copying are violations of Federal Law.

Reading Strategy

Unit 2 — Answer Key — Answer Key — Answer Key

Who's the strongest of them all?

Directions: Use the table below to fill in facts about Batman and Iron Man.

	Secret Identity	Background/ Creation	Costume	Gadgets	Enemies	Miscellaneous	Creators
BATMAN	Bruce Wayne. Rich businessman who gives to charity. Deceased parents. Acts scatterbrained to hide his identity.	Parents killed when he was a child. Trained in many areas to fight crime. When trying to figure out superhero identity, a bat flew into his room.	Wears hood with pointed bat-like ears. Also wears cape that looks like bat wings. Gray and blue colored.	Belt holds batarangs, grappling hook, small explosive devices to create diversions, and other tools to fight crime. Also famous for modes of transportation.	Joker, Penguin, Riddler, and his parents' murderers.	Teams up with other superheroes to fight crime in the world. Sometimes dark persona makes it difficult to separate desire to do good from desire to take vengeance on those who do wrong to others.	DC Comics
Iron man	Tony Stark. Intelligent and rich son of deceased parents. Inherited Stark Enterprises.	An evil warlord forced him to create weapons for enemy army. Created iron suit to protect himself.	Red and yellow armor covers entire body. Slits for eyes.	Always creates new suits. Suit speeds up reaction time. Can withstand bullets and rockets. Can fire rays from his hands.	Black Widow, Mandarin, Iron Monger, Hawkeye, and personal demons such as alcohol.	Being a superhero doesn't make someone's life perfect.	Marvel Comics

Based on the facts in the completed table, which superhero would you say is the strongest?

Answers will vary.

30

©2008 PRINCIPLE WOODS, INC. Removal of copyright notice and copying are violations of Federal Law.

Answer Key — Answer Key — Answer Key   **Batman** vs. **Iron Man**

Interpreting the Data

PART I

Which superhero packs the biggest box office punch?

Who do you think is more powerful: Batman or Superman? The Hulk or Spider-Man? These types of questions have entertained comic book fans for years. While we may never know who is truly the toughest, we can at least look at box office statistics to determine which superhero packs the biggest punch in the entertainment industry.

Begin by making a prediction. Based on what you know, rank the following superheroes in order of popularity, with "A" being the most popular and "F" being the least popular. We'll then look at the amount of money their movies earned to see how close we are with our predictions.

Prediction: Superheroes ranked by popularity.
A. Answers will vary for A–F.
B.
C.
D.
E.
F.

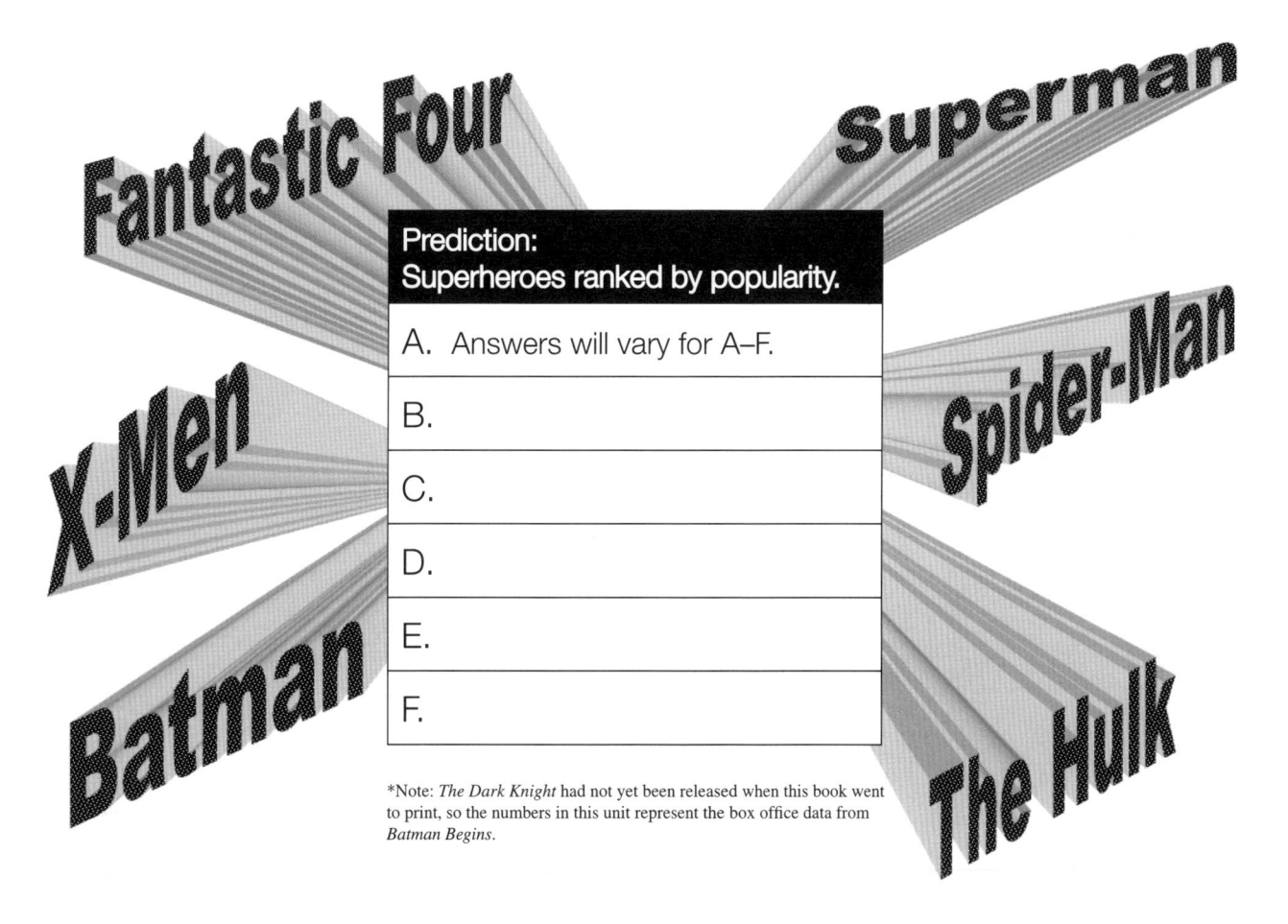

Note: The Dark Knight had not yet been released when this book went to print, so the numbers in this unit represent the box office data from *Batman Begins.*

Figure 1 displays the amount of money grossed worldwide by six popular superhero movies. The dollar amount is given in millions of dollars and rounded to the nearest whole million. Also included is the budget for each movie. The budget is the amount of money the producers said they needed to create the movie.

©2008 PRINCIPLE WOODS, INC. Removal of copyright notice and copying are violations of Federal Law.

Unit 2

Answer Key — Answer Key — Answer Key

Figure 1. The amount of money grossed and budgeted by popular superhero movies

Superman Returns
Release Date: 2006
Worldwide Gross: $391M
Budget: $204M
After Budget: **$187M**

Batman Begins
Release Date: 2005
Worldwide Gross: $372M
Budget: $159M
After Budget: **$213M**

Fantastic Four
Release Date: 2005
Worldwide Gross: $329M
Budget: $88M
After Budget: **$241M**

Superhero Movies

The Hulk
Release Date: 2003
Worldwide Gross: $245M
Budget: $137M
After Budget: **$108M**

Spider-Man
Release Date: 2002
Worldwide Gross: $822M
Budget: $139M
After Budget: **$683M**

X-Men
Release Date: 2000
Worldwide Gross: $296M
Budget: $75M
After Budget: **$221M**

15. Rank the movies by the amount budgeted:	16. Rank the movies by the amount grossed:	17. Rank the movies by the amount earned after the budget is subtracted from the gross:
A. *Superman Returns*	A. *Spider-Man*	A. *Spider-Man*
B. *Batman Begins*	B. *Superman Returns*	B. *Fantastic Four*
C. *Spider-Man*	C. *Batman Begins*	C. *X-Men*
D. *The Hulk*	D. *Fantastic Four*	D. *Batman Begins*
E. *Fantastic Four*	E. *X-Men*	E. *Superman Returns*
F. *X-Men*	F. *The Hulk*	F. *The Hulk*

18. Using the data in Figure 1, determine which superhero is the highest money-maker after budget when compared to the other movies. Explain your conclusion using data from at least two movies.

ANALYZE EVALUATE EXPLAIN

Student answers could contain facts such as the following:

Spider-Man is the highest moneymaker. After the budget for the film is subtracted, *Spider-Man* earned $683 million, while the next closest superhero movie, *Fantastic Four*, earned only $241 million—a difference of $442 million.

Use the short-response rubric to reference the criteria required for an acceptable answer and to determine the points to award.

©2008 PRINCIPLE WOODS, INC. Removal of copyright notice and copying are violations of Federal Law.

Answer Key — Answer Key — Answer Key **Batman vs. Iron Man**

PART II

Which comic book superhero packed the most punch on opening weekend?

Table 1. Opening weekend statistics for eight of the most popular comic-book-based movies

	Spider-Man	X-Men	Teenage Mutant Ninja Turtles (TMNT)	Batman (Begins)	Fantastic Four	Superman (Returns)	Transformers	Iron Man
(a) 1st weekend gross (millions)	$114.8	$54.5	$25.4	$48.7	$56.1	$52.5	$70.5	$102.1
Budget (in millions)	$139	$75	$13.5	$150	$87.5	$204	$151	$186
(b) % of budget grossed on the first weekend	$114.8M/$139M= .825899= 82.6%	19. 72.7%	20. 188.1%	21. 32.5%	22. 64.1%	23. 25.7%	24. 46.7%	25. 54.9%
# of theaters	3,615	3,025	2,006	3,858	3,602	4,065	4,011	4,105
(c) $ grossed per theater on 1st weekend	$114.8M/3,615 theaters= $31,757	$54.5M/3,025 = 26. $18,017	27. $12,662	28. $12,623	29. $15,575	30. $12,915	31. $17,577	32. $24,872

The Great Tournament: Determine which superhero movie had the greatest take-off by comparing the opening weekend numbers for the different movies. Complete the math and fill in the tournament bracket. Use the data to determine which comic book superhero would have been victorious when paired up with another. Then determine which hero defeats the next at each subsequent round of the "tournament."

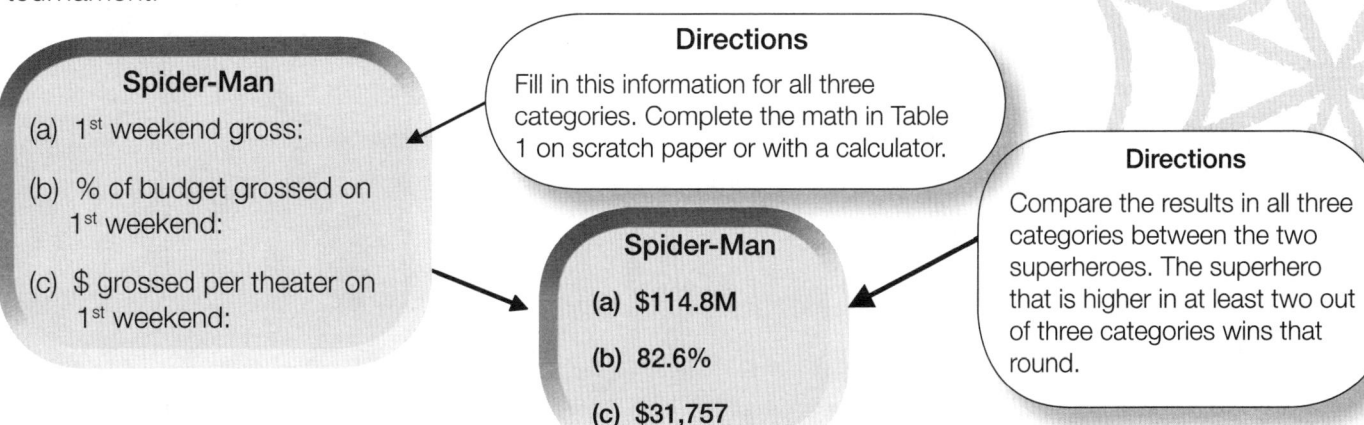

Spider-Man
(a) 1st weekend gross:
(b) % of budget grossed on 1st weekend:
(c) $ grossed per theater on 1st weekend:

Directions
Fill in this information for all three categories. Complete the math in Table 1 on scratch paper or with a calculator.

Spider-Man
(a) $114.8M
(b) 82.6%
(c) $31,757

Directions
Compare the results in all three categories between the two superheroes. The superhero that is higher in at least two out of three categories wins that round.

©2008 PRINCIPLE WOODS, INC. Removal of copyright notice and copying are violations of Federal Law.

Answer Key — Answer Key — Answer Key

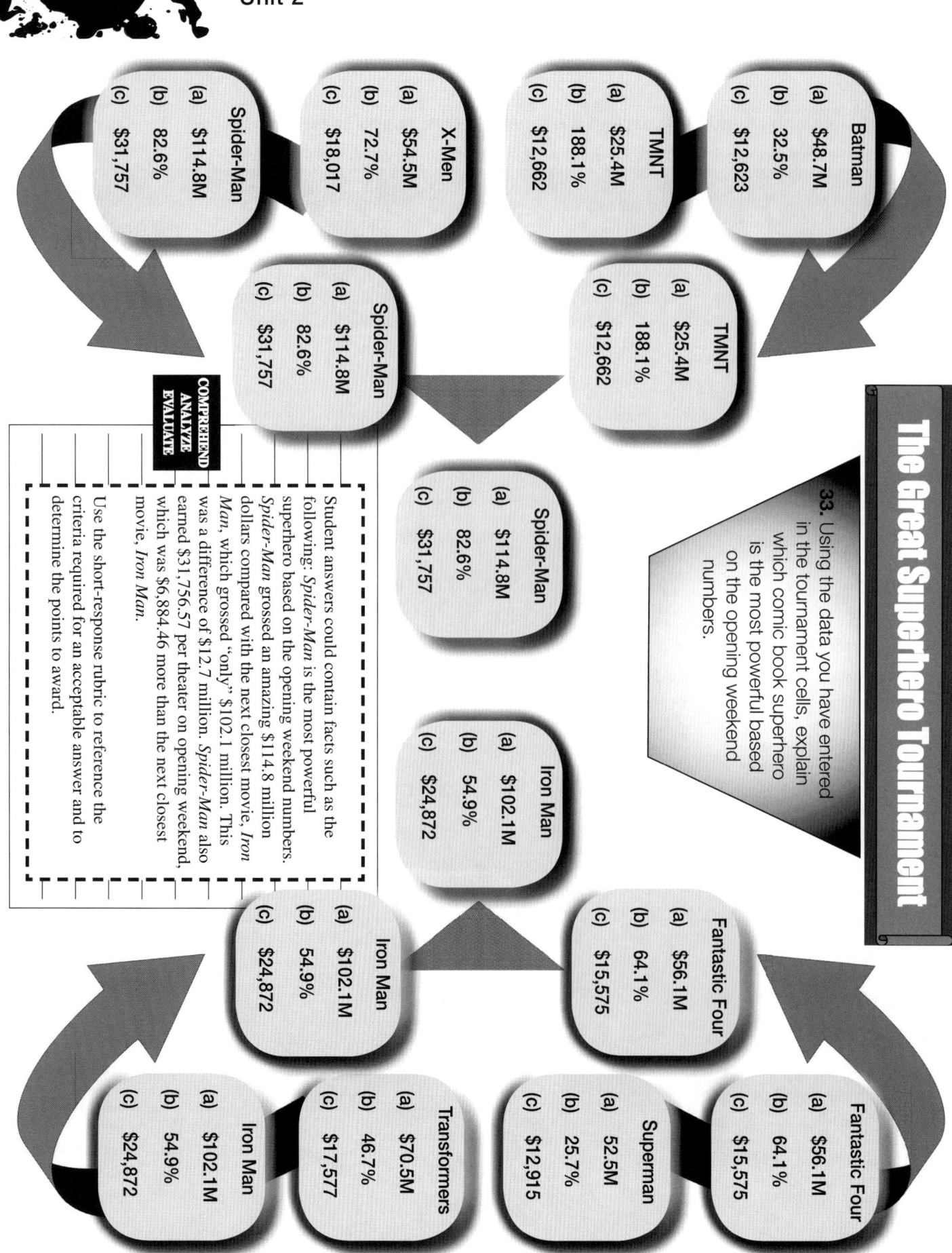

Unit 2

The Great Superhero Tournament

33. Using the data you have entered in the tournament cells, explain which comic book superhero is the most powerful based on the opening weekend numbers.

Batman
(a) $48.7M
(b) 32.5%
(c) $12,623

TMNT
(a) $25.4M
(b) 188.1%
(c) $12,662

X-Men
(a) $54.5M
(b) 72.7%
(c) $18,017

Spider-Man
(a) $114.8M
(b) 82.6%
(c) $31,757

Spider-Man
(a) $114.8M
(b) 82.6%
(c) $31,757

TMNT
(a) $25.4M
(b) 188.1%
(c) $12,662

Spider-Man
(a) $114.8M
(b) 82.6%
(c) $31,757

Iron Man
(a) $102.1M
(b) 54.9%
(c) $24,872

Iron Man
(a) $102.1M
(b) 54.9%
(c) $24,872

Fantastic Four
(a) $56.1M
(b) 64.1%
(c) $15,575

Iron Man
(a) $102.1M
(b) 54.9%
(c) $24,872

Transformers
(a) $70.5M
(b) 46.7%
(c) $17,577

Superman
(a) 52.5M
(b) 25.7%
(c) $12,915

Fantastic Four
(a) $56.1M
(b) 64.1%
(c) $15,575

COMPREHEND / ANALYZE / EVALUATE

Student answers could contain facts such as the following: *Spider-Man* is the most powerful superhero based on the opening weekend numbers. *Spider-Man* grossed an amazing $114.8 million dollars compared with the next closest movie, *Iron Man*, which grossed "only" $102.1 million. This was a difference of $12.7 million. *Spider-Man* also earned $31,756.57 per theater on opening weekend, which was $6,884.46 more than the next closest movie, *Iron Man*.

Use the short-response rubric to reference the criteria required for an acceptable answer and to determine the points to award.

©2008 PRINCIPLE WOODS, INC. Removal of copyright notice and copying are violations of Federal Law.

Answer Key — Answer Key — Answer Key   **Batman** vs. Iron Man

Reflect and Respond

34. Superheroes have superpowers. Some can fly. Some can become invisible. Some can shoot webs. Some can even move faster than a speeding bullet. Most importantly, they have the character to know how and when to use these powers. Write a few paragraphs that explain which superpowers you would like to have and which character traits (e.g., honesty, courage, patience, maturity, dependence, dependability) you would need to strengthen in yourself in order to be a true superhero.

> Answers may vary, but students should address each part of the question. The question is meant to elicit strong classroom conversation about character. Students should be able to demonstrate an ability to examine themselves for the types of character traits they believe they possess and those they need to improve upon.
>
> Use the character education rubric to reference the criteria and number of points to award.

Unit 2

Answer Key — Answer Key — Answer Key

Reading Instructional Guide for Technical Extension

BEFORE READING

Looking at the Words

Determining How the Word Sounds (Phonics)
Technical texts often necessitate the use of multisyllabic words that are unfamiliar to students. Use the Syllable Guide to help students decode any words they might have trouble reading.

Determining What the Word Means (Vocabulary)

Words to Study	Breaking into Syllables	Short Definition
consult	con-sult	(v.) to ask guidance from
deface	de-face	(v.) to disfigure or mark on
demon	de-mon	(n.) an evil influence
genre	gen-re	(n.) a kind of a work of art
inexpensive	in-ex-pen-sive	(adj.) not high in price
manageable	man-age-a-ble	(adj.) that can be controlled

Activating Background Knowledge

Graphic Organizer
Either individually or in groups, students may brainstorm about the important factors to remember when selling a used comic book recalling anything previously learned and any prior experience with the subject. Next, encourage students to see the relationships between their ideas by having them complete a cycle graphic organizer to demonstrate what they already know about rating the condition and evaluating the price of a used comic book.

The Process of Reselling a Comic Book

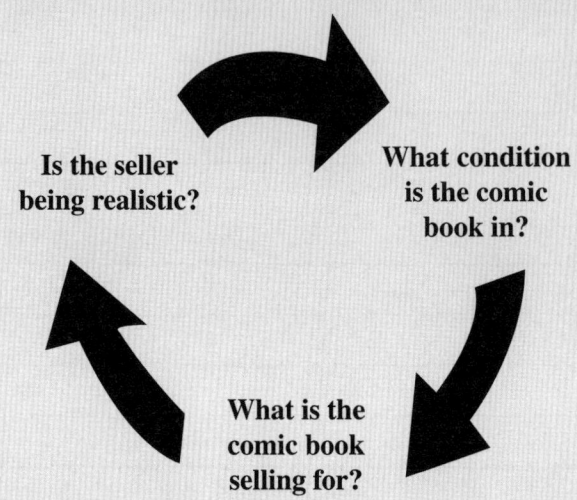

- What condition is the comic book in?
- What is the comic book selling for?
- Is the seller being realistic?

Answer Key — Answer Key — Answer Key   Batman vs. Iron Man

Starter Questions
After completing the Graphic Organizer, generate a group or class discussion to come up with questions about the subject, a prediction about the article, and at least one learning goal. The first question has been provided for you.

Question: Why do you think people enjoy collecting comic books?

Question: _____

Prediction: _____

Goal: _____

DURING READING
Use the Reading Instructional Guide Template found in the front of the book.

AFTER READING
After reading, you may teach reading strategy use by giving students opportunities to do the following:
- Review, paraphrase, and summarize
- Participate in main-idea discussions by describing the information in their own words
- Reflect on concept maps and generate additional discussion starter questions based on the mappings
- Participate in small-group discussions using discussion starter questions

Discussion Starter Questions

The first question has been provided for you.

1. How does the condition of a comic book affect the resale value?

2. _____

3. _____

Unit 2

Answer Key — Answer Key — Answer Key

Technical Extension

The Case for Comics

Comic book heroes like Batman and Iron Man entertain us with their adventures as they face their enemies and their inner demons. Our personal struggles seem more manageable when we read their stories. Adults and children alike read and collect comic books. The books themselves started out as collections of strips that had already appeared in newspapers.

Detective Comics, now known as DC, published the first book of original comics in 1935. Writer Major Malcolm Wheeler-Nicholson put together *New Fun: The Big Comic Magazine* #1. The "birth" of Superman occurred in *Action Comics* #1 in 1938. DC readers were hooked by the action of this first superhero. They eagerly bought the next issue as soon as it hit the newsstands. Superman was soon followed by Batman and other superheroes such as Flash, the Green Lantern, Captain Marvel, and Wonder Woman. Batman was created by cartoonist Bob Kane. He realized that he could gain more readers by switching from traditional cartoons to the new genre of superheroes. He wanted to create a costumed hero with a simple design that was easily recognized. His design was inspired by artist Leonardo da Vinci's drawing of a bat-like flying machine. Then, in May 1939, Batman was born in *Detective Comics* #27.

Marvel Comics introduced Iron Man, "a cool exec with a heart of steel," in *Tales of Suspense* #39 in March 1963. Marvel brings its characters alive through movies and video games. Clothing, toys, and collectibles also highlight favorite characters.

The appeal of comic books is easy to understand. People like to read stories that are accompanied by illustrations. Comic books have been around longer than VCRs or DVDs even existed. Comic books are a versatile form of entertainment. They can be read anytime, anywhere, and they can be read over and over. Most are also relatively inexpensive.

Collecting comic books has become big business. In the 1970s, small independent comic book stores began to open in strip shopping centers. Most of these stores were operated by adults who read and collected the books themselves. Older readers (the average DC reader is 25) are able to purchase more comic books than younger readers because they make more money. There is also a growing respect for comic books as an art form. Professional people in the arts, such as book editors, directors, publishers, and musicians, enjoy the genre of comics.

Sometimes this means the books have an increase in value. However, just because the owner of a comic book thinks it is valuable doesn't mean that it can be sold for a lot of money. The collector needs to know the following things about the book to be sold:

- What condition is it in? How does the cover look, and are the inside pages faded or yellowed?

- Has the seller consulted a price guide?

- What is the comic book currently selling for on auction sites like eBay?

- Is the seller being realistic? The popularity of the book, how quickly the seller needs to sell it, and the condition it is in all must be considered.

The most important thing to remember, though, is that a book's value depends on how much someone is willing to pay for it.

Some people have been willing to pay incredibly high prices. One person paid $135,000 for a 1940 Batman edition. It was in near-mint condition, meaning that someone kept it protected for many years before it was sold. In 2006 a comic book auction brought in over $2.19 million on comic books in just one weekend. *Action Comics* #1, the first appearance of Superman, is thought to be the world's most valuable comic book. Its value is estimated at $400,000 if in near-mint condition. Keep in mind, though, that many comics are not protected. Most books sell for their original cover price or less, depending on their condition.

Someone who collects comic books usually builds a collection based on what is important to him or her. Some people want to own all the books about a certain character, like Batman or Iron Man. Others want to collect all issues from a certain company, like DC or Marvel. This means that many collectors will buy books that are considered "lower grade" in order to complete a collection.

Collectors who collect to make money will only purchase comics in perfect or near-perfect condition. Their goal is to resell the books later for more money. There is also the issue of searching for signed copies of the comics. Some collectors look for these, while others consider it a defacement of the book since there are markings on the pages or cover.

Comic books provide hours of reading entertainment to millions of people around the world. They offer an escape from everyday problems. Often they teach lessons of courage and character. In recent years, those who collect comics have been able to create an enjoyable hobby for themselves. Many have even turned their collections into a lucrative business.

Unit 2 — Answer Key — Answer Key — Answer Key

Reading Comprehension

After reading "The Case for Comics," choose the options that best answer questions 1–11.

1. Read this sentence.
   This means that many collectors will buy books that are considered "lower grade" in order to complete a collection.

   What is the meaning of the word *grade* as it is used in this sentence?
   A. mark
   B. quality
   C. difficulty
   D. popularity

2. Read this sentence.
   Comic books are a versatile form of entertainment.

   What is the meaning of the word *versatile* as it is used in this sentence?
   F. limited
   G. flexible
   H. virtuous
   I. well-loved

3. What is the MOST important factor in determining the value of a comic book?
   A. the cover
   B. how much someone will pay
   C. how much it is selling for on eBay
   D. whether or not the writer has signed the book

4. What phrase BEST describes the overall popularity of comic books?
   F. They always increase in value.
   G. They are portable and can be read anywhere.
   H. They are sold in stores that are easily accessible to both young people and adults.
   I. They provide entertainment and escape, and sometimes they can be turned into cash.

5. The author organizes the article by
   A. outlining the history of all comic book makers.
   B. discussing how to sell comic books in order to make money.
   C. discussing DC and Marvel Comics and then outlining how collectors make money on comics.
   D. telling the history of Batman and Iron Man and then discussing why people of all ages like to read comic books.

Answer Key — Answer Key — Answer Key

Batman vs. Iron Man

6. What is the main idea of the fourth paragraph?
   F. **Comic books are appealing.**
   G. DVDs took the place of comic books.
   H. Comic books are too expensive to collect.
   I. Once companies began to tape comic books, they became more popular.

7. Why did Bob Kane, the creator of Batman, change his career path?
   A. **He realized that he could gain more readers.**
   B. His job as a cartoonist was eliminated, so he needed work.
   C. Marvel Comics hired him to create Batman but then ran out of money.
   D. He had an idea for a costumed superhero, and he wanted to sell it to a major company.

8. Comic books are compared to VCRs or DVDs because
   F. they are all inexpensive.
   G. **they are visual presentations.**
   H. the person using them can share them with others.
   I. some people collect comic books as well as VCR tapes and DVDs.

9. Which fact from the article BEST supports the author's point that collecting comic books can become a money-making operation?
   A. **A Batman comic from 1940 sold for $135,000.**
   B. Many comics are not protected after they are purchased and read.
   C. Price guides must be consulted in order to determine a comic's true worth.
   D. Hard-core collectors will only consider comic books that are in perfect or near perfect condition.

10. If you want to become a comic book collector, what would be MOST important to know?
    F. Books are often sold on auction sites.
    G. Comic books tell stories of courage and character.
    H. Comic book hobbyists make it difficult to collect books in good condition.
    I. **The value of a comic book is determined by a number of things, but especially by what someone is willing to pay for it.**

11. If a comic book needs to be sold quickly, what must the owner understand?
    A. The owner must sell for the amount first offered.
    B. An auction site may be offering the book for less money.
    C. **The book may sell for less money due to the quick time frame.**
    D. It may not sell at all due to factors like the condition of the cover and pages.

Unit 2

Answer Key — Answer Key — Answer Key

Technical Writing Prompt

12. Imagine that you are a collector of a comic book series and that you have decided to sell your complete series. You have contacted the owner of a comic book store, and she is interested in buying your series. Write a business letter to give her more specific information about your collection. Be sure to include how many comics are in the series, what series it is, what condition the books are in, the price, and the steps you took to figure out the price.

> Student answers may vary.
>
> The student should address the question to the best of his/her ability using the article and personal experience. The question is meant to prepare students to be active citizens who can accurately and effectively use written communication skills.
>
> Use the technical writing rubric to reference the criteria and determine the number of points to award.

Vocational Extension

HELP WANTED:
Motion picture company is hiring animators to work with a creative team to develop a new character for launch in 1–2 years. Applicants must have a degree in fine arts and have at least one year of experience in animation. Salary is flexible depending on years of experience and work history. Apply in person at the Human Resources department on the studio lot.

Can you imagine drawing a cartoon or comic strip as a job? Maybe all that drawing you have been doing in the margins of your homework can pay off in the future! Artists do just that for comics and other kinds of books, magazines, movies, television shows, and advertisements.

There are dozens of different kinds of jobs in the field of art. So if you want to put your creativity to work, you may choose from some of these careers:

- <u>Animators</u> create the pictures of movement for characters like Batman and Iron Man.
- <u>Cartoonists</u> develop characters for cartoons using drawings and words. Some of these comic strips appear in newspapers.
- <u>Mural artists</u> design and paint very large drawings on walls and buildings. Graffiti artists, known as "taggers," could turn graffiti into a legal career by painting murals instead.
- <u>Graphic designers</u> do hundreds of different art jobs. Some examples are designing logos and websites for companies and illustrating three-dimensional images for computer games and then bringing them to life.
- <u>Art directors</u> are in charge of teams of artists that create designs we all see in magazines and on billboards, products, and television.

Successful artists must be creative, organized, and able to follow directions. Because clients often have a specific design in mind, the artist must be able to bring it to life. Some artists work with teams of other creative people, so they must be able to work successfully in a group.

Many artists today also rely heavily on computers. Some work on computers to develop characters and then put them in motion. These artists must have knowledge of various software programs in order to make their characters "real" to the audience.

Artists work in many places. Some work alone at home or in a studio, and others work in offices of large companies. Salaries for artists also have a wide range. Experienced art directors may earn over $100,000 per year, while many self-employed artists do not make enough money to support themselves without other sources of income. Average salaries range from $20,000 to $80,000 per year.

A good place to start perfecting your skills as an artist is in school art classes. The next step would be to earn a college degree in fine arts. This education will increase your chances of being hired as an artist in the future. Artists start collecting work for their portfolio early in their careers, so why not begin now? Get out your drawing pencils or paints and start preparing for a creative career in the field of art!

Answer Key — Answer Key — Answer Key

Unit 2

Looking Forward

13. Imagine that you are pursuing a career in art. Artists work in many different fields. Using your personal experience and information from the article, select a specific job listed in the article and explain why you think you would be suited for this position. What experience, expertise, and assets would you bring to this field?

> Student answers may vary.
>
> The student should address the question to the best of his/her ability using the article and personal experience. The question is meant to encourage students to explore areas of interest for their future and begin to determine how they will prepare for a future career.
>
> Use the extended-response rubric to reference the criteria and determine the number of points to award.

Ethical Dilemma

14. A wealthy art collector has approached you to create a mural for her home. She is willing to pay a great deal of money, but she needs it done in a very short period of time. You already have ongoing commitments to several small art galleries to help with shows over the next few months. The work you do for these galleries helps pay your bills each month. If you accept the art collector's commission, you will have to break your commitment to the galleries, but the money you make will be enough to live on for six months. Do you accept the art collector's commission? Is there any compromise you could offer the galleries?

> Student answers may vary.
>
> The student should address the question to the best of his/her ability using background knowledge from the article as well as personal opinion and experience. The question is meant to encourage students to contemplate scenarios and make ethical decisions.
>
> Use the character education rubric to reference the criteria and determine the number of points to award.

©2008 PRINCIPLE WOODS, INC. Removal of copyright notice and copying are violations of Federal Law.

Answer Key — Answer Key — Answer Key   **Batman** vs. **Iron Man**

Unit Vocabulary Assessment

Matching
Match each word in Column I to its definition in Column II.

Column I
- **B** 1. demon
- **D** 2. avenger
- **E** 3. miscellaneous
- **A** 4. manageable
- **C** 5. shrapnel

Column II
a. that can be controlled
b. an evil influence
c. a shell containing lead pellets
d. someone who inflicts punishment
e. consisting of different kinds

Multiple Choice
Choose the word that MOST NEARLY replaces the underlined word in each sentence.

6. Romance is my favorite movie <u>genre</u>.
    A. event
    B. subject
    C. general
    D. literature

7. Superheroes sometimes seek <u>vengeance</u> on those who hurt others.
    A. evil
    B. help
    C. revenge
    D. guidance

8. Walking through the haunted house was a <u>frightful</u> experience.
    A. fun
    B. scary
    C. uneventful
    D. unforgettable

9. We found a program that is relatively <u>inexpensive</u>.
    A. cheap
    B. exclusive
    C. intolerable
    D. interesting

Word Bank
consult
deface
emblem
inherited

Fill in the Blank
Choose a word from the word bank to fill in the blank in the sentence below.

10. Jamey **inherited** several antique chests when his grandmother passed away.

11. We will **consult** an expert in order to get a better diagnosis.

12. The **emblem** on the flag signifies the people's freedom.

13. Please take care not to **deface** any of the property in the classroom.

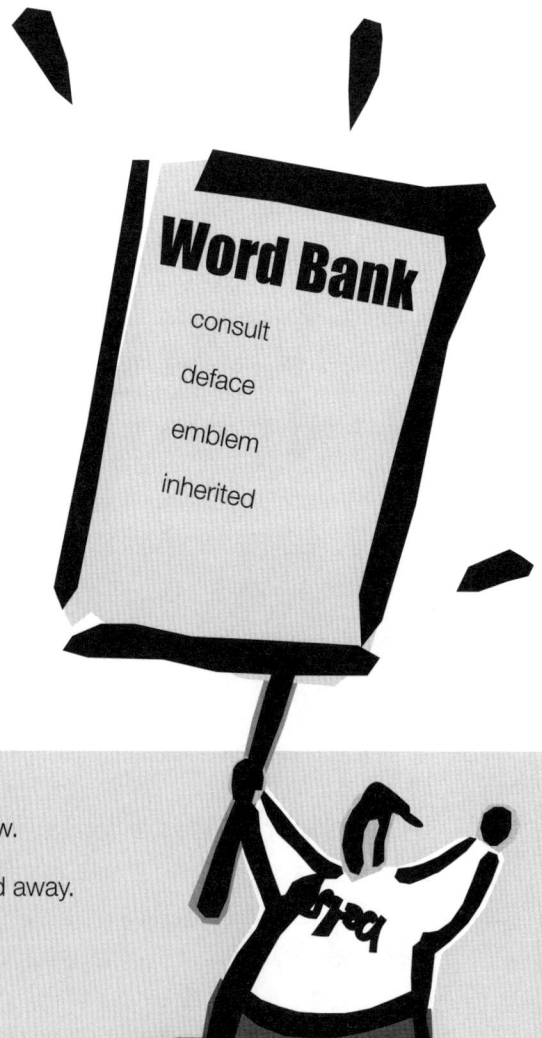

Answer Key — Answer Key — Answer Key   **Batman** vs. **Iron Man**

45

©2008 PRINCIPLE WOODS, INC. Removal of copyright notice and copying are violations of Federal Law.

Unit 2 — Answer Key — Answer Key — Answer Key

Authentic Assessment

Students will create a comic strip based on the unit "Batman vs. Iron Man." This activity combines the authentic components of writing, symbolic thinking, and creativity linked to the comprehension of a written text. Students will be given access to examples of comic strips and should discuss some of the elements included in creating a well-planned comic strip.

Instructions for Creative Story

1. **Prompt.** Students will be given the following prompt: "Imagine that you are a superhero attempting to save the world. Write and illustrate a comic strip based on your adventures."

2. **Story plan.** Before students begin the comic strips, they should brainstorm story ideas. Storylines should be interesting and informative but simple enough to take up only six panels. Students may use information from the unit "Batman vs. Iron Man" and may research other comics for more information. Students should write a draft of their story and submit it to the teacher for approval. Here are a few questions students might want to address in the stories:
   a. What is your background?
   b. What special abilities do you have?
   c. What is your costume?
   d. Who are your enemies or villains?
   e. What are your flaws?
   f. Who needs your help?

3. **Comic strip planner.** After the story is approved, students may begin planning the comic strip. They should completely fill in the comic strip planner provided. Following are items to consider when planning a comic:
   a. What do you want the caption to express?
   b. What action is occurring, and who is involved?
   c. How can you make the transition from one panel to another?

4. **Comic strip.** Once the comic strip planner is completed and approved, students may begin working on their actual comic strip. Text and illustrations included must effectively tell the story written in the story plan. Students may be given the option to create their comic strips on the computer by using software.

5. **Assessment.** The comic strip will be assessed with the rubric from the following page.

Answer Key — Answer Key — Answer Key **Batman vs. Iron Man**

Comic Strip Planner

Scene	Actions Occurring	Characters Present	Background	Caption
1				
2				
3				
4				
5				
6				

Comic Strip Rubric

Requirement	8–10 Points	4–7 Points	0–3 Points	Points Earned
Story Plan	The student creates an interesting and informative story plan that is well written.	The student creates a story plan that lacks some interest or information.	The student does not create a story plan, or the plan is incomplete.	
Comic Strip Planner	The student fully completes each element of the comic strip planner.	The student completes most elements of the comic strip planner.	The student does not complete the comic strip planner or completes only a small portion.	
Comic Strip	The comic strip is neatly drawn/written, with no errors in spelling, punctuation, or grammar.	The comic strip is neatly drawn/written, with a few errors in spelling, punctuation, or grammar.	The comic strip is not completed, is difficult to read, or has many errors in spelling, punctuation, or grammar.	
Content	The comic strip tells a complete story and follows it through an adventure.	The comic strip tells a story that is mostly complete and follows it through an adventure.	The comic strip does not tell a complete story and does not include a fluid adventure.	

©2008 PRINCIPLE WOODS, INC. Removal of copyright notice and copying are violations of Federal Law.

— Unit 3 —
Image : UNattainable
Reading Instructional Guide for High-Interest Article

BEFORE READING

Front-Loading Background Knowledge through Read Aloud/Think Aloud

Search the Internet for recent articles on health and body image and use them to model the effective habits of readers through a Read Aloud/Think Aloud.

Check out articles at the following websites to determine if they would be appropriate for your RATA:

- United States Department of Agriculture. MyPyramid.gov. http://www.mypyramid.gov/.
- The Nemours Foundation. "Eating Disorders: Anorexia and Bulimia." *TeensHealth*. http://www.kidshealth.org/teen/your_mind/mental_health/eat_disorder.html.

(Please keep in mind that it is the responsibility of the teacher to determine if articles from suggested sites are appropriate. The sites may have changed content since this publication. The publisher takes no responsibility for the current content of the site.)

Looking at the Words

Determining How the Word Sounds (Phonics)
Using the Syllable Guide and the Reading Instructional Guide Template found in the beginning of the book, follow the steps to help students learn how to break a word into manageable parts.

Determining What the Word Means (Vocabulary)

Words to Study	Breaking into Syllables	Short Definition
alter	al-ter	(v.) to change
analyze	an-a-lyze	(v.) to examine closely
endorse	en-dorse	(v.) to support
frantically	fran-ti-cal-ly	(adv.) excitedly or rapidly
intense	in-tense	(adj.) showing extreme effort
project	pro-ject	(v.) to communicate or convey
sculpt	sculpt	(v.) to shape
unattainable	un-at-tain-a-ble	(adj.) impossible to achieve

Activating Background Knowledge

Anticipation Guide
Have students mark each of the following statements True or False:

1. ____ Being too thin can hurt someone's health as much as being overweight can.

2. ____ Body mass index is a formula used to count daily calories.

Answer Key — Answer Key — Answer Key   Image : UNattainable

3. ____ The bodies of celebrities and athletes do not influence the way people view their own bodies

4. ____ A person's heart can be affected by improper eating.

5. ____ Fashion designers have made attempts to discourage models from eating improperly.

Starter Questions
After completing the Anticipation Guide, have a group or class discussion with the students using the following questions:

1. What is body mass index (BMI)?

2. What are some improper methods athletes have used to lose weight?

3. Who is Luisel Ramos?

4. What body type does society tend to associate with celebrities?

5. What do Jennifer Hudson and America Ferrera have in common?

Make a prediction about what you think the article will be about.

DURING READING
Use the Reading Instructional Guide Template found in the front of the book.

AFTER READING

Discussion Starter Questions

1. Why do you think our society continually focuses on the physical image of an individual?

2. How could athletes assist with promoting healthier body types?

3. Should the fashion industry across the world be encouraged to comply with the standards set forth by fashion shows in Madrid? Why or why not?

4. To prevent future health problems, how can we educate society on eating disorders and improper dieting techniques?

5. What role does the media play in the way we view body image? How can we use the media to assist with promoting healthier body images?

Teacher Reflection

Use the Reading Instructional Guide Template found in the front of the book.

Image : UNattainable

Sometimes it seems that there isn't much a celebrity can do to please the public when it comes to her body. Newspapers and television shows say she's either too big or too thin. Every inch of her body is analyzed and criticized. Is this fair? Should someone in the spotlight expect this? Does the attention given to the bodies of celebrities give the rest of us unrealistic goals?

Recently, actress Jennifer Love Hewitt was criticized by the media after pictures of her on vacation were printed with hurtful comments. Hewitt was celebrating her engagement in Hawaii when a photographer caught a shot of her in a bathing suit. The photo showed that her body isn't perfectly sculpted. In reality, Hewitt is an attractive woman who has done modeling in the past. She was caught in a private moment at an unfavorable angle. However, she didn't just sit back and let the media talk about her. She answered back. She said that the constant criticism of women's bodies was damaging to girls who struggle with their body image. Hewitt serves as a positive example of someone who projects a love for her body just the way it is.

Visit almost any runway show, and the models are much smaller than the average person. The fashion industry endorses an image that is dangerously thin. In fact, many fashion designers do not make clothes bigger than a size 2 or 4. Only a tiny fraction of women would fit into this clothing. Psychologists are afraid that seeing this dangerously thin image may make young women try to copy it, even if it's unhealthy. In fact, research suggests that seeing these thin images can add to the development of eating disorders such as anorexia and bulimia.

Those in fashion and entertainment aren't the only ones affected. This issue also touches the athletic world. It makes sense that athletes would have healthy appetites because of the amount of energy they use. However, many work out at an intense level but limit what they eat to keep a certain weight. And this problem doesn't affect just girls. This trend is common in wrestling. Wrestlers often starve themselves and exercise frantically before a match weigh-in. Then they eat unhealthy amounts after the match is over. Trying to control the body's natural metabolism this way is dangerous. It can lead to heart problems and even death. In addition, some athletes use steroids and other illegal drugs as a way to improve body

> "The promotion of the [thin] ideal in our culture has created a situation where the majority of girls and women don't like their bodies. And body dissatisfaction can lead girls to participate in very unhealthy behaviors to try to control weight."
>
> —Body-image researcher Sarah Murnen, Professor of Psychology at Kenyon College in Gambier, Ohio

Answer Key — Answer Key — Answer Key

Image : UNattainable

The Skinny on Weight

With television and magazines portraying such extremes of weight, it can be difficult for the average person to identify what "healthy" looks like. Both extremes of weight, too thin and obese, are unhealthy.

Body mass index (BMI) is one way to measure if a person's weight is healthy or not. BMI is determined by a simple formula, but understanding the meaning of a teen's BMI is not as simple as it is for an adult. Because teens continue to grow and develop, doctors consider a teen's gender and age when looking at BMI. Determining if your weight is in the healthy range should be done with the help of your doctor.

The media, and therefore our culture, generally believes that skinny is good and fat is bad. But the line gets shaky when the extremes of either are promoted as something to be achieved.

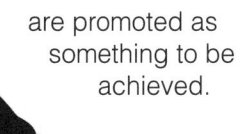

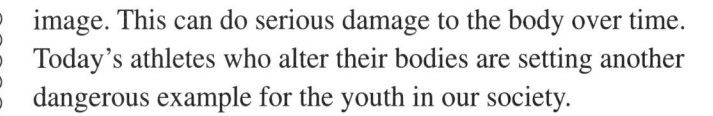

image. This can do serious damage to the body over time. Today's athletes who alter their bodies are setting another dangerous example for the youth in our society.

Recently, things have begun to change. Several fashion companies in Europe have recognized the body image trend as a serious problem. They have made strides to ban thin models. Fashion shows in Madrid have even set some concrete standards. They won't allow models with a body mass index below 18 to participate on the runway. 18 is the mark for malnutrition. This new rule stems from stories such as that of Luisel Ramos. Ramos was a young model from Uruguay who died of heart failure resulting from low weight. Ramos was told by her modeling agency that she would have a better career if she lost weight. She started following a diet of only salads and Diet Coke. Then one day, just moments after leaving the catwalk, she collapsed and died. Tragic stories like this one not only show the dangers of being too thin, but also lead us to think about what body types we should look at as healthy.

Some media outlets have also made an effort to promote "normal" body images, especially among women. Large strides have been made with many actresses such as *Dreamgirls*' Jennifer Hudson and *Ugly Betty*'s America Ferrera. Women like his have proved that beauty comes in all shapes and sizes. And yet the idea still exists that skinniness is a symbol of success, happiness, and control.

If we as a society truly believe that it's what's on the inside that counts, then why do we continue to focus on what's on the outside of ourselves and others? Being healthy, including the way we eat, exercise, and treat our bodies, is important. However, it seems that our culture continues to show body image standards that are unattainable and even dangerous.

Unit 3

Answer Key — Answer Key — Answer Key

Reading Comprehension

After reading "Image: Unattainable," choose the options that best answer questions 1–14.

1. Read this sentence.
   Does the attention given to the bodies of celebrities give the rest of us unrealistic goals?

   What is the meaning of the word *unrealistic* as it is used in the sentence?
   A. true
   B. hopeful
   C. authentic
   D. not practical

2. Read this sentence.
   Some media outlets have also made an effort to promote "normal" body images, especially among women.

   What is the meaning of the word *promote* as it is used in the sentence?
   F. support
   G. sacrifice
   H. contribute
   I. discourage

3. According to the article, why might society's fascination with body image hurt young women and athletes?
   A. Peer pressure may cause others to dress like celebrities and athletes.
   B. Young women and athletes may act like celebrities in order to make friends.
   C. Young women and athletes may take unhealthy measures to try to achieve an ideal body type.
   D. Young women and athletes may follow in the footsteps of some celebrities by using alcohol and drugs.

4. What change did fashion shows in Madrid make to encourage healthier body types?
   F. Models are now encouraged to have a doctor's evaluation prior to modeling.
   G. Models are now required to spend time with a dietician to learn how to eat properly.
   H. Runway models that are considered to be malnourished are no longer allowed to model.
   I. Models now participate in education programs to learn about the consequences of eating disorders.

5. With which statement would the author most likely agree?
   A. Female celebrities and athletes are the only ones who fall victim to eating disorders.
   B. The media does not have an effect on the ideal image that is presented to young women.
   C. Statistics show that there is a decline in the number of people who become victims of eating disorders.
   D. The more society is exposed to impractical body images, the more likely we are to adopt unhealthy eating patterns.

6. The author organizes the article by
   F. presenting research on eating disorders.
   G. describing the problem and presenting examples.
   H. providing an interview with victims of eating disorders.
   I. illustrating the pros and cons of modeling in our society.

52

©2008 PRINCIPLE WOODS, INC. Removal of copyright notice and copying are violations of Federal Law.

Answer Key — Answer Key — Answer Key

Image: UNattainable

7. Why does the author include Jennifer Hudson and America Ferrera in this article?
   A. to inspire others to go into acting
   B. to explain that they are from the same hometown
   C. to demonstrate that beauty does not require having a thin body
   D. to discuss two successful actresses who have won several awards

8. If the article were published in a newspaper, what would be the most informative headline?
   F. Time to Eat Better
   G. An Athlete's Quest
   H. The Life of a Celebrity
   I. Suffering from Society's Standards

9. What is the tone of this article?
   A. serious
   B. amused
   C. sarcastic
   D. very angry

10. Why do some wrestlers starve themselves prior to beginning a match?
    F. They are unable to handle the anxiety of competing.
    G. They feel they are overweight and are unhappy with their physical appearance.
    H. They feel they can perform better in a wrestling event if they have an empty stomach.
    I. They stop eating before weighing in to make sure they are allowed to compete in a competition.

11. What comparison does the author make between wrestlers and models?
    A. Wrestlers are healthier than models.
    B. Both wrestling and modeling require hard work.
    C. Both wrestlers and models alter their bodies at the expense of good health.
    D. Wrestlers actually have a more valid reason for starving themselves and altering their body image.

12. Which statement about body mass index (BMI) is LEAST accurate?
    F. Gender is not a factor in calculating BMI.
    G. A doctor should be involved in discussing a teen's BMI.
    H. Malnutrition is indicated when a person's BMI falls below 18.
    I. BMI measures whether a person's weight is in the healthy range.

13. People who read this article will learn
    A. how to help someone who has an eating disorder.
    B. how athletes are handling the stress of competing.
    C. to understand the symptoms of an eating disorder and how to confront a friend with the problem.
    D. that celebrities, athletes, and models are just some of the people in our society who are affected by eating disorders.

14. According to this article, why do many girls feel unhappy about their physical appearance?
    F. Young girls continually feel peer pressure to be thin.
    G. Being thin is heavily advertised in our society, so young girls feel they need to maintain that image.
    H. Young girls are athletic and therefore feel they need to be thin in order to perform well in various sporting events.
    I. Young girls become upset when they cannot fit into some of the designer clothes that appear in fashion magazines.

©2008 PRINCIPLE WOODS, INC. Removal of copyright notice and copying are violations of Federal Law.

Unit 3 — **Answer Key — Answer Key — Answer Key**

Reading Strategy

Directions: Choose three of the most important ideas from the body of the article. Use the ice cream scoops below to organize those ideas to help identify the topic and main idea of the article. Use the space under each spoon to list supporting details for each of the ideas.

Idea #3: Athletes also set a dangerous example by altering their bodies.

Idea #2: The fashion & entertainment world portrays unhealthy body types.

Idea #1: The public analyzes and criticizes celebrities' bodies.

Topic: Body image

Supporting Details for Idea #3
- intense workouts and limiting what they eat to maintain weight
- affects males and females, especially male wrestlers
- weigh-in weight and binge eating
- steroids and other illegal drugs

Supporting Details for Idea #2
- dangerously thin models
- clothes no bigger than size 4
- thin image from media could create eating disorders (anorexia or bulimia)

Supporting Details for Idea #1
- media criticism of Hewitt's bathing suit photo
- says media comments damaging to girls
- role model of healthy body image
- projects a love for her body just the way it is

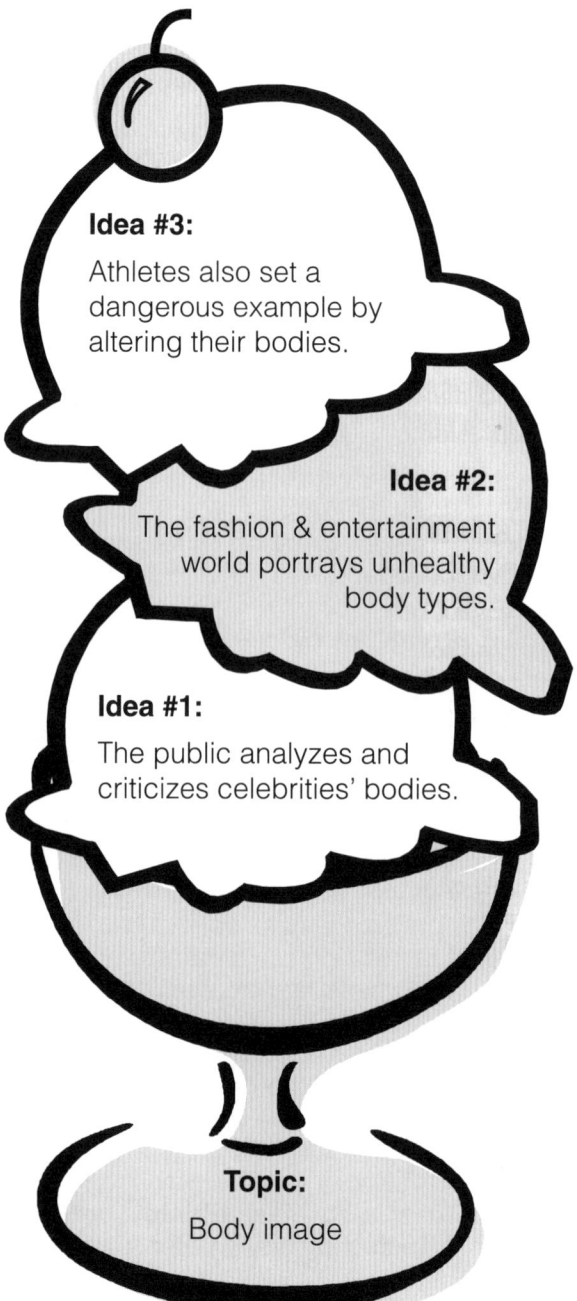

Write a one-sentence summary of the overall main idea of the article in the space below.
Our culture shows body image standards that are unattainable and even dangerous.

Answer Key — Answer Key — Answer Key Image : UNattainable

Interpreting the Data

PART I

Which group in the population has the biggest issues with body weight?

Body mass index (BMI) is the relationship between a person's height and weight. It can be used to determine if someone is at a healthy or unhealthy weight. Table 1 includes information on people 18 years of age and over and their BMIs.

Table 1. Percentage of the population at given body mass index ranges in 2004

Group	Under-weight (<18.5)	Healthy weight (18.5–24.9)	Above healthy weight — Total	Over-weight (25.0–29.9)	Obese (≥30)
Total (includes all races and ethnicities)	1.8	32.9	65.3	33.7	31.6
Age					
18 to 44 years old	2.7	38.0	59.3	29.5	29.8
45 to 64 years old	(B)	26.0	73.1	37.2	35.9
65 to 74 years old	(B)	25.5	74.0	39.4	34.6
75 years and over	0.8	33.3	65.9	42.4	23.5
Gender					
Male	1.5	28.5	69.9	39.2	30.7
Female	2.0	36.6	61.5	28.7	32.8
Gender and race/ethnicity					
Not Hispanic or Latino:					
White, male	1.5	27.8	70.7	39.6	31.1
White, female	2.2	39.2	58.6	28.4	30.2
Black alone or African-American, male	(B)	31.3	67.0	33.7	33.3
Black alone or African-American, female	(B)	18.3	80.3	27.3	53.0
Mexican or Mexican-American, male	(B)	26.3	73.4	42.0	31.4
Mexican or Mexican-American, female	(B)	27.2	72.1	32.6	39.5

15. Which race/gender combination has the largest percentage of underweight members?
    A. White male
    B. White female
    C. Black/African-American male
    D. Black/African-American female

16. According to the data, which age group appears to be the healthiest?
    A. 18 to 44 years old
    B. 45 to 64 years old
    C. 65 to 74 years old
    D. 75 years and over

©2008 PRINCIPLE WOODS, INC. Removal of copyright notice and copying are violations of Federal Law.

Answer Key — Answer Key — Answer Key
Unit 3

17. Circle the letter of the pie graph that correctly illustrates the percentages of total people in the categories of underweight, healthy weight, and above healthy weight as shown in Table 1.

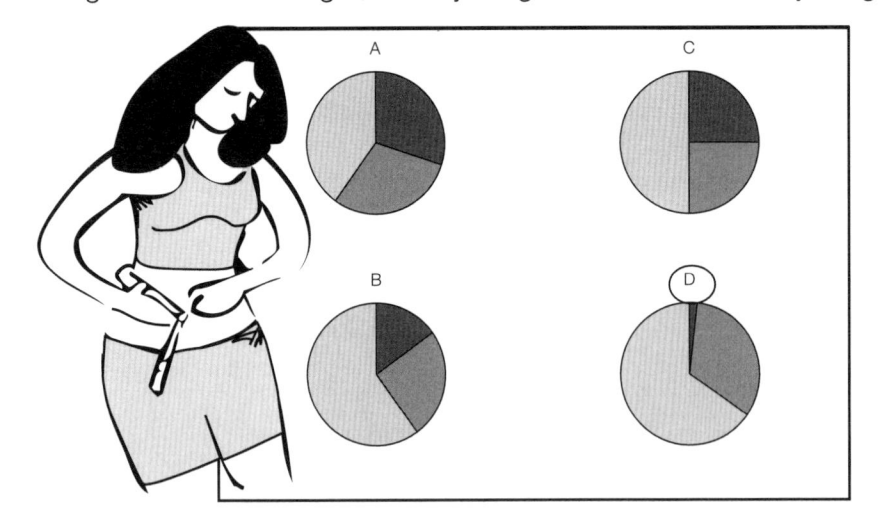

   (D is circled)

   - Underweight
   - Healthy weight
   - Above healthy weight

18. Study Table 1, focusing especially on gender and age. Based on the data, which group appears to be the unhealthiest? Use data to explain your answer.

   COMPREHEND ANALYZE EVALUATE

   Student answers could contain facts such as the following:

   Males and people ages 45 to 74 appear to be the unhealthiest. According to the table, 69.9% of males are above a healthy weight and 1.5% are below a healthy weight, for a total of 71.4% outside the healthy range. That is nearly 8% more than females. By comparison, 59.3% of people ages 18 to 44 are over a healthy weight, and 2.7% are under a healthy weight, for a total of 62% outside the healthy range. That is over 10% lower than either of the next two age groups listed, which are around the 73–74% range.

   Use the extended-response rubric to reference the criteria required for an acceptable answer and to determine the points to award.

PART II

Is there a correlation between the amount of soda we as a country have consumed over the last 25 years and the increasing amount of overweight people in our country?

Figure 1 shows bar graphs that illustrate the number of states with given percentages of people that are considered obese (extremely overweight). In 1995, for instance, 27 states had a population in which 15%–19% of their people were obese and 23 of the states had a population in which 10%–14% of their citizens were obese.

Answer Key — Answer Key — Answer Key   Image : UNattainable

Figure 1. Number of states with certain percentages of their populations considered obese (1985–2000)

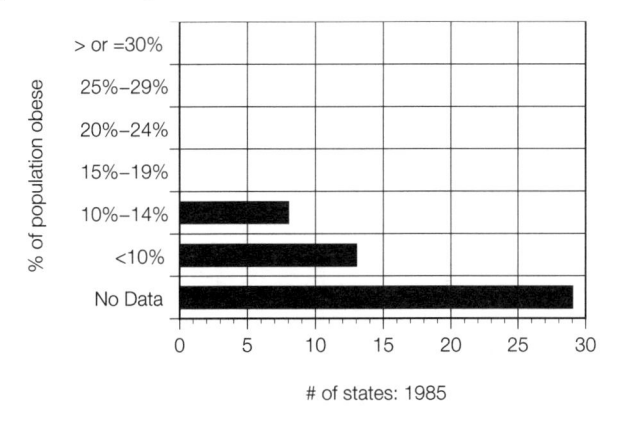

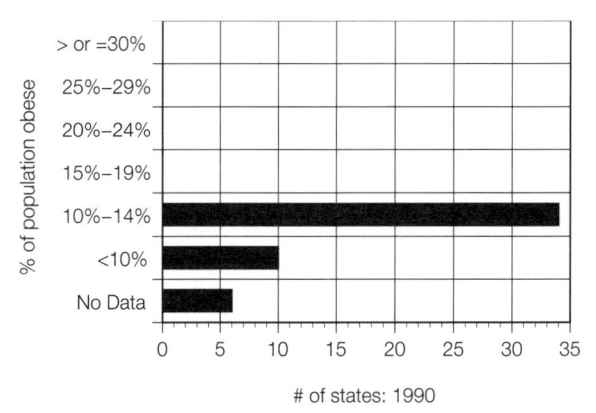

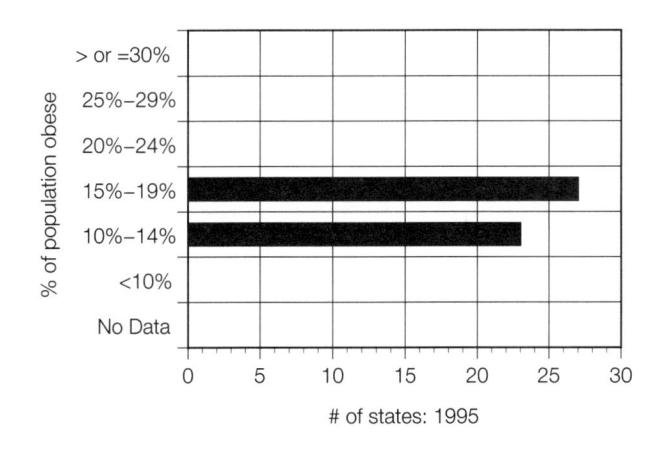

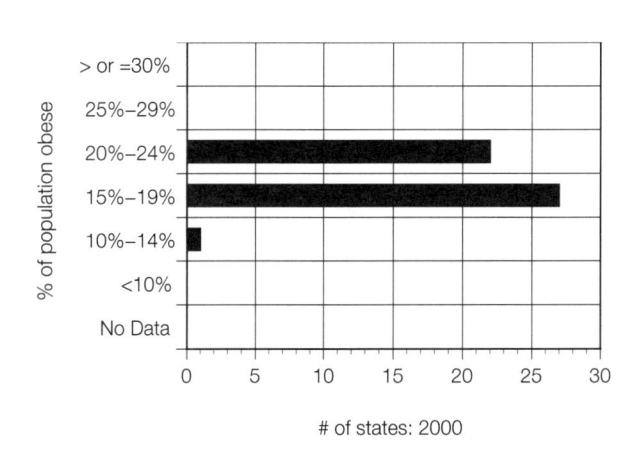

1985: No Data ≈ 29; <10% ≈ 13; 10%–14% ≈ 8.

1990: No Data ≈ 6; <10% ≈ 10; 10%–14% ≈ 34.

1995: 10%–14% ≈ 23; 15%–19% ≈ 27.

2000: 10%–14% ≈ 1; 15%–19% ≈ 27; 20%–24% ≈ 22.

19. Which of the following statements is most correct based on the data in Figure 1?
    A. There were more overweight citizens in 1995 than in 2000.
    B. Overall, citizens in the United States are becoming healthier as time passes.
    C. Overall, states had more citizens that were obese in 2000 than in any other year.
    D. There were nearly 35 states with obese citizens in 1990 compared with only about 25 in 2000.

Figure 2. Number of states with certain percentages of their populations considered obese (2005)

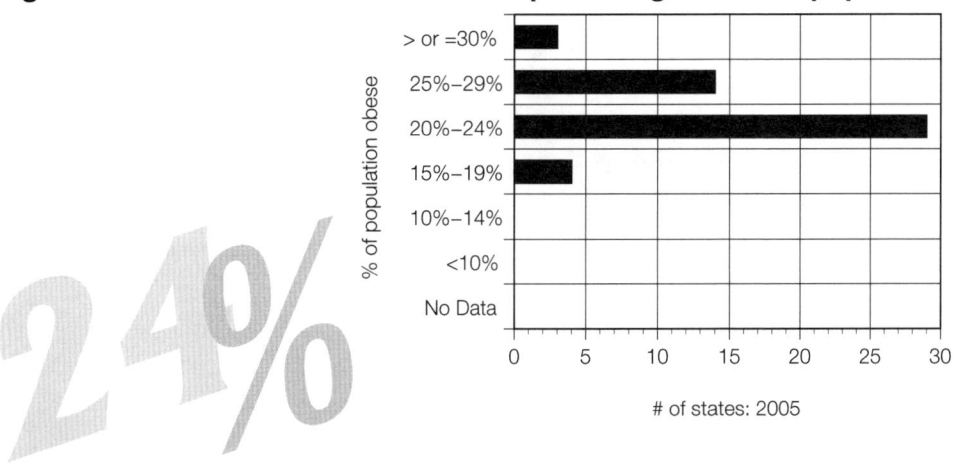

2005: 15%–19% ≈ 4; 20%–24% ≈ 29; 25%–29% ≈ 14; >or =30% ≈ 3.

©2008 PRINCIPLE WOODS, INC. Removal of copyright notice and copying are violations of Federal Law.

Unit 3 — *Answer Key — Answer Key — Answer Key*

20. In Figure 2, look at the number of states in which 15%–19% of their populations were considered obese in 2005 and compare it with 2000 from Figure 1. Determine if the bar graphs indicate that the population of the United States is getting less obese or more obese. Explain your answer.

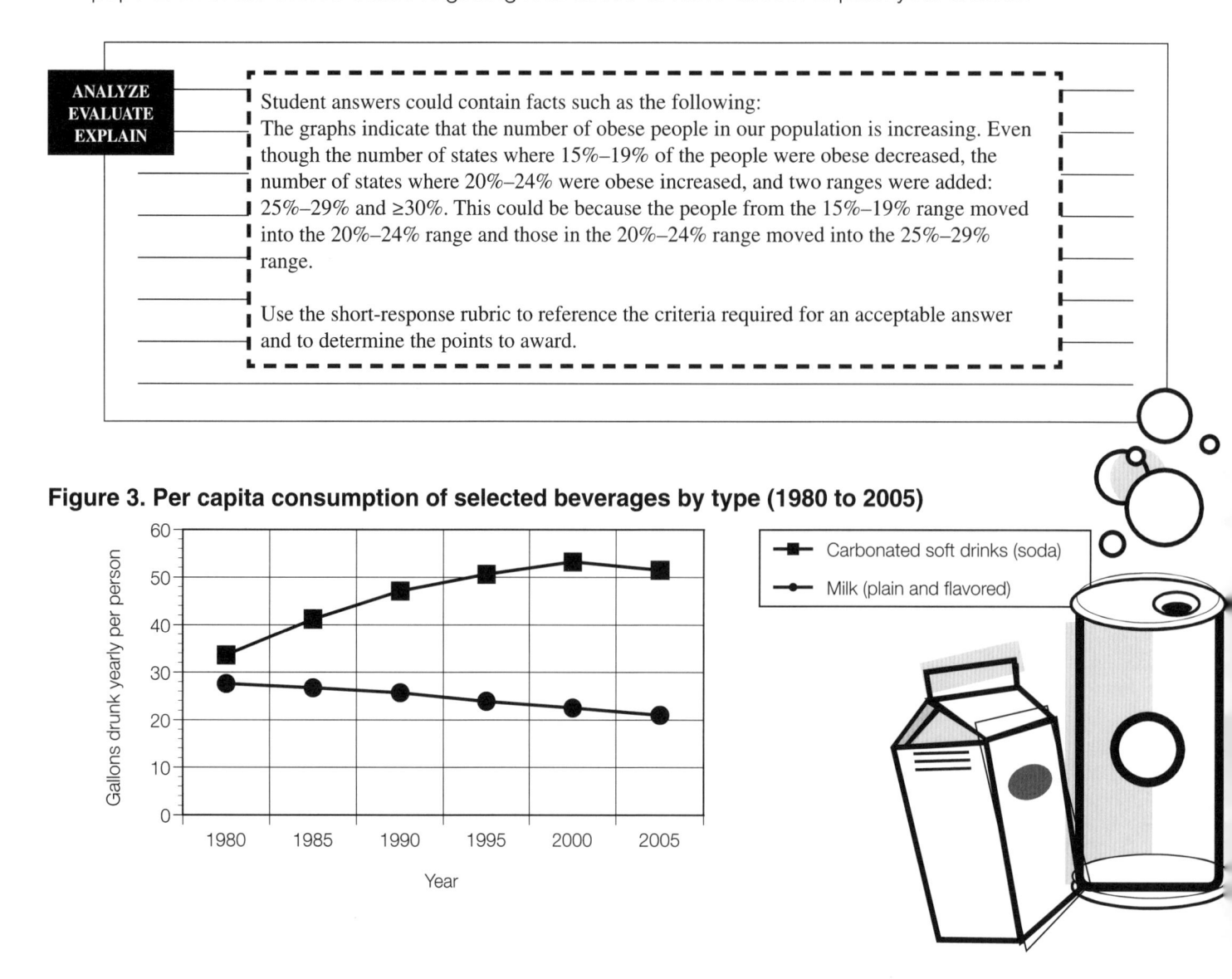

ANALYZE EVALUATE EXPLAIN

Student answers could contain facts such as the following:
The graphs indicate that the number of obese people in our population is increasing. Even though the number of states where 15%–19% of the people were obese decreased, the number of states where 20%–24% were obese increased, and two ranges were added: 25%–29% and ≥30%. This could be because the people from the 15%–19% range moved into the 20%–24% range and those in the 20%–24% range moved into the 25%–29% range.

Use the short-response rubric to reference the criteria required for an acceptable answer and to determine the points to award.

Figure 3. Per capita consumption of selected beverages by type (1980 to 2005)

21. According to Figure 3, what has happened to the amount of soda drunk per person over the last 25 years compared to the amount of milk?

    A. The amount of soda drunk has decreased while the amount of milk drunk has increased.

    B. The amount of soda drunk has increased while the amount of milk drunk has decreased.

    C. The amount of soda drunk has increased while the amount of milk drunk has stayed the same.

    D. The amount of soda drunk has stayed the same while the amount of milk drunk has decreased.

58

©2008 PRINCIPLE WOODS, INC. Removal of copyright notice and copying are violations of Federal Law.

Answer Key — Answer Key — Answer Key

Image : UNattainable

22. Compare Figures 1 through 3. What correlation can you make between the number of overweight people in our country and the amount of soft drinks consumed yearly? Use data to explain your answer.

ANALYZE EVALUATE EXPLAIN

Student answers could contain facts such as the following:
Over the period shown, the country has increased in the amount of soda consumed and in the number of obese people. When these two factors are looked at in isolation, one could conclude that as we drink more soda, we are becoming unhealthier. (The teacher may want to point out that there is no specific cause-and-effect relationship proven here, but there does appear to be a correlation. The teacher could also discuss the implication of drinking more soda and less milk. Maybe we are taking less care of ourselves as a whole, thus resulting in the increase in unhealthy weight levels.)

Use the short-response rubric to reference the criteria required for an acceptable answer and to determine the points to award.

Reflect and Respond

23. Think of a famous celebrity that you like, and think about why you like that person. What are at least three things you like better about yourself? Using those three characteristics, tell why it is better for you to be who you are than to be that celebrity.

Reflect & Respond

Answers may vary, but students should address each part of the question. The question is meant to elicit strong classroom conversation about character. Students should be able to demonstrate an ability to find valuable characteristics in themselves.

Use the character education rubric to reference the criteria and number of points to award.

Unit 3 — *Answer Key — Answer Key — Answer Key*

Reading Instructional Guide for Technical Extension

BEFORE READING

Looking at the Words

Determining How the Word Sounds (Phonics)
Technical texts often necessitate the use of multisyllabic words that are unfamiliar to students. Use the Syllable Guide to help students decode any words they might have trouble reading.

Determining What the Word Means (Vocabulary)

Words to Study	Breaking into Syllables	Short Definition
calculation	cal-cu-la-tion	(n.) determination of something using mathematical methods
circumstance	cir-cum-stance	(n.) a condition or fact to be considered
interpret	in-ter-pret	(v.) to bring out the meaning
nutrient	nu-tri-ent	(n.) a source of nourishment
psychological	psy-cho-log-i-cal	(adj.) mental

Activating Background Knowledge

Graphic Organizer
Either individually or in groups, students may brainstorm about body mass index (BMI), recalling anything previously learned and any prior experience with the subject. Next, encourage students to see the relationships between their ideas by having them complete the KWHL (what you know, what you want to learn, how can you learn it, what you learned) to demonstrate what they already know about how body mass index is calculated and used to help people.

Body Mass Index (BMI)

What do you already know about BMI?	What do you want to learn about BMI?	How can you find more information about BMI?	What did you learn about BMI?

©2008 PRINCIPLE WOODS, INC. Removal of copyright notice and copying are violations of Federal Law.

Answer Key — Answer Key — Answer Key

Image : UNattainable

Starter Questions
After completing the Graphic Organizer, generate a group or class discussion to come up with questions about the subject, a prediction about the article, and at least one learning goal. The first question has been provided for you.

Question: How do you determine what a healthy body weight is?

Question: _____

Prediction: _____

Goal: _____

DURING READING
Use the Reading Instructional Guide Template found in the front of the book.

AFTER READING
After reading, you may teach reading strategy use by giving students opportunities to do the following:
- Review, paraphrase, and summarize
- Participate in main-idea discussions by describing the information in their own words
- Reflect on concept maps and generate additional discussion starter questions based on the mappings
- Participate in small-group discussions using discussion starter questions

Discussion Starter Questions

The first question has been provided for you.

1. What advice would you give a friend or classmate who is struggling with his/her weight and needs to know where to seek help?

2. _____

3. _____

©2008 PRINCIPLE WOODS, INC. Removal of copyright notice and copying are violations of Federal Law.

Unit 3

Answer Key — Answer Key — Answer Key

Technical Extension

Whose Body Is It?

What is a healthy weight for you? Do you know? You can find dozens of articles about celebrities who strive for a body image that is lean and thin, but what is "normal" for ordinary people? Many young people struggle each day with the unrealistic and often unhealthy images put out by the media. Some practical information would be helpful.

Body mass index (BMI) is a good place to start for anyone who falls into the trap of comparing themselves to models and celebs. This calculation uses a person's height and weight to estimate how much fat the body contains. A table then shows if the person falls within the normal range. Most doctors will answer questions and help determine BMI as well as develop a healthy eating plan. Doctors would rather work with patients to set goals than see them in the hospital after they develop an eating disorder. So teens shouldn't be shy about asking an adult to set an appointment with a doctor or health clinic to get started.

Calculating BMI starts with a measurement of a person's weight and height. The results of a BMI are interpreted differently for teens than they are for adults. It's normal and healthy for teens to go through periods of time when there is sudden rapid growth. Their bodies are also producing hormones that affect muscle growth, fat, and bone density. During this time of life, an average person can grow as much as 10 inches before reaching adult height! Rates of growth are also different for boys and girls, as well as for individuals. Two best friends who are the same height might have a different weight, yet both could still be in the "normal" range.

Once BMI is figured, the next step is to discuss the results with someone who knows how to interpret them. This process considers individual body type and circumstances. Again, a doctor is a good place to start, so teens shouldn't feel uncomfortable asking. A nurse at school may also be able to suggest someone qualified to help, like a dietician or nutritionist. Many of these sources of help are free or low cost. The most important thing in the whole process is to focus on a healthy lifestyle for each individual person. People should not focus on the lifestyle of celebrities who may also be unsatisfied with the way they look.

If a doctor does recommend losing weight in order to be healthy, there are easy ways to start. Most Americans eat larger portions of food compared to other people around the world. Just cutting back on the amount of each item eaten can result in weight loss without much work. Teens need to eat at least 1600 calories from a variety of foods each day to maintain a level of healthy nutrients in the body, so it's not safe to go below that level. Exercise is also effective. A toned

©2008 PRINCIPLE WOODS, INC. Removal of copyright notice and copying are violations of Federal Law.

Answer Key — Answer Key — Answer Key

Image : UNattainable

Anorexia affects your whole body

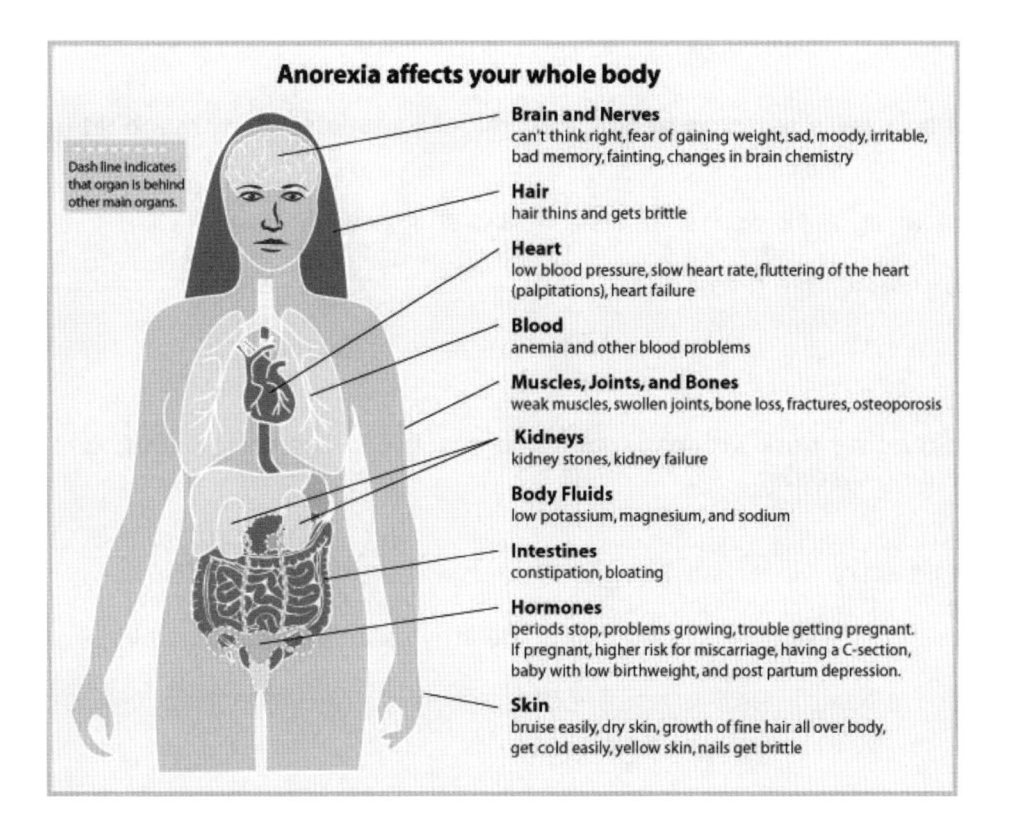

Dash line indicates that organ is behind other main organs.

Brain and Nerves
can't think right, fear of gaining weight, sad, moody, irritable, bad memory, fainting, changes in brain chemistry

Hair
hair thins and gets brittle

Heart
low blood pressure, slow heart rate, fluttering of the heart (palpitations), heart failure

Blood
anemia and other blood problems

Muscles, Joints, and Bones
weak muscles, swollen joints, bone loss, fractures, osteoporosis

Kidneys
kidney stones, kidney failure

Body Fluids
low potassium, magnesium, and sodium

Intestines
constipation, bloating

Hormones
periods stop, problems growing, trouble getting pregnant. If pregnant, higher risk for miscarriage, having a C-section, baby with low birthweight, and post partum depression.

Skin
bruise easily, dry skin, growth of fine hair all over body, get cold easily, yellow skin, nails get brittle

body can be achieved by adding a small amount of exercise to the daily routine. You might walk for 10–15 minutes each day or take the stairs instead of an elevator.

Teens who try too hard to diet may develop conditions like anorexia nervosa and bulimia. These eating disorders can result in long-term harm to the body. They might include the inability to have children, dental problems that cause loss of teeth, and even death. People who lack a strong sense of self-esteem or feel out of control in some way can develop anorexia and bulimia. They are trying to look a certain way whether or not it is realistic for their body type. Or they may feel that controlling their food intake is the only thing they can control in their lives. Once these disorders develop, they are difficult to correct without medical and psychological help.

Simple things can lead to an obsession with weight too. Did you ever wonder why you often have to buy different sizes of clothing during the same trip to the mall? Clothing manufacturers have no standard for the sizing of clothing. Some of them have found creative ways to make sure their customers feel good about themselves while shopping in their stores. One shopper may wear a size 4 in Gap jeans, for example, but those same jeans would be labeled a size 6 in other stores. So customers may believe that size 4 is the ideal size and then do whatever it takes to maintain that small body type when the sizing measurements are not consistent!

Celebrity watching will always be a source of entertainment, but we all need to be aware that Hollywood is a different world. It's one that is the subject of extreme media attention. Our first concern must be to stay healthy, both for today and for our future. We can do this by being aware of what is truly normal at each stage of our lives and then having a healthy plan to maintain or reach those goals.

Unit 3 — *Answer Key — Answer Key — Answer Key*

Reading Comprehension

After reading "Whose Body Is It?" choose the options that best answer questions 1–11.

1. Read this sentence.
   This calculation uses a person's height and weight to estimate how much fat the body contains.

   What is the meaning of the word *estimate* as it is used in this sentence?
   A. to weigh an item precisely
   B. to make an educated guess
   C. to determine the exact cost of an item
   D. to compute the size of an object or item by using its measurements

2. Read this sentence.
   Doctors would rather work with patients to set goals than see them in the hospital after they develop an eating disorder.

   According to this sentence, doctors
   F. don't treat people with eating disorders who are in hospitals.
   G. know that most teens with eating disorders will eventually be in a hospital.
   H. would prefer to teach people how to be healthy rather than to treat illnesses like anorexia or bulimia.
   I. are unable to determine whether a specific person has an eating disorder based on the person's BMI and psychological profile.

3. According to this article, why is body mass index (BMI) a useful tool in determining how to stay healthy?
   A It takes a person's age into consideration.
   B. It provides a starting point in building healthy eating habits.
   C. It doesn't require any specific knowledge to interpret the results.
   D. BMI calculations factor in an eating plan for each individual person.

4. BMI results are interpreted differently for teens because
   F. teens' bodies are still developing.
   G. adults don't have changes in their hormonal levels.
   H. bone density calculations are important only for adults.
   I. a person's rate of growth isn't a factor at any stage of life.

5. The author organizes the article by
   A. outlining various scientific methods of weighing our bodies.
   B. explaining that BMI as the most important way to determine overall health.
   C. focusing on anorexia and bulimia and outlining their effects on a person's body.
   D. discussing BMI as an accurate method for teens to know what is healthy for them as individuals.

6. What is the main idea of this article?
   F. Celebrities don't know about tools like BMI.
   G. Eating disorders are the result of not using a tool such as BMI.
   H. Teenagers need to have realistic information about normal body size for healthy people.
   I. The clothing industry helps people of all ages, but especially teens, feel comfortable with their body type.

Answer Key — Answer Key — Answer Key   Image : UNattainable

7. Why do some clothing stores purposely label their sizes smaller than other stores?
   A. Their customers demand it.
   B. They want to make their customers believe they wear smaller sizes.
   C. The clothing manufacturers could not agree on standards for various sizes.
   D. Some American clothing companies use foreign measurements to encourage their customers to wear smaller sizes.

8. What is true of BOTH anorexia and bulimia?
   F. Long-term harm can result from both.
   G. BMI is unimportant in diagnosing either disorder.
   H. Bulimia has more negative results on the human body.
   I. Anorexia is an eating disorder that results from low self-esteem, while bulimia comes from feeling out of control.

9. Which statement about BMI is LEAST accurate?
   A. Anorexia and bulimia can have long-term effects on your body.
   B. Your BMI today will help you determine an eating plan for every stage of your life.
   C. An average person needs to eat about 1600 calories a day from various food groups to maintain health.
   D. Teenagers sometimes attempt to look like their favorite celebrities even if it leads to unhealthy eating habits.

10. According to the text box "Anorexia affects your whole body," which statement is NOT true?
    F. Bones are not affected by anorexia.
    G. Fainting is a result of this eating disorder.
    H. Anorexia may cause you to grow hair all over your body.
    I. Anorexia could affect your ability to have children in the future.

11. Based on the information in this article, which of these conclusions is accurate?
    A. Anorexia and bulimia are easily treated.
    B. Celebrities use personal trainers to stay healthy.
    C. Doctors would rather treat a disease than help prevent it.
    D. Teenagers cannot compare their bodies to anyone else's.

©2008 PRINCIPLE WOODS, INC. Removal of copyright notice and copying are violations of Federal Law.

Unit 3 — *Answer Key — Answer Key — Answer Key*

Technical Writing Prompt

12. Imagine that you a college student majoring in psychology. You have just completed a research paper on the psychological impact of unrealistic body images on adolescent girls. Write a persuasive letter to the media explaining the dangers of portraying dangerously thin images to young people. Urge the media to stop portraying ultra-thin body images and explain what they could do to support a healthier body image. Use specific examples from your research (the articles in this unit) as well as your own experience to answer the prompt.

Technical Writing

Student answers may vary.

The student should address the question to the best of his/her ability using the article and personal experience. The question is meant to prepare students to be active citizens who can accurately and effectively use written communication skills.

Use the technical writing rubric to reference the criteria and determine the number of points to award.

Vocational Extension

HELP WANTED:

Fabulous Fitness Spa and Gym is looking for a certified personal trainer to add to our team. Candidates must be at least 18 years old and hold current certification from a qualified organization. Valid CPR certification is also required. Potential team members must be healthy and fit and have the desire to help others achieve their personal fitness goals. To inquire contact Janice @fabulousfitness.com.

Celebrities don't maintain their fit bodies by accident. It takes a great deal of work and is usually done with the help of a personal trainer. Trainers dedicate their lives to teaching people how to stay as healthy as they can be. Celebrities use trainers to stay healthy and thin, but so do teachers, heads of companies, pilots, and folks from any other profession or job that you can imagine. The demand for personal trainers will grow each year as more people look for health, fitness, weight loss, and nutrition information. Could this be the career for you?

The most important requirement is the need to help people. Trainers can make a good income after working a few years, but that won't happen if the trainer doesn't like working with people. Trainers must be kind to all their clients, especially those who are overweight or maintain an unhealthy lifestyle. Clients must stay with a program until they reach their goals. A good trainer will spend time motivating clients and adjusting to their needs. Trainers must also develop personalized maintenance plans to keep their clients healthy and fit.

Fitness professionals must have the knowledge to build an exercise plan and nutrition program for each client. They must constantly update their information and stay current with medical progress that affects fitness and nutrition. This is especially important for those clients who have physical disabilities that must be accommodated.

A college degree is not necessary, although many trainers do obtain degrees in courses of study like health science or sports medicine. However, all trainers must receive professional certification. This is available through a number of organizations and companies. If you are interested in entering this field, you should talk to managers at local gyms and health clubs to find the best certification for your area.

According to the American Council on Exercise, personal trainers can make from $24,000 to $55,000 per year. Salaries can depend on where they live and how many hours they work each day. More than 70% of trainers recently surveyed are paid on an hourly basis. They make $28 to $46 per hour. One drawback of making a living as a personal trainer is the lack of benefits, such as health insurance. Less than 30% of full-time trainers receive any kind of benefits.

If fitness and health are important to you, you might start now by stopping by a local gym or health spa and meeting some personal trainers. They will be able to answer your questions, and they might even help you get started on the path to your future career!

Unit 3 — Answer Key — Answer Key — Answer Key

Looking Forward

13. One of the most important jobs of a personal trainer is motivating someone to strive for his/her best. If you were a personal trainer, you would need to continually observe and meet with your client as well as research new methods to assist your client. Using personal experience and information from the article, devise a plan or system that includes how you would support and motivate your client in order to maximize your client's potential.

> Student answers may vary.
>
> The student should address the question to the best of his/her ability using the article and personal experience. The question is meant to encourage students to explore areas of interest for their future and begin to determine how they will prepare for a future career.
>
> Use the extended-response rubric to reference the criteria and determine the number of points to award.

Ethical Dilemma

14. You are one of several personal trainers at a local health club, and you work individually with a number of regular clients. One of your female clients recently asked you to develop a diet for her with a goal weight that you know is unhealthy. If you refuse, you are sure that she will just go to the other trainers until she finds one who will do what she asks. If you lose this client, you will also lose the income from working with her. Do you develop the diet as she requests? What are some other options?

> Student answers may vary.
>
> The student should address the question to the best of his/her ability using background knowledge from the article as well as personal opinion and experience. The question is meant to encourage students to contemplate scenarios and make ethical decisions.
>
> Use the character education rubric to reference the criteria and number of points to award.

Answer Key — Answer Key — Answer Key   Image : UNattainable

Unit Vocabulary Assessment

Matching
Match each word in Column I to its definition in Column II.

Column I

<u> C </u> 1. unattainable
<u> D </u> 2. calculation
<u> A </u> 3. intense
<u> B </u> 4. nutrient

Column II

a. showing extreme effort
b. a source of nourishment
c. impossible to achieve
d. a determination using mathematics

Multiple Choice
Choose the word that MOST NEARLY replaces the underlined word in each sentence.

5. To serve in the military, you must pass a psychological exam.
   A. mental
   B. science
   C. physical
   D. weapons

6. The mother searched frantically for her missing child.
   A. slowly
   B. carefully
   C. excitedly
   D. methodically

7. She went to the gym three times a week in order to sculpt her body.
   A. know
   B. shape
   C. detail
   D. secure

8. There are several circumstances where keeping a secret isn't acceptable.
   A. areas
   B. series
   C. productions
   D. occurrences

9. We analyzed the poem to fully understand its meaning.
   A. read
   B. wrote
   C. recited
   D. examined

Word Bank

alter

endorse

interpret

project

Fill in the Blank
Choose a word from the word bank to fill in the blank in the sentence below.

10. Because of the new weekend schedule, we had to **alter** our plans.

11. President Bush will **endorse** John McCain as his potential successor.

12. Julia will **project** her love for the environment at the demonstration.

13. How do you make meaning of the numbers and **interpret** the results of the election?

Unit 3 — Answer Key — Answer Key — Answer Key

Authentic Assessment

Students will create a personal nutrition and exercise plan based on the unit "Image: Unattainable." This activity combines the authentic components of research and analysis linked to the comprehension of a written text. Creating a plan will help students identify personal habits while reflecting on health and wellness in their lives.

Instructions for Creating a Nutrition and Exercise Plan

1. **Samples.** Students will be given a sample of the food pyramid to view (see resource list). Then they will look at sample daily exercise options (see resource list).

2. **Journal.** Students will create a health and wellness journal to record the evolution of their plan. The journal should have each of the components listed below. See below for specific requirements of each section.

    a. Food pyramid
    b. Daily food intake
    c. Daily exercise
    d. Plan for wellness
    e. Reflection

3. **Food pyramid.** The food pyramid will be provided by the teacher. Students should graph the pyramid on a pie chart, estimating the percentages of each of the food groups.

4. **Daily food intake and exercise.** Students should spend at least one day journaling their food intake and any exercise that takes place. These should be neatly charted. Students should take care to represent a typical day in their lives.

5. **Plan for wellness.** Students should create a food plan and exercise plan to live a well-balanced life. A sample food plan should include a one-day menu for each meal of the day. The exercise plan should include what exercise will take place, where it will take place, and how long it will last.

6. **Reflection.** Students should write a short response for each of the questions below. Instruct them to write the question before the response and answer using information from the activity, the unit, and personal experience or opinion.

    a. If your current food intake journal doesn't match up to the food pyramid, what can you do to change that?
    b. Why is it important to learn to eat and exercise responsibly?
    c. What might happen if you make poor health decisions as a teenager?
    d. What might happen if you make poor health decisions as an adult?
    e. Do you think that most young adults seriously consider eating and exercising well?

7. **Assessment.** The plan will be assessed using the rubric on the following page.

Answer Key — Answer Key — Answer Key Image : UNattainable

Resource List

United States Department of Agriculture:
http://www.mypyramid.gov/

The Food Guide:
http://www.kidshealth.org/kid/stay_healthy/food/pyramid.html

Exercise and Teens:
http://life.familyeducation.com/teen/exercise/29461.html

Information for Teens:
http://www.kidshealth.org/PageManager.jsp?dn=familydoctor&lic=44&article_set=20488

Nutrition and Exercise Rubric

Requirement	8–10 Points	4–7 Points	0–3 Points	Points Earned
Food Pyramid	The student uses data provided to correctly create a pie graph of the food pyramid.	The student uses data provided to create a pie graph of the food pyramid but makes a few mistakes.	The student either does not create a pie graph or makes up data to create an incorrect pie graph.	
Daily Student Food Intake and Exercise	The student completely and neatly keeps a record.	The student nearly completely or somewhat neatly keeps a record.	The student does not keep a record.	
Plan for Wellness	The student creates an accurate and thoughtful wellness plan.	The student creates a wellness plan that is moderately thought-out and accurate.	The student either does not create a wellness plan or does not put thought into it.	
Reflection	The reflection thoughtfully and clearly answers all of the questions.	The reflection is thoughtful but incomplete.	The reflection is missing or mostly incomplete.	

©2008 PRINCIPLE WOODS, INC. Removal of copyright notice and copying are violations of Federal Law.

Unit 4
Circle of Friends

High-Interest Article for Reading Instructional Guide

BEFORE READING

Front-Loading Background Knowledge through Read Aloud/Think Aloud

Search the Internet for recent articles on choosing friends and use them to model the effective habits of readers through a Read Aloud/Think Aloud.

Check out articles at the following websites to determine if they would be appropriate for your RATA:
- "Parents Can Help Teens Choose 'Good' Friends, Study Finds." Ohio State University, Research Communications. Updated August 12, 2005. http://researchnews.osu.edu/archive/adolfrnd.htm.
- "Making Friends." Shykids.com. http://www.shykids.com/shykidsfriends.htm.

(Please keep in mind that it is the responsibility of the teacher to determine if articles from suggested sites are appropriate. The sites may have changed content since this publication. The publisher takes no responsibility for the current content of the site.)

Looking at the Words

Determining How the Word Sounds (Phonics)
Using the Syllable Guide and the Reading Instructional Guide Template found in the beginning of the book, follow the steps to help students learn how to break a word into manageable parts.

Determining What the Word Means (Vocabulary)

Words to Study	Breaking into Syllables	Short Definition
admirable	ad-mi-ra-ble	(adj.) deserving approval
endorsement	en-dorse-ment	(n.) the act of supporting products or services
engage	en-gage	(v.) to involve
multimillionaire	mul-ti-mil-lion-aire	(n.) a person who has a fortune worth many millions of dollars
questionable	ques-tion-a-ble	(adj.) open to doubt
suspicion	sus-pi-cion	(n.) the condition of being suspected, especially of a crime
underprivileged	un-der-priv-i-leged	(adj.) lacking opportunities or advantages; needy

Activating Background Knowledge

Anticipation Guide
Have students mark each of the following statements True or False:

1. ____ Michael Vick formerly played for the Atlanta Falcons.

Answer Key — Answer Key — Answer Key

Circle of Friends

2. _____ Michael Vick grew up in Virginia.

3. _____ Dogfighting operations are legal.

4. _____ Sean Taylor is an example of someone who took a stand and changed his life for the better.

5. _____ Sean Taylor's child positively influenced his life.

Starter Questions
After completing the Anticipation Guide, have a group or class discussion with the students using the following questions:

1. What position did Michael Vick play?

2. Michael Vick was recently found guilty of what crime?

3. "Ookie" is an alias for what famous athlete?

4. Who is Sean Taylor?

5. How was Sean Taylor's life cut short?

Make a prediction about what you think the article will be about.

DURING READING
Use the Reading Instructional Guide Template found in the front of the book.

AFTER READING

Discussion Starter Questions

1. What influences might have led Michael Vick to choose involvement in crime?

2. Do you think Michael Vick received a fair sentence? Why or why not?

3. What changes did Sean Taylor make in his life?

4. What do you think Venjah Hunte could have done differently to change the outcome of his life-changing night?

5. What qualities do you look for in a friend?

Teacher Reflection

Use the Reading Instructional Guide Template found in the front of the book.

Circle of Friends

#7— Shining Bright

He was blessed with speed. His left arm was nearly a weapon, firing rockets down the football field. He was the first player selected in the NFL draft the year he left college. The record books were ready to be rewritten as #7, Michael Vick, took the field.

He was not normal. No quarterback had ever rushed for 1,000 yards in a single season. No quarterback had ever rushed for 8.4 yards per carry. None. Michael Vick was in a league of his own. He changed the role of the quarterback in professional football.

In 2004 he signed a 10-year contract for $130 million with a $37 million signing bonus. He would receive millions more for doing endorsements with Nike, EA Sports, Coca-Cola, and other companies. He went from the neighborhoods of Newport News, Virginia to multimillionaire. Not bad. Not bad at all.

His friends included people like Warrick Dunn, one of the NFL's ultimate "good guys." Dunn played with him for the Atlanta Falcons. They partnered in charity events. Dunn has praised Vick, saying that "his love for his family, children and community is truly admirable."

Hank Aaron, Major League Baseball's home run king, described Vick as an "impressive young man." He praised him for his work off the field with underprivileged children.

Hardly anyone's star shone brighter than Vick's when he first broke into the league. Dan Reeves, the Hall of Fame coach of the Atlanta Falcons, was impressed with Vick's style of play and his inner strength.

Ookie

Ookie was a man who hung out at Bad Newz Kennels on Moonlight Road in Virginia. His friends had spent time in jail for various charges related to drugs. These friends, known as P-Funk, Q, and T, helped Ookie keep up the dogfighting operation he paid for.

Police raided the house at Moonlight Road on suspicion of drug activity. There they found the equipment and materials used to run the dogfighting operation. Law enforcement found that this group of men had been training pit bulls to kill other dogs. They had been traveling around, engaging their dogs in brutal battles with dogs from other fighting operations. They discovered that the men had badly mistreated the dogs, even killing those that didn't perform well.

Ookie had been friends with this group of men nearly all of his life. On December 10, 2007, Ookie was sentenced to 23 months in prison as punishment for the crimes they committed together. His friends had similar sentences.

The especially tragic side of the story is the real name that appeared above the alias "Ookie" in the criminal court papers: Michael Vick.

Could It Be Happily Ever After?

"God Forgive Me." These words were tattooed on the left arm and shoulder of Sean Taylor. The life led by the star cornerback of the Washington Redskins certainly had required a great amount of forgiveness. Arrests, fines, and questionable activities were a big part of one of the hardest hitters in the NFL. From the moment the Redskins drafted him, Taylor had a difficult time staying out of trouble. He skipped a mandatory meeting for rookies. He was often fined for unsportsmanlike plays. Finally, he was involved in an argument with men who reportedly tried to steal one of his cars. He pulled a gun and found himself in trouble. However, the judge in the case went easy on him and sentenced Taylor to probation only.

Then he became a father, and things began to change. He had a new baby daughter, a family who loved him, and supportive teammates. They helped to pull him out of the hole he'd dug for himself over the years. His teammates said he became a new person. Renaldo Wynn, a player for the Redskins, recalled a turning point. Taylor moved his locker from the end of the locker room where the younger, wilder players hung out to the end where the more conservative ones were. Wynn felt that Taylor was trying to take steps toward growing up. He slowly began to be a positive influence in the locker room. Teammate Chris Samuels complimented Taylor's new maturity. Taylor said, "I'm just focused on my job and staying out of trouble and doing all the right things." After his transformation, one of his coaches even described him as "radiant" as well as "positive and energetic."

Taylor was a model for young kids who have been in trouble. His life had been low, and his friends had been rough. But he was strong enough to begin to become a new person.

Four Boys Out for a Ride

Four boys ages 17, 18, 19, and 20 drove to a ritzy Miami neighborhood wondering what to do. Fancy cars in a driveway reportedly led one to ask who lived there. Another bragged that he knew whose home it was. It belonged to a famous football player. He said he knew the man kept $200,000 in a bag in his bedroom. Once he'd once stolen $5,000 from the house. After a while, the four returned to the home. The football star was supposed to be traveling with the team.

One of the boys, Venjah Hunte, claims he stayed in the car. He supposedly didn't know his friends had brought a gun. After the others broke into the house, one ran out, scared because he'd heard noises. But another talked him into going back inside. Then Hunte says he heard a gunshot and a scream. His friends came running out, got in the car, and they drove off together.

A day later, Hunte would learn that Sean Taylor had not been traveling with the team. He was hurt, so he was home with his one-year-old baby. Hunte would find out that one of his friends had shot Taylor after surprising him during the break-in. Taylor died a couple of days later. Police eventually caught up with Hunte and the other young men. They were charged with the murder of Sean Taylor.

Hunte's life changed forever that night because he'd been along for the ride with a circle of friends he should have chosen more wisely.

The Circle of Friends

Michael Vick. Venjah Hunte. Sean Taylor. Three tragic stories of lives influenced by circles of friends. One lost millions. One may lose his freedom forever following his trial. And one's life was tragically cut short. Ironically, he'd been the one that had finally found happiness thanks to good decisions about his circle of friends.

Look at their stories. Look at your own. Where is your circle of friends taking you?

Where is your circle of friends taking you?

Unit 4 — Answer Key — Answer Key — Answer Key

Reading Comprehension

After reading "Circle of Friends," choose the options that best answer questions 1–14.

1. Read this sentence.
   After his transformation, one of his coaches even described him as "radiant" as well as "positive and energetic."

   What is the meaning of the word *transformation* as it is used in the sentence?
   A. rest
   B. change
   C. decoration
   D. staying the same

2. Read this sentence.
   He was often fined for unsportsmanlike plays.

   What is the meaning of the word *unsportsmanlike* as it is used in the sentence?
   F. being kind to other players
   G. following the rules of the game
   H. not displaying good character qualities in games
   I. engaging in illegal activities while playing in games

3. According to the article, Michael Vick was
   A. a talented athlete.
   B. a basketball player.
   C. a famous football coach.
   D. an athlete who had difficulty controlling his temper.

4. How can friendships affect a person's choices in life?
   F. One should not listen to a friend's advice.
   G. Friends can often influence the choices we make.
   H. Friends do not have any effect on the choices we make.
   I. Friends will always encourage us to make the best decisions in life.

5. What aspect of Sean Taylor's life does the author seem to admire the most?
   A. his relationship with his friends
   B. his relationship with his parents
   C. his ability to positively change his life
   D. the records he broke while playing in the NFL

6. The author organizes the article by
   F. providing research on the impact of friends
   G. comparing the statistics of two infamous football players
   H. presenting questions and answers of recent interviews with famous athletes
   I. illustrating examples of people whose lives were impacted by a group of friends

Answer Key — Answer Key — Answer Key

Circle of Friends

7. Why does the author write about Sean Taylor?
    A. to portray the life of a famous football player
    B. to encourage the reader to become a Washington Redskins fan
    C. to show that famous athletes still have time in their busy schedules to make friends
    D. to show how an innocent person's life can be affected by someone else's wrong choice

8. Which title BEST fits the article?
    F. How to Make Friends
    G. Choosing Your Circle
    H. How to Become an Athlete
    I. Football Is the Best Sport to Play

9. If Michael Vick were given the opportunity to change his life, what decision would he probably make?
    A. to become a football coach
    B. not to engage in dogfighting
    C. to stay in school and further his education
    D. not to become a professional football player

10. Why did the police initially decide to investigate Michael Vick's home in Virginia?
    F. burglary
    G. drug suspicion
    H. cheating on taxes
    I. domestic violence

11. Michael Vick and Venjah Hunte are similar in that
    A. they drive the same kind of car
    B. they attended the same high school
    C. they are both famous football players
    D. they were both found guilty of committing crimes

12. Which sentence from the article offers the BEST evidence that Vick was a talented football player?
    F. He was not normal.
    G. His friends included people like Warrick Dunn, one of the NFL's "good guys."
    H. In 2004 he signed a 10-year contract for $130 million with a $37 million signing bonus.
    I. The especially tragic side of the story is the real name that appeared above the alias "Ookie" in the criminal court papers: Michael Vick.

13. How does the author organize the first two paragraphs of the passage?
    A. by explaining Michael Vick's accomplishments
    B. by comparing and contrasting famous football athletes
    C. by providing information on how the reader can join an athletic team
    D. by listing the reasons why Michael Vick should be released from jail early

14. Which statement about Venjah Hunte is LEAST accurate?
    F. Hunte was involved in a crime that resulted in murder.
    G. Hunte selected a group of friends that displayed strong values.
    H. Hunte stated that he did not know his friends brought a gun with them.
    I. Hunte is currently serving jail time for the murder of a famous football player.

Unit 4 — Answer Key — Answer Key — Answer Key

Reading Strategy

Directions: Using information from the article and personal experience with your friends, fill in the hot air balloon with traits or examples of good friends that would help you succeed. Then fill in the anvil with traits or examples of friends that would bring you down.

How are YOU influenced by your friends?

- Supportive
- Loving
- Caring
- Help you when you make mistakes
- Help you study for tests
- Help you make good decisions
- Positive influence
- Reliable

- Involved in criminal activity
- Careless
- Bad influence
- Selfish
- Unkind
- Bullying
- Dishonest

Answer Key — Answer Key — Answer Key

Circle of Friends

Interpreting the Data

What made you do it, Michael Vick?

Below are summarized excerpts from the court papers filed against Vick and his friends involved with Bad Newz Kennels. You will read the legal charges and answer the questions that follow.

Federal Indictment for Criminal Conspiracy
In the **spring of 2002**, PEACE, PHILLIPS, and TAYLOR traveled from Virginia to North Carolina with a male pit bull named **Seal** to participate in a dogfight against a male pit bull named **Maniac**, owned by an individual from **North Carolina**. The purse for the dogfight was established at approximately **$500** per side. PEACE, PHILLIPS, and TAYLOR lost the purse when Maniac prevailed over Seal.
In **late 2002**, an individual traveled from **North Carolina** to Virginia with a male pit bull named **Maniac** to participate in a dogfight against a pit bull named **Zebro**, owned by an unknown person. Bad Newz Kennels established the purse at approximately **$1,000** per side. An unknown person, aided and assisted by TAYLOR and VICK, lost the purse when Maniac prevailed over Zebro.
In **late 2002**, individuals traveled from **Alabama** to Virginia with a **male pit bull** to participate in a dogfight against a male pit bull named **Chico**, owned by Bad Newz Kennels. Bad Newz Kennels established the purse at approximately **$1,000** per side. Bad Newz Kennels **won** the purse when Chico prevailed over the male pit bull from Alabama.
In **late 2002**, PEACE, PHILLIPS, TAYLOR, and another individual traveled from Virginia to Maryland with a female pit bull named **Jane** to participate in a dogfight against a **female pit bull** owned by Show Biz Kennels of **New York**. The purse was established at approximately **$1,000** per side. Bad Newz Kennels won the purse when Jane prevailed over the female pit bull owned by Show Biz Kennels.
In the **spring of 2003**, PEACE, PHILLIPS, TAYLOR, VICK, and two other individuals traveled from Virginia to **North Carolina** with a female pit bull named **Jane** to participate in a dogfight against a **female pit bull** owned by unknown individuals. The purse was established at approximately **$1,500** per side. Bad Newz Kennels won the purse when Jane prevailed over the female pit bull from North Carolina.
In the **spring of 2003**, an individual traveled from **South Carolina** to Virginia with **a male pit bull** to participate in a dogfight against a male pit bull named **Big Boy**, owned by Bad Newz Kennels. The purse was established at approximately **$1,000** per side. Bad Newz Kennels won the purse when Big Boy prevailed over the male pit bull from South Carolina.
In **March of 2003**, Cooperating Witness (C.W.) #2 traveled from **North Carolina** to Virginia with his 35-pound female pit bull and a 47-pound male pit bull to participate in the dogfights against members of Bad Newz Kennels. In **March of 2003**, PEACE, VICK, and other individuals sponsored a **female pit bull** in a dogfight against the 35-pound female pit bull owned by C.W. #2. The purse was established at approximately **$13,000** per side. Bad Newz Kennels lost the purse when the 35-pound **female pit bull** owned by C.W. #2 prevailed over the Bad Newz Kennels pit bull.

©2008 PRINCIPLE WOODS, INC. Removal of copyright notice and copying are violations of Federal Law.

Unit 4 — Answer Key — Answer Key — Answer Key

In **March of 2003**, PEACE, VICK, and other individuals sponsored a **male pit bull** in a dogfight against the 47-pound **male pit bull** owned by C.W. #2. The purse was established at approximately **$10,000** per side. Bad Newz Kennels lost the purse when the 47-pound male pit bull owned by C.W. #2 prevailed over the Bad Newz Kennels pit bull.

In **March of 2003**, PEACE, VICK, and other individuals sponsored a **female pit bull** in a dogfight against a female pit bull named **Cleo**, owned by an individual from **New York**. The purse was established at approximately **$3,000** per side. Bad Newz Kennels lost the purse when **Cleo** beat the Bad Newz Kennels female pit bull.

In **late 2003**, PEACE, PHILLIPS, TAYLOR, and VICK traveled from Atlanta, Georgia to **South Carolina** with a male pit bull named **Big Boy** to participate in a dogfight against a **male pit bull** owned by an individual from South Carolina. The purse was established at approximately **$3,600** per side. Bad Newz Kennels won the purse when Big Boy prevailed over the male pit bull from South Carolina.

In **late 2003**, PEACE, PHILLIPS, TAYLOR, and another individual traveled from Virginia to **New Jersey** with a female pit bull named **Jane** to participate in a dogfight against a **female pit bull** owned by individuals unknown to the Grand Jury. The purse was established at approximately **$5,000** per side. Bad News Kennels won the purse when Jane prevailed over the female pit bull.

In the **fall of 2003**, PEACE, PHILLIPS, TAYLOR, and VICK traveled from Atlanta, Georgia to **South Carolina** with a male pit bull named **Magic** to participate in a dogfight against a **male pit bull** owned by individuals from South Carolina. The purse was established at approximately **$1,500** per side. Bad Newz Kennels won the purse when Magic prevailed over the male pit bull from South Carolina.

In the **fall of 2003**, Cooperating Witness Number 3 (C.W. #3) traveled to Virginia with a **male pit bull** from **North Carolina** to participate in a dogfight against a male pit bull named **Tiny**, owned by Bad Newz Kennels. The purse was established at approximately **$3,500** per side. Bad Newz Kennels won the purse when Tiny prevailed over the male pit bull owned by C.W. #3.

In **late 2003**, Cooperating Witness Number 4 (C.W. #4) traveled to Virginia with a female pit bull named **Trouble**, a dog that originally came from **Florida**, to participate in a dogfight against a **female pit bull** owned by Bad Newz Kennels. The purse was established at approximately **$7,000** per side. PEACE placed a side-bet with C.W. #4 of approximately **$4,000** on the Bad Newz Kennels dog to win the fight. Bad Newz Kennels lost the purse when Trouble prevailed over the Bad Newz Kennels pit bull. **VICK paid C.W. #4** the purse money of approximately **$7,000** and approximately **$4,000** for the side-bet entered by PEACE.

In the **spring of 2004**, individuals traveled from **New Jersey** to Virginia with a **male pit bull** to participate in a dogfight against a male pit bull named **Big Boy**, owned by Bad Newz Kennels. The purse was established at approximately **$1,500** per side. Bad Newz Kennels won the purse when Big Boy prevailed over the male pit bull from New Jersey.

In **early 2004**, individuals traveled from **Maryland** to Virginia with a **male pit bull** to participate in a dogfight against a male pit bull named **Too Short**, owned by Bad Newz Kennels. The purse was established at approximately **$3,000** per side. Bad Newz Kennels **won** the purse when Too Short prevailed over the male pit bull from Maryland.

At various times from late **2004 through 2005**, PEACE, PHILLIPS, VICK, and others known and unknown to the Grand jury continued operation of the animal fighting venture at 1915 Moonlight Road and hosted approximately 10 dogfights on the property. In **early 2007**, PEACE, PHILLIPS, VICK, and others known and unknown to the Grand Jury continued operation of the animal fighting venture at 1915 Moonlight Road.

Answer Key — Answer Key — Answer Key

Circle of Friends

To answer questions 15–25, use the information in the summarized charges to fill in the shaded boxes to complete Table 1. You will determine how much money Vick and Bad Newz Kennels won or lost with their dogfighting scheme.

Table 1. Data on Bad Newz Kennel's dogfighting operation

When fight took place (ex., "late 2002")	Description and/or name of Bad Newz Kennel's dog (ex., "Seal" or "female pit bull")	Description of opponent's dog (name, gender, state of origin if given)	$ Bad Newz Kennels won	$ Bad Newz Kennels lost
Spring 2002	Seal	Maniac- NC		$500
Late 2002	Zebro	Maniac- NC		$1,000
Late 2002	Chico	Male pit bull- AL	$1,000	
Late 2002	Jane	Female pit bull- NY	$1,000	
15. Spring 2003	**Jane**	Female pit bull- NC	$1,500	
16. Spring 2003	**Big Boy**	Male pit bull- SC	$1,000	
17. March 2003	Female pit bull	**Female pit bull- NC**		**$13,000**
18. March 2003	Male pit bull	**Male pit bull- NC**		**$10,000**
19. March 2003	**Female pit bull**	Cleo- NY		$3,000
20. Late 2003	Big Boy	**Male pit bull- SC**	$3,600	
Late 2003	Jane	Female pit bull- NJ	$5,000	
Fall 2003	Magic	Male pit bull- SC	$1,500	
21. Fall 2003	**Tiny**	**Male pit bull- NC**	$3,500	
22. Late 2003	**Female pit bull**	Trouble- FL		**$11,000**
23. Spring 2004	**Big Boy**	Male pit bull- NJ	$1,500	
Early 2004	Too Short	Male pit bull- MD	$3,000	
		Totals	**24.** $22,600	**25.** $38,500

26. How much money did Bad Newz Kennels and Michael Vick lose overall on the fights described in the court papers?

$15,900

27. When were Bad Newz Kennels and Michael Vick most active in dogfighting?

Spring 2003 and late 2003

©2008 PRINCIPLE WOODS, INC. Removal of copyright notice and copying are violations of Federal Law.

Unit 4 — *Answer Key — Answer Key — Answer Key*

Figure 1 illustrates the number of games Michael Vick started and played over the course of his career. Each of the football seasons took place in the fall, or the late part of the year.

Figure 1. Number of games Michael Vick played and started each season

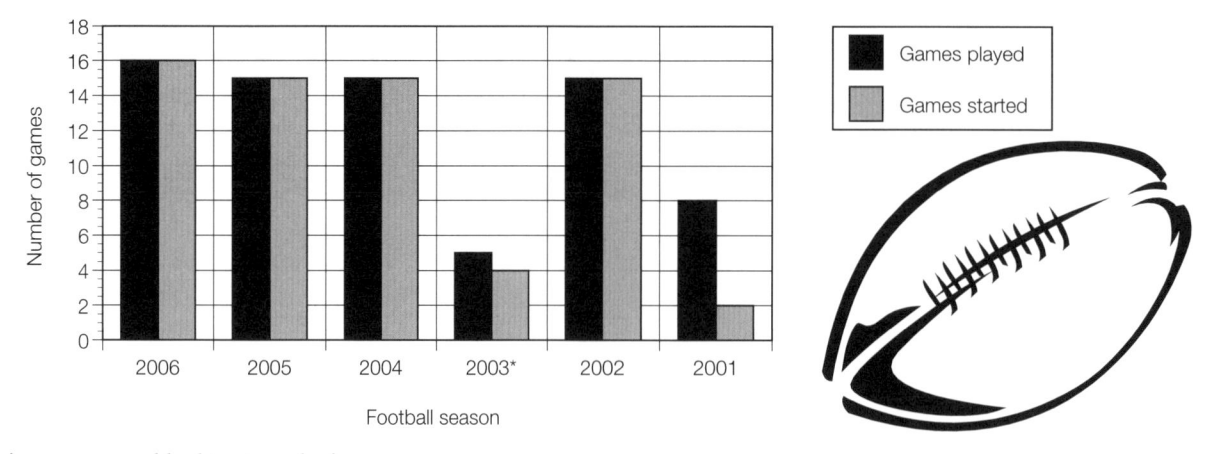

Football season	Games played	Games started
2006	16	16
2005	15	15
2004	15	15
2003*	5	4
2002	15	15
2001	8	2

*Injured during season and had to stop playing.

28. Use Table 1 to determine when Michael Vick was most active in dogfighting. After looking at Figure 1 illustrating the number of games he started and played, explain why you think he was so active in dogfighting during that part of his football career.

ANALYZE EVALUATE EXPLAIN

Student answers could contain facts such as the following.

According to the court papers, Michael Vick was most active in dogfighting in the spring of 2003 and the fall of 2003. Figure 1 tells us that he was injured during the 2003 football season and couldn't play (except for five games). Since the football season takes place in the late part of the year, we might assume that Michael Vick became more active in dogfighting because he wasn't able to play football and wanted to have something to do with his time.

Use the extended-response rubric to reference the criteria required for an acceptable answer and to determine the points to award.

Answer Key — Answer Key — Answer Key

Circle of Friends

Reflect and Respond

29. Think about the following questions:

- Why do you think people who earn a lot of money sometimes get in trouble?

- Do you find yourself getting in trouble for the same reasons?

- How important is it for you to stay busy in order to stay out of trouble?

- Name three things in which you participate that actually keep you from getting into trouble.

Now write a letter to Michael Vick giving him advice on how to change his life so that he can stay out of trouble after he is released from prison.

> Answers may vary, but students should address each part of the question. The question is meant to elicit strong classroom conversation about character. Students should be able to make text-to-self connections based on the situations illustrated in this unit. They should then be able to use those connections to teach a lesson through the letter they write.
>
> Use the character education rubric to reference the criteria and number of points to award.

Unit 4

Answer Key — Answer Key — Answer Key

Reading Instructional Guide for Technical Extension

BEFORE READING

Looking at the Words

Determining How the Word Sounds (Phonics)
Technical texts often necessitate the use of multisyllabic words that are unfamiliar to students. Use the Syllable Guide to help students decode any words they might have trouble reading.

Determining What the Word Means (Vocabulary)

Words to Study	Breaking into Syllables	Short Definition
character	char-ac-ter	(n.) moral or ethical strength; integrity
constitute	con-sti-tute	(v.) to equal to something
detrimental	det-ri-men-tal	(adj.) damaging
incident	in-ci-dent	(n.) an event or occurrence
integrity	in-teg-ri-ty	(n.) following moral principles
represent	rep-re-sent	(v.) to act on behalf of

Activating Background Knowledge

Graphic Organizer
Either individually or in groups, students may brainstorm about character, recalling anything previously learned and any prior experience with the subject. Next, encourage students to see the relationships between their ideas by having them complete a pie chart to demonstrate what they already know about adjectives to describe a person who demonstrates positive character.

Adjectives That Describe Positive Character

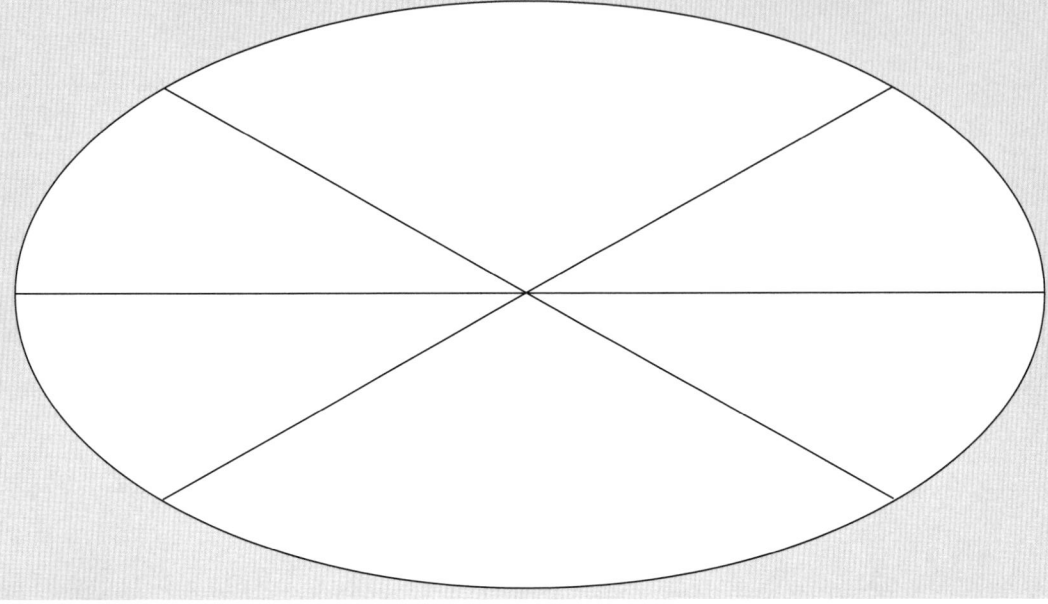

©2008 PRINCIPLE WOODS, INC. Removal of copyright notice and copying are violations of Federal Law.

Answer Key — Answer Key — Answer Key

Circle of Friends

Starter Questions
After completing the Graphic Organizer, generate a group or class discussion to come up with questions about the subject, a prediction about the article, and at least one learning goal. The first question has been provided for you.

Question: What is integrity?

Question: _____

Prediction: _____

Goal: _____

DURING READING
Use the Reading Instructional Guide Template found in the front of the book.

AFTER READING
After reading, you may teach reading strategy use by giving students opportunities to do the following:
- Review, paraphrase, and summarize
- Participate in main-idea discussions by describing the information in their own words
- Reflect on concept maps and generate additional discussion starter questions based on the mappings
- Participate in small-group discussions using discussion starter questions

Discussion Starter Questions

The first question has been provided for you.

1. Is it fair for the National Football League to impose its own penalties on players who commit crimes, or should the league just let the judicial system penalize the players? Explain.

2. _____

3. _____

Technical Extension

Integrity On and Off the Field

"Engaging in violent and/or criminal activity is unacceptable and constitutes conduct detrimental to the integrity of and public confidence in the National Football League." These are the words of the new conduct policy put in place by National Football League Commissioner Roger Goodell in 2007. It was the result of a 2006 season when more than 50 players were arrested. NFL players have been hot topics recently. But not all of the attention has been about their talent on the football field. What exactly is *integrity*? Should a player's off-field behavior be a factor in his career and his paycheck?

Integrity is defined as "unwavering following of a strict moral or ethical code." How does that relate to how football players or other athletes behave on or off their fields of play? Former Buffalo Bills player Jim Kelly believes that it's past time for the NFL to strengthen its code for player conduct. "Players got to understand they represent the National Football League and what that means, and they also represent their namesake and their families. If you're not doing the right thing, you don't need to be a part of it," Kelly said in an interview. Kelly's statement shows that he thinks "doing the right thing" at all times is a mark of a person's integrity, or what is sometimes referred to as character.

Commissioner Goodell clearly agrees. Fines and other disciplinary actions will be given from now on as a part of the new conduct policy in order to "protect the integrity of the NFL." Several high-profile players can confirm that the new NFL policy means business. Adam "Pacman" Jones was suspended for the entire 2007 season for a barroom incident. Chris Henry was benched for the first half of the same season for off-the-field issues. Michael Vick is currently serving a prison term for lying about his involvement in a dogfighting operation. He may never play football again.

Some teams seem to do a better job of drafting players of positive character. San Diego Chargers general manager says, "We judge players on these things: on-the-field production, off the field and work ethic." The St. Louis Rams appear to hold to this standard also, as they have dealt with only 3 incidents involving a total of 2 players. On the other hand, the Minnesota Vikings and the Cincinnati Bengals have had a combined total of at least 44 incidents involving their players since 2000.

There are others within the sport who don't believe a player's character off the field should affect his job. Former player Thurman Thomas said he has been disappointed that the players union hasn't waited for the legal system to complete its process before imposing heavy fines or discipline. He points out that although Pacman Jones had been arrested several times before his suspension, he had never been convicted. "You want your players to behave," Thomas said. "But you've also got to protect them. I don't think someone who hasn't been convicted should be suspended for an entire season." Former player Deion Sanders believes that players should be required to continue to report to work, without pay, so they can get whatever assistance the team and league feels would be helpful, such as counseling in anger management.

Despite these differing opinions, one thing everyone agrees on is that the media leaves players no margin for error. The cameras are always rolling, and many of the players are barely out of college or high school. They have fancy cars and make a lot of money. Partying is a part of our culture for many young men in any occupation. Football players are followed everywhere by the cameras. If they make a mistake, everyone is going to know it by the next morning's news.

Character is sometimes defined as "doing the right thing even when you believe no one is looking." Due to the tougher NFL conduct policy, professional football players have been put on notice that character does matter both on and off the field, whether they think anyone is watching them or not.

National Football League Conduct Policy

General Policy	Engaging in violent and/or criminal activity is unacceptable….Such conduct alienates fans on whom the success of the league depends and has negative and sometimes tragic consequences…
Prohibited Conduct	…violent and/or criminal activity. Examples include: use of threat of physical violence; use of a deadly weapon in the commission of a crime; involvement in "hate crimes" or domestic violence; theft, larceny, or other property crimes; sex offenses; racketeering; money laundering; obstruction of justice; resisting arrest; violent or threatening conduct.
Persons Charged with Criminal Activity	Any covered person arrested for or charged with conduct prohibited will be required to undergo an immediate, mandatory clinical evaluation, and, if directed, appropriate counseling.
Persons Convicted of Criminal Activity	Any covered person convicted of or admitting to a criminal violation will be subject to discipline as determined by the Commissioner. Such discipline may include a fine, suspension without pay and/or banishment from the NFL.
Persons Engaged in Violent Activity in the Workplace	Criminal conduct in the workplace or against other employees is prohibited. Any covered person who commits or threatens violent acts against coworkers, regardless of whether an arrest is made or criminal charges are brought, shall be subject to evaluation, counseling and discipline, including termination of employment.
Duty to Report	The obligation to report an arrest or criminal charge extends to both the person involved and to the club or league entity for which he or she works. Failure to report an incident will constitute conduct detrimental and will be taken into consideration in the final determination of discipline under this policy.

Unit 4 — Answer Key — Answer Key — Answer Key

Reading Comprehension

After reading "Integrity On and Off the Field," choose the options that best answer questions 1–11.

1. Read this sentence.
   Kelly's statement shows that he thinks "doing the right thing" at all times is a mark of a person's integrity, or what is sometimes referred to as character.

   According to this sentence, what is the meaning of the word *integrity*?
   A. character
   B. work ethic
   C. impaired judgment
   D. a mark on the player's record

2. Read this sentence.
   Despite these differing opinions, one thing everyone agrees on is that the media leaves players no margin for error.

   What does the author mean by this sentence?
   F. The media sees all the player's mistakes.
   G. The media often misrepresents what actually happens.
   H. The media reports players' actions, but often with many errors.
   I. The media represent many different opinions on what should be reported about football players.

3. According to this article, what effect does the media have on player behavior?
   A. The media has no effect.
   B. Players are not allowed to talk to the media.
   C. Any behavior issues are immediately known by everyone.
   D. The media and the NFL agree on the number of articles that can be printed about player behavior.

4. What is the purpose of the new conduct policy of the NFL?
   F. to please the media
   G. to ease tensions between players
   H. to protect the integrity of the NFL
   I. to ensure that the teams draft players of good character

5. The author organizes the article by
   A. defining integrity.
   B. giving statistics of arrests of NFL players.
   C. providing different perspectives of those involved in the NFL.
   D. comparing the former NFL conduct policy with the new conduct policy.

6. What is the main idea of the article?
   F. Integrity is unimportant in football.
   G. The new NFL conduct policy has increased player arrests.
   H. Some think players should not be punished by the NFL unless they have been convicted of a crime.
   I. The tougher NFL conduct policy has alerted players that their behavior on and off the field is important.

Answer Key — Answer Key — Answer Key

Circle of Friends

7. The new NFL conduct policy was adopted because
   A. there was a high number of player arrests.
   B. the media coverage of player behavior had increased.
   C. the draft system was not effective in determining which players should be drafted.
   D. several players had sued the NFL in recent years for unfair enforcement of the old conduct policy.

8. How do Thurman Thomas and Jim Kelly differ in their opinions about the code of conduct and player behavior?
   F. Kelly believes the conduct policy is too strict.
   G. Thomas believes the conduct policy should be enforced only after any legal proceedings are complete.
   H. Kelly thinks that the players union is the only organization that has the right to discipline players.
   I. Thomas believes that a player's off-the-field behavior should not be considered in any way in issuing discipline.

9. Which of the following facts from the article BEST supports the need for the NFL's new conduct policy?
   A. Some teams draft only players who have good character.
   B. Jim Kelly believes it is past time for the NFL to strengthen their conduct policy.
   C. The St. Louis Rams have dealt with only 3 behavior incidents involving a total of 2 players.
   D. Before his suspension in 2007, Pacman Jones had been arrested several times, but he had never been convicted in a court of law.

10. People who read this article will learn
    F. how the NFL draft affects player behavior.
    G. how the media causes poor behavior by players.
    H. that integrity and character are unimportant in the new NFL conduct policy.
    I. that the new NFL conduct policy considers a player's character both on and off the field when issuing discipline.

11. According to the article and the text box, which of the following is true?
    A. Fans may be disciplined under the conduct policy.
    B. The team must agree before discipline is issued by the NFL.
    C. A player who is found guilty of a crime will automatically be banned from football for life.
    D. An NFL player who is merely charged with a crime can be disciplined and must undergo a clinical evaluation.

Unit 4

Answer Key — Answer Key — Answer Key

Technical Writing Prompt

12. Write an e-mail to the commissioner of the NFL to voice your opinion about the personal conduct policy. Explain why you agree or disagree with the policy. Urge the commissioner either to continue the strict policy or to make it more lenient. Use specific facts from the article as well as your own experience to support your opinion. The commissioner's time is precious, so keep your e-mail to the point.

Technical Writing

Student answers may vary.

The student should address the question to the best of his/her ability using the article and personal experience. The question is meant to prepare students to be active citizens who can accurately and effectively use written communication skills.

Use the technical writing rubric to reference the criteria and determine the number of points to award.

Answer Key — Answer Key — Answer Key

Circle of Friends

Vocational Extension

> **HELP WANTED:**
> Position for head football coach open at state university. Master's degree and previous experience as assistant head coach necessary. Must be organized and able to motivate young people. Salary negotiable based on experience. Contact Darrell Jones, Athletic Director, at the Human Resources office on campus.

Athletic coaches are responsible for much more than winning or losing. Coaches teach the basics of their sport first, including the rules and strategies. They also mold the character of their players by teaching them good sportsmanship. They teach them what is expected both on and off the field. This provides the young people on the team a solid foundation for their game and for life.

People who coach in their community, such as at local YMCAs, only need a love of their sport and the desire to help children learn to play it. Coaches at the public school level often teach an academic subject and coach one or more sports at the school. College studies that lead to a coaching career are exercise and sports science, nutrition and fitness, physical education, and sports medicine.

Many of the men and women who coach teams begin their careers as assistant coaches. Coaches must have good communication and leadership skills. Successful coaches keep a positive attitude and share their own enthusiasm for the game with their players. A big part of coaching is encouraging players to be the best that they can be. One player may not be motivated the same way as another. Coaches must know the players individually so that they can use the method that works best with each one.

There is no such thing as a "typical day" in the life of an athletic coach! A day at work might include the following:

- Teaching the rules
- Showing players how to reach their physical "best"

©2008 PRINCIPLE WOODS, INC. Removal of copyright notice and copying are violations of Federal Law.

- Leading practice sessions
- Coaching during games
- Teaching good sportsmanship and teamwork
- Making sure their team has the proper equipment and supplies
- Evaluating opposing teams before competitions
- Working with the other coaches and staff
- Determining team strategy

The workweek might be longer than a five-day week too. Games often take place on weekends. However, the job usually requires more than a "normal" 40-hour workweek. Once a game is over, the coach must begin preparing for the next one right away.

There is a wide range of salaries for coaches. In 2004 the median yearly salary for coaches at the community level was $19,020, while colleges and universities paid an average of $36,610 per year. Some larger universities pay much more. They also offer many other sources of income for their coaches, like free housing, cars, jets, and a percentage of ticket sales. Several coaches at schools like these make millions of dollars from salaries and the other benefits.

Coaches have the opportunity to work in a sport that they love while also helping young people to enjoy that sport. If you are involved in a competitive sport today, you might be able to build it into a career for your future!

Answer Key — Answer Key — Answer Key

Circle of Friends

Looking Forward

13. In addition to teaching the fundamentals of the sport, a good athletic coach instills positive sportsmanship and motivation in the athletes. Imagine that you have just been hired to coach a high school athletic team. Explain how you will develop character and success in your athletes. Use personal experience (as an athlete or as an observer) and information from the article to answer the question.

> Student answers may vary.
>
> The student should address the question to the best of his/her ability using the article and personal experience. The question is meant to encourage students to explore areas of interest for their future and begin to determine how they will prepare for a future career.
>
> Use the extended-response rubric to reference the criteria and determine the number of points to award.

Ethical Dilemma

14. You are an assistant coach at one of the large state universities. One of your jobs is to monitor the academic performance of the team members. You discover that one of the star players is nearly failing a required course and has hired someone to take tests in his place. No one else knows about this yet. Without this player, the team will probably lose all important games for the rest of the season. List two or three actions that you might take and the possible consequences of each one. Which choice do you think is best? Which one will you choose?

> Student answers may vary.
>
> The student should address the question to the best of his/her ability using background knowledge from the article as well as personal opinion and experience. The question is meant to encourage students to contemplate scenarios and make ethical decisions.
>
> Use the character education rubric to reference the criteria and determine the number of points to award.

©2008 PRINCIPLE WOODS, INC. Removal of copyright notice and copying are violations of Federal Law.

Unit 4 — Answer Key

Unit Vocabulary Assessment

Matching
Match each word in Column I to its definition in Column II.

Column I
- **D** 1. underprivileged
- **C** 2. endorsement
- **B** 3. constitute
- **A** 4. admirable
- **E** 5. questionable

Column II
- a. deserving approval
- b. to equal to
- c. the act of supporting
- d. lacking opportunities or advantages
- e. open to doubt

Multiple Choice
Choose the word that MOST NEARLY replaces the underlined word in each sentence.

6. The <u>incident</u> on the football field ended with both players being suspended.
   - A. ethics
   - **B. event**
   - C. action
   - D. energy

7. Cigarette smoking is <u>detrimental</u> to one's health.
   - A. helpful
   - B. destined
   - **C. damaging**
   - D. equivocal

8. Over the summer, Jacob was <u>engaged</u> in many activities.
   - A. readied
   - B. paid for
   - C. invested
   - **D. involved**

9. They promised to run the campaign with <u>integrity</u>.
   - A. need
   - **B. morals**
   - C. interest
   - D. support

Fill in the Blank
Choose a word from the word bank to fill in the blank in the sentence below.

Word Bank: character, multimillionaire, represent, suspicion

10. It was Carol's **character** that gave her strength in hard times.

11. Her wise investments have made her a **multimillionaire**.

12. John was arrested on **suspicion** of robbery.

13. The lawyer will go to court and **represent** our interests.

Answer Key — Answer Key — Answer Key

Authentic Assessment

Students will write a journal entry based on the unit "Circle of Friends." This activity combines the authentic components of hypothesis and writing linked to the comprehension of a written text. Participating in this activity will allow students to identify with someone making a difficult decision and to explore that through writing.

Instructions for a Journal Entry

1. **Choice of subject.** Students will choose a person from the article or someone else from popular culture who has had to make a difficult decision about the crowd they associate with.

2. **Synopsis.** Students will write a one-paragraph synopsis about how the person's choice of friends affected his or her life, including job, social life, family, etc.

3. **Research.** Students will then research the person further, using newspapers, magazines, and the Internet. They should use a minimum of three sources to support their writing.

4. **Journal entry.** Next, students will write a one-page journal entry about a hypothetical event in the person's life. They should write in first person. The entry should include the following components:
   a. Details of one hypothetical event that clearly shows how the person's circle of friends affected that particular event.
   b. A hypothetical description of emotions that the person feels about the event, his or her circle of friends, and how the two interact with one another.
   c. A well-written account, using appropriate writing conventions, facts from the article, and personal knowledge.

5. **Assessment.** The entry will be assessed using the rubric below.

Rubric for Journal Entry

Requirement	8–10 Points	4–7 Points	0–3 Points	Points Earned
Sources	The student uses at least three sources, one of which is the assigned text. Facts are gathered from each source and used accurately in the exhibit.	The student uses between one and two sources. Facts are gathered from each source and used somewhat accurately in the exhibit.	The student does not list sources or makes up facts with no basis.	
Event Details	The student provides a detailed account of the hypothetical event.	The student provides a somewhat detailed account of the hypothetical event.	The student provides little detail of the hypothetical event.	
Emotional Description	The student provides a detailed emotional description, clearly showing the effect of the circle of friends.	The student provides a somewhat detailed emotional description, generally showing the effect of the circle of friends.	The student provides little detail of emotional reaction or does not show the effect of the circle of friends.	
Quality of Writing	The writing is clear and follows appropriate writing conventions.	The writing is somewhat clear, and most conventions are correct.	The writing is unclear, and the conventions are incorrect or misused.	

Unit 5

RIDING DUBS

Reading Instructional Guide for High-Interest Article

BEFORE READING

Front-Loading Background Knowledge through Read Aloud/Think Aloud

Search the Internet for recent articles on accessorizing cars and use them to model the effective habits of readers through a Read Aloud/Think Aloud.

Check out articles at the following websites to determine if they would be appropriate for your RATA:

- Bierman, Fred. "NBA Accessorizing: Supersize My Ride." *New York Times*, December 24, 2006.
  http://www.newyorktimes.com/.
- Reich, Holly. "Women Customize Cars Too!" Edmunds.com, January 2, 2007.
  http:www.edmunds.com/apps/vdpcontainers/do/vdp/articleId=119034/pageNumber=1.

(Please keep in mind that it is the responsibility of the teacher to determine if articles from suggested sites are appropriate. The sites may have changed content since this publication. The publisher takes no responsibility for the current content of the site.)

Looking at the Words

Determining How the Word Sounds (Phonics)
Using the Syllable Guide and the Reading Instructional Guide Template found in the beginning of the book, follow the steps to help students learn how to break a word into manageable parts.

Determining What the Word Means (Vocabulary)

Words to Study	Breaking into Syllables	Short Definition
accessorize	ac-ces-so-rize	(v.) to furnish with objects that make something more attractive or convenient
amateur	am-a-teur	(adj.) lacking professional skill or expertise
credibility	cred-i-bil-i-ty	(n.) the quality of being believable
custom	cus-tom	(adj.) made to order
luxury	lux-u-ry	(n.) something that is very expensive but not needed
persona	per-so-na	(n.) one's public image
unique	u-nique	(adj.) being the only one of its kind; original
valet	val-et	(n.) a person who parks cars for customers

Activating Background Knowledge

Anticipation Guide

Have students mark each of the following statements True or False:

1. ____ Some people embellish their cars to show their individuality.
2. ____ The number of companies that provide automobile accessories is declining.

Answer Key — Answer Key — Answer Key   RIDING DUBS

3. ____ Hip-hop fans expect their musical artists to have cars that are adorned with many gadgets and added features.

4. ____ Hip-hop artists often duplicate others when accessorizing their vehicles.

5. ____ In addition to decorating a car's exterior, hip-hop artists often fix up a car's engine and internal systems.

Starter Questions
After completing the Anticipation Guide, have a group or class discussion with the students using the following questions:

1. What hobby do many hip-hop artists have?

2. Why do hip-hop artists choose to accessorize their vehicles?

3. What are some ways people can embellish their own cars?

4. Who is Will Castro?

5. What type of events does *DUB Magazine* sponsor?

Make a prediction about what you think the article will be about.

DURING READING
Use the Reading Instructional Guide Template found in the front of the book.

AFTER READING

Discussion Starter Questions

1. Why do you think hip-hop artists think they can gain fans by displaying accessorized cars?

2. How are hip-hop artist Twista and business entrepreneur Will Castro similar?

3. Why do you think hip-hop artists use their vehicles to illustrate their success?

4. How do you think others can learn from Will Castro's accomplishments?

5. Do you think Twista would be as popular today if he did not have a customized car? Why or why not?

Teacher Reflection

Use the Reading Instructional Guide Template found in the front of the book.

©2008 PRINCIPLE WOODS, INC. Removal of copyright notice and copying are violations of Federal Law.

RIDING DUBS

Will Castro:

Will Castro is the owner of Unique Autosports. The company customizes cars for celebrities such as Busta Rhymes, Pam Anderson, LeBron James, and Tony Stewart. Castro's work is displayed on a Speed Channel show called *Unique Whips*. This show brings attention to the car industry, specifically celebrity cars. Based out of New York, the show debuted in 2005. Castro's work as a valet led him to pursue his dream of making money doing what he loves most—cars. He is Puerto Rican and wants "to prove to the world that a minority can run a [successful business] and be respected." So far, he makes his clients happy, and his business continues to grow.

DUB Magazine Car Show and Concerts:

DUB Magazine writes about popular entertainers and their vehicles. They sponsor the annual DUB Custom Auto Show and Concert Tour. The tour has traveled to cities such as Los Angeles, Dallas, Atlanta, and Miami. At each show there is a display of cars of famous celebrities. Imagine a sea of chrome wheels, paint jobs, and video and audio packages. Visitors are treated to a remarkable visual display. At the same time they are being entertained by the sounds of artists such as Twista, Sean Kingston, Jim Jones, and Chamillionaire. At each stop on the tour, there are between 14,000 and 30,000 people in attendance. Each event displays the connection between hip-hop music, the auto world, and fans of both.

Pulsing vibes pound off the street. High-tech Alpine speakers ride above 20 inch sterling silver Tyndarides rims.[1] Poppa G rides low, leaning back in his seat. His left arm hangs out the open window of his Mercedes GL550 SUV. His right arm rests on the steering wheel. This isn't any ordinary car, and he isn't any ordinary person. His music has changed the hip-hop world, making him instant millions. This car is a luxury. It's a part of his persona. In his world, his whips[2] and dubs[3] tell who he is.

No more riding in used cars, bruised cars, or loser cars.

This is *his* car—at least on Friday nights. On Saturdays, Poppa G rolls in his BMW 760Li. It has 20" chrome rims with his name on them. And on Sundays, his 1970 Chevy Chevelle convertible shows the world what he is all about.

Monday through Thursday, he is all business in his Lexus LS Hybrid 08. It looks professional, but the luxury shows anyone watching that he is the king. There are no ordinary horse and buggies in his kingdom. To feel like royalty, he has to live like royalty.

The hip-hop world has no real Poppa G, but it is full of artists just like him. To them, their cars have a value much greater than what they pay for them. They buy. They accessorize. They special order. And they search for an original look. Everything must be unique. To ride in a car that looks like someone else's would be like two girls showing up at the prom in the same dress. Their cars display their personality. They say, "Look at me. You want to be me!"

Companies that specialize in car accessories are growing in popularity. The companies provide anything you could ever want on a car. There are chrome wheels, spinners,[4] and stereo systems with speakers that could entertain an NFL stadium. They make doors that open out like wings, paint jobs that make the ceiling of the Sistine Chapel[5] look like amateur work, and on and on. Where does it end? It doesn't. As long as there are people out there with extra money to spend, they will stay in business.

Fancy rides are the business side of the hip-hop world. Artists use their fancy cars to show their fans how hard they work. They also hope to grab the attention of new fans who will bring them more money. The cars portray the lifestyle that fans expect to see. Otherwise, the credibility of the artists goes down. If they are to survive, they need to play the game. And this game involves expensive toys. When that lifestyle is how they succeed, it makes sense to spend money on the finest ride possible.

However, putting the cart before the horse can get dangerous. One has to work hard to earn that lifestyle before living it. For the kid working at McDonald's, spending $3,000 on a set of chrome alloy wheels makes no sense. That money could be better spent on college or training that will prepare him for the future. Then, when he has enough money to afford what he needs, he can focus on what he wants.

One hip-hop artist who has been smart on his way to success is Cavalier Terrell Mitchell, otherwise known as Twista. He worked harder than most hip-hop artists to get where he is today. He was 30 years old before he had his first major hit album, *Kamikaze*, in 2004. To celebrate the album's success, he decked out his 2003 Hummer H2 with custom wheels called Kamikazes.

Twista's cars display to the world how far he has come. When he stands alone in an empty parking lot, he is the same person he has always been. But looking in the reflection of his glossy cars, he sees a new person. This person spent countless hours practicing, singing, making calls, and being rejected on the road to fame. His cars didn't get him *to* his goals. His cars *became* part of the goals. This made them more valuable once he'd earned them. Now he can enjoy the role his cars play in helping him maintain his ranking in the hip-hop music world.

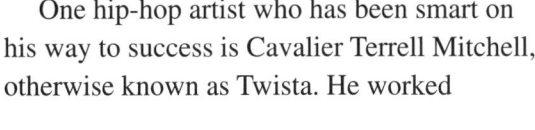

---

[1]Tyndarides rims: Expensive rims that cost about $500 each.

[2]Whip: A fancy, expensive car.

[3]Dubs: Rims on a car's tires that are 20" in diameter.

[4]Spinners: Rims that spin independently of the tires.

[5]Sistine Chapel: The main chapel in the Vatican at Rome, famous for its ceilings with detailed paintings by Micheangelo.

Unit 5 — **Answer Key — Answer Key — Answer Key**

Reading Comprehension

After reading "Riding Dubs," choose the options that best answer questions 1–14.

1. Read this sentence.
   This car is a luxury. It's a part of his persona.

   What is the meaning of the word *persona* as it is used in this sentence?
   A. love
   B. wealth
   C. engine
   D. public image

2. Read this sentence.
   However, putting the cart before the horse can get dangerous.

   What is the meaning of the sentence in the context of the article?
   F. Carts and buggies are an old way of driving.
   G. It is dangerous to ride in a cart pulled by a horse.
   H. Buying expensive car parts before you have the money isn't smart.
   I. The cars designed by celebrities are unique like carts and horses once were.

3. From this article, the reader can tell that
   A. adorning cars is not a hobby for the hip-hop world.
   B. it is easy for anyone to fix a car's interior and exterior.
   C. adorning cars is a way of life in the hip-hop industry.
   D. adorning a car is not an expensive hobby for someone to begin.

4. According to the article, which of these is likely to occur?
   F. The fascination with accessorizing cars will continue to follow a downward trend.
   G. Accessorizing a car's interior will become more popular than decorating a car's exterior.
   H. The number of speakers sold will begin to surpass the number of rims sold at auto shows.
   I. Companies that help people accessorize cars will continue to make money by selling the accessories.

5. What aspect of Cavalier Terrell Mitchell's life does the author seem to admire MOST?
   A. his singing
   B. his work ethic
   C. his knack for picking out trendy rims
   D. his financial ability to purchase a Hummer H2

6. The author organizes the article by
   F. providing the positive and negative points of accessorizing a car.
   G. listing the reasons why everyone should consider accessorizing cars.
   H. explaining accessorizing cars and presenting examples of its significance in society.
   I. providing biographical information on hip-hop stars who have chosen to adorn their vehicles.

7. Why does the author begin the article with a detailed description of an accessorized car?
   A. to give the reader a vivid visual image
   B. to explain the importance of accessorizing a car
   C. to inspire the reader with ways to accessorize a car
   D. to discourage the reader from adding accessories to a car

©2008 PRINCIPLE WOODS, INC. Removal of copyright notice and copying are violations of Federal Law.

Answer Key — Answer Key — Answer Key   RIDING DUBS

8. Which title best fits the article?
   F. Hipper Cars
   G. Hip-Hop Artists
   H. Car Shows Galore
   I. Specializing Our Music

9. What attitude does Twista appear to have about his cars?
   A. bored
   B. proud
   C. embarrassed
   D. disinterested

10. Why do hip-hop artists, athletes, and celebrities choose to create different looks for their cars?
    F. to present their own unique style
    G. to give fans different perspectives
    H. to motivate fans to accessorize their own cars
    I. to encourage fans to view the different cars at car shows

11. The author contrasts Poppa G's accessorized cars with "mundane horse and buggies" because the cars
    A. are faster than horse and buggies.
    B. are more expensive than horse and buggies.
    C. are fancier and more intricate than horse and buggies.
    D. are as important to today's society as horse and buggies were in the past.

12. Which of these supports the idea that *DUB Magazine* car shows have helped the hip-hop industry?
    F. The shows introduce fans to new artists.
    G. The shows give hip-hop artists proceeds from the ticket sales.
    H. The shows reaffirm the close relationship between the industry and fans.
    I. The shows provide additional ideas for ways hip-hop artists can adorn their cars in the future.

13. According to the text box, Will Castro has successfully proven that
    A. a minority can be successful.
    B. anyone can create a car accessorizing company.
    C. he understands the different styles of hip-hop artists and athletes.
    D. he has helped to increase the popularity of accessorizing vehicles.

14. Based on the information about both *DUB Magazine* and Will Castro, which of these conclusions is accurate?
    F. Will Castro appears to be more successful with his business than *DUB Magazine*.
    G. More celebrities attend the *DUB Magazine* car shows than watch Will Castro's *Unique Whips*.
    H. *DUB Magazine* and Will Castro both discourage people from adorning the exterior and interior of their vehicles.
    I. Both *DUB Magazine* and Will Castro benefit from the relationship between fans and celebrities who accessorize cars.

Unit 5 — **Answer Key — Answer Key — Answer Key**

Reading Strategy

REFLECTIVE WHEEL

Directions: Reflective questions are written in the question wheel. Interactive readers ask reflective questions while reading to connect to text. Answer the reflective questions in the answer wheel below.

Questions

1. How has Poppa G's life changed since he became famous?
2. What do hip-hop stars look for when choosing their cars?
3. How does a car represent a person?
4. What do Twista's shiny chrome wheels represent in his life?
5. Did Will Castro use his cars to get to his goals, or did they become a part of his goals?
6. Why do you think celebrities want to be a part of *DUB Magazine's* car shows and concerts?

Answers

1. Poppa G has different cars for different days of the week. He no longer drives used cars.
2. The stars are looking for custom cars that showcase their uniqueness and individuality.
3. Cars are customized for each individual to portray the lifestyle that fans come to expect.
4. They represent his new life of fame after spending countless hours singing, rhyming, making calls, and being rejected.
5. Both. His job as a valet led him into the business, and now he profits from the business by creating new looks for each celebrity.
6. This attention creates opportunity for artists to showcase their talent and attract new fans.

©2008 PRINCIPLE WOODS, INC. Removal of copyright notice and copying are violations of Federal Law.

Answer Key — Answer Key — Answer Key **RIDING DUBS**

Interpreting the Data

PART I

Does it make sense to pay more money for a car that will use less gas?

Environmentally Friendly vs. Economical. Use the information in this section to determine whether Americans should start buying hybrid automobiles.

Table 1. Glossary of automobile terms

Term	Definition
Hybrid car	A car that runs on a combination of a gasoline-powered motor and an electrically-powered motor, causing it to use less gasoline and be friendlier to the environment.
Ford Escape Hybrid	Ford Motor Company's version of the hybrid car. It runs on a gasoline motor at high speeds and an electric motor at low speeds. It is meant to save gasoline.
Ford Escape	A car that is almost identical to the Ford Escape Hybrid, but runs solely on a gasoline engine.
Combined miles per gallon	The amount of miles a car can travel on one gallon of gas (on average) when highway and city miles are combined.
MSRP	Manufacturer's Suggested Retail Price. The price that the manufacturer of the car suggests that the dealer charge for the car.

Table 2. Comparison of the Ford Escape and the Ford Escape Hybrid

Car Model	Combined miles per gallon	MSRP
Ford Escape	21	$18,770
Ford Escape Hybrid	30	$26,265

15. After looking at Table 2, one reason to buy the Escape Hybrid instead of the Escape would be that
    A. it costs less.
    B. it costs more.
    C. it gets less combined miles per gallon.
    D. it gets more combined miles per gallon.

16. Table 2 shows that
    A. the Escape costs less and gets more miles per gallon.
    B. the Escape costs more and gets less miles per gallon.
    C. the Escape Hybrid costs more and gets less miles per gallon.
    D. the Escape Hybrid costs more and gets more miles per gallon.

©2008 PRINCIPLE WOODS, INC. Removal of copyright notice and copying are violations of Federal Law.

Unit 5

Answer Key — Answer Key — Answer Key

17. How much more does the Escape Hybrid cost than the Escape?

    $7,495

According to the Environmental Protection Agency, Americans drive an average of 231 miles per week. With 52 weeks in a year, this averages to about 12,000 miles per year. Study Figure 1 to see how much money the average American would save over a 16-year period by driving the Ford Escape Hybrid 12,000 miles per year instead of driving the Ford Escape (non-hybrid). The graph assumes that the average cost of gasoline will remain at $4.00 per gallon each year over the next 16 years.

Figure 1. Gas money saved driving the Escape Hybrid instead of the Escape

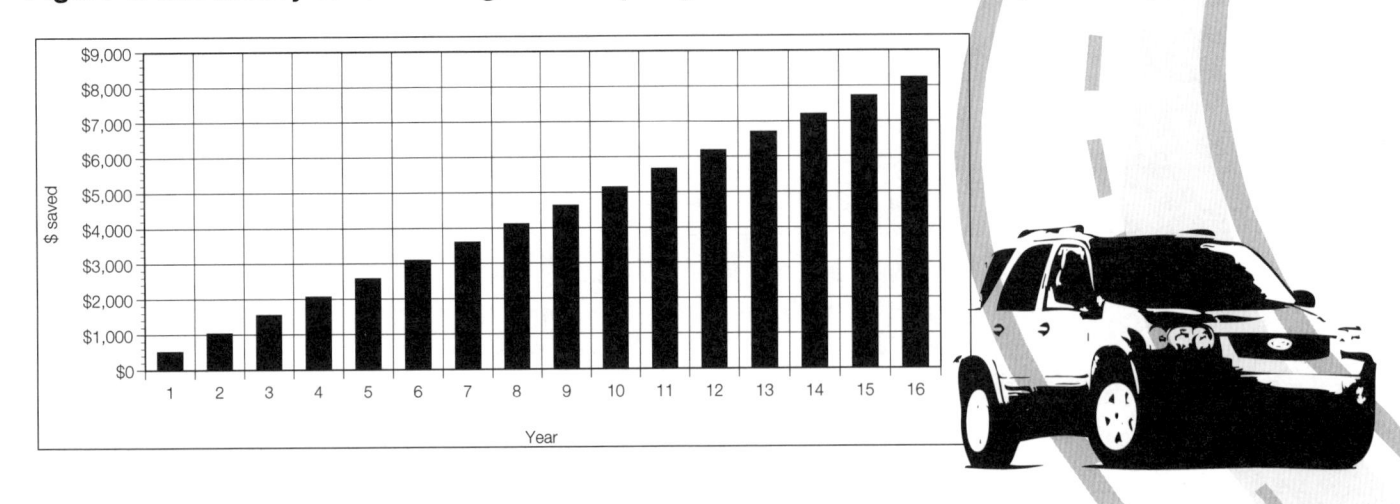

18. According to Figure 1, at least how many years of driving the Escape Hybrid would it take before you would save $1,000 in gas money?

    A. 1
    B. 2
    C. 3
    D. 4

19. According to Figure 1, at least how many years of driving the Escape Hybrid would it take for the gas savings to make up for the extra money you would have paid to purchase the Escape Hybrid instead of the Escape?

    A. 1
    B. 8
    C. 11
    D. 15

20. At 12,000 miles per year, how many miles would you have to drive the Ford Escape Hybrid before the gas savings would make up for the extra money you would have paid to purchase the Escape Hybrid instead of the Escape? Complete your work in the box below:

11 years to save $7,495   X   12,000 miles per year:
12,000
X   11
132,000 miles   Answer: **132,000 miles**

©2008 PRINCIPLE WOODS, INC. Removal of copyright notice and copying are violations of Federal Law.

Answer Key — Answer Key — Answer Key   RIDING DUBS

21. Using the answers you have provided so far and the data from Table 2 and Figure 1, explain which of the cars seems like the better deal economically.

ANALYZE EVALUATE EXPLAIN

Student answers could contain facts such as the following:

The non-hybrid car looks like it might be the better deal economically. If someone were to pay the higher price to purchase the hybrid car, it would take approximately 11 years or 132,000 miles of driving to earn the extra money back in gas savings. Trying to earn back money on something like a car over a 11-year period doesn't seem to be the best way to try to save money. (Of course, students could point out that if the price of gasoline continues to increase at high rates over the next 11 years, then purchasing the hybrid car may be the better deal.)

Use the short-response rubric to reference the criteria required for an acceptable answer and to determine the points to award.

PART II

Is it important for Americans to try to use less gasoline?

Fuel Use. The amount of gasoline purchased by the United States has steadily increased over the last 60 years. The gasoline purchased is measured in units called barrels. Table 3 displays the rise in the amount of gasoline needed by Americans over the last six decades.

Table 3. Amount of gasoline purchased by the United States

Year	Barrels per day
1945	1,587,000
1955	3,463,000
1965	4,593,000
1975	6,675,000
1985	6,831,000
1995	7,789,000
2005	9,159,000

22. Study Table 3. About how much more gas did the U.S. purchase in 2005 than in 1945?
    A. **six times as much**
    B. two times as much
    C. nine times as much
    D. three times as much

Unit 5 — Answer Key — Answer Key — Answer Key

Figure 2 shows the rise in the average retail price of gasoline in the United States over the past 17 years. The prices have been adjusted for inflation using the Consumer Price Index for the value of money in the year 2006. The "$ per gallon" prices on the graph are in 2006 dollars. (For instance, the average price for gas in 1992 was actually $1.04, which equals $1.49 in 2006 dollars.)

Figure 2. Average retail cost of gasoline over the past 17 years

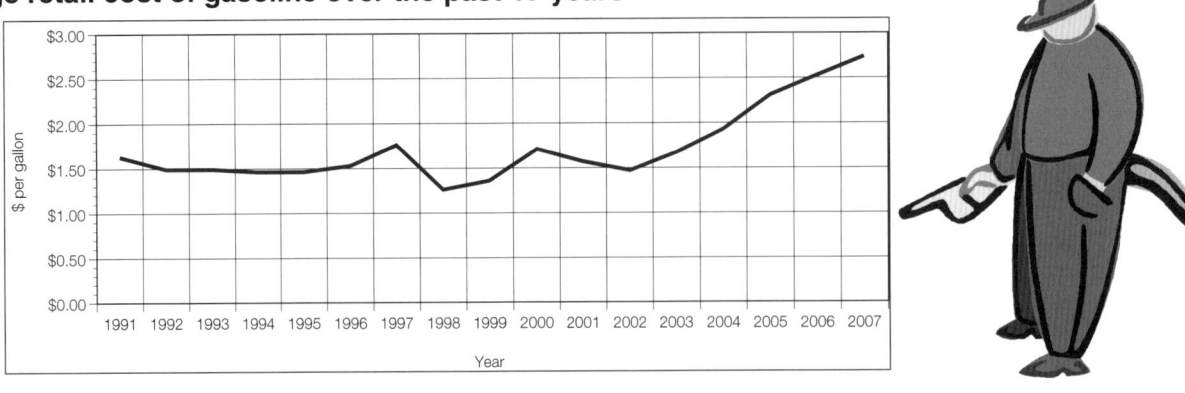

23. Study Figure 2. What has happened to the cost of gasoline over the last 17 years?

    Other than dropping between 1997 and 1998 and between 2000 and 2002, the cost of gasoline has increased overall since 1991—most sharply since 2002.

24. Look at Table 3 and Figure 2. What has happened to the cost of gasoline as the amount purchased has increased?

    In general, as the amount of gasoline purchased has gone up, so has the price.

25. Based on the information provided in this unit, should Americans begin purchasing hybrid automobiles, or should they continue to purchase regular automobiles? Explain the value of purchasing one type of car over the other. Use data from this unit to support your answer.

    ANALYZE SYNTHESIZE EXPLAIN

    Student answers could contain facts such as the following:

    If our need for gasoline and the price of gasoline continue to rise in the future, then it would be important for Americans to start purchasing hybrid cars to save gasoline and hopefully decrease the price of gas. If we continue to purchase regular automobiles, we are doing nothing to save on gas, which could be considered wasteful. We have multiplied our supply of gasoline over the last six decades by six times, which can't be considered environmentally sound.

    Students who are not concerned with the environmental factor may write answers based on economical facts such as those in question 21.

    Use the extended-response rubric to reference the criteria required for an acceptable answer and to determine the points to award.

Answer Key — Answer Key — Answer Key

Reflect and Respond

26. Assume that you have a part-time job that will enable you to earn just enough money to purchase a slightly used car that is not too fancy. You won't be able to afford many accessories. Your parents have agreed that you can purchase a car, but they won't be able to help you with the payments. What will your list of priorities be as you shop? Make a list of the top five items that you will consider as you begin looking, and briefly explain why each of those things is important to you.

Here is a list of the types of things you might want to consider:

-low insurance	-low payments	-good stereo	-nice rims/wheels
-gas mileage	-2- or 4-door	-2- or 4-wheel drive	-big/fast engine
-exterior appearance	-interior appearance	-number of miles	-repairs needed

> Answers may vary, but students should address each part of the question.
>
> The question is meant to elicit strong classroom conversation about character. Students should be able to demonstrate the ability to keep their desire to make a style statement from getting in the way of their ability to make sound financial decisions.
>
> Use the character education rubric to reference the criteria and number of points to award.

Unit 5 — Answer Key — Answer Key — Answer Key

Reading Instructional Guide for Technical Extension

BEFORE READING

Looking at the Words

Determining How the Word Sounds (Phonics)
Technical texts often necessitate the use of multisyllabic words that are unfamiliar to students. Use the Syllable Guide to help students decode any words they might have trouble reading.

Determining What the Word Means (Vocabulary)

Words to Study	Breaking into Syllables	Short Definition
consumer	con-sum-er	(n.) a person who buys things
commission	com-mis-sion	(n.) a fee or percentage given to a sales agent for providing a service
depreciation	de-pre-ci-a-tion	(n.) a loss in value
interest	in-ter-est	(n.) a sum paid for borrowing money
profit	prof-it	(n.) the amount made after expenses are met
warranty	war-ran-ty	(n.) a written promise for a buyer that states a company will make repairs free of charge for a specific time period

Activating Background Knowledge

Graphic Organizer
Either individually or in groups, students may brainstorm about the car buying process, recalling anything previously learned and any prior experience with the subject. Next, encourage students to see the relationships between their ideas by having them complete a basic flow chart demonstrate what they already know about the necessary sequential steps to buying a car.

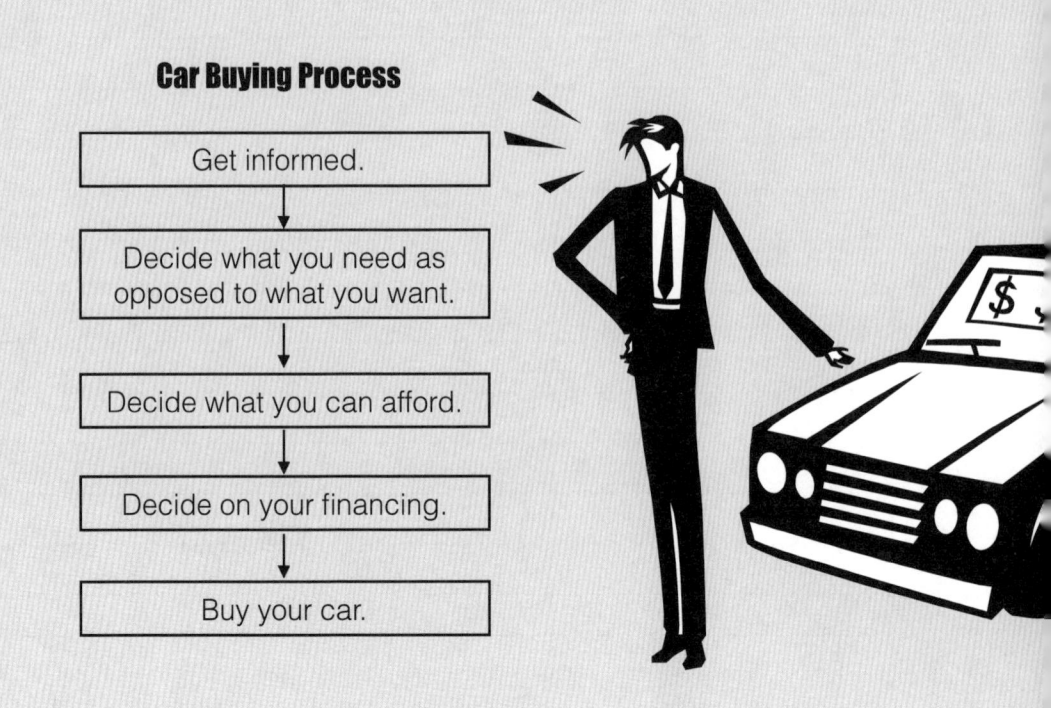

Car Buying Process

Get informed.
↓
Decide what you need as opposed to what you want.
↓
Decide what you can afford.
↓
Decide on your financing.
↓
Buy your car.

Answer Key — Answer Key — Answer Key   RIDING DUBS

Starter Questions
After completing the Graphic Organizer, generate a group or class discussion to come up with questions about the subject, a prediction about the article, and at least one learning goal. The first question has been provided for you.

Question: Name some ways people can obtain information about a car prior to purchasing it.

Question: _____

Prediction: _____

Goal: _____

DURING READING
Use the Reading Instructional Guide Template found in the front of the book.

AFTER READING
After reading, you may teach reading strategy use by giving students opportunities to do the following:
- Review, paraphrase, and summarize
- Participate in main-idea discussions by describing the information in their own words
- Reflect on concept maps and generate additional discussion starter questions based on the mappings
- Participate in small-group discussions using discussion starter questions

Discussion Starter Questions
The first question has been provided for you.

1. What are the advantages and disadvantages of buying a car that is 2–3 years old as opposed to buying a new car?

2. _____

3. _____

©2008 PRINCIPLE WOODS, INC. Removal of copyright notice and copying are violations of Federal Law.

Unit 5

Answer Key — Answer Key — Answer Key

Technical Extension

CAR BUYING 101

Buying a car isn't as easy as it might seem, especially today. As a future consumer, you can learn the basics about the car buying process now. Then you can look forward to getting the best deal *for you* on your very first ride. There are many ways that salespeople make money on a car besides the sticker price on the window. They must make a profit to stay in business, but you can be smart about it too.

You should be as educated as possible before you buy a car. The Internet is a great place to start learning about car buying in general. It can also help you learn about that model you have your heart set on. Also, talking with adults who have already bought cars might help you learn from their mistakes.

Salespeople make commission off of the cars they sell. This sometimes makes them try to get you to buy extra things that are already included in the price. For example, they might try to sell you rustproofing or a warranty. So, it's important to read everything in the contract. The contract may look scary to read, but you need to take the time to do that. The phrase "buyer beware" really does apply here.

While celebrities may be able to pay for a new car in cash, most of the rest of us have to get a loan and make a payment each month. With a loan comes interest. It's important to know how much you can afford each month for your car payment. In order to figure that out, you need to have a budget. How much do you have available for things like clothes, food, rent, and electricity? And don't forget that your car payment is not the only expense that comes along with buying a car. You will also have to pay for insurance, gas, and upkeep. Accessories can also cost a bundle.

Now, let's get back to the dealership to buy your car. Car dealerships will quickly offer to loan you the money to buy your car. They will give you a Retail Installment Sales Contract, or RISC. But beware—it's not your best deal. The dealership's loan will have a very high interest rate. The dealer gets to keep the extra interest as profit. To avoid the RISC, get a loan from a bank before you even go to buy the car.

Did you know that some new cars are worth only half of what you paid for them after the first year? This is called depreciation. It means that you won't be able to sell or trade your car in for as much as you owe on the loan. If you plan to drive the car a long time, this is less important to you. However, if you like to have a new car often, it might be better to get a used car that has already been driven for more than a year.

Maybe you didn't realize that there was so much involved in buying a car. But it's important that you take your time and educate yourself before buying your first new ride. Then go out and enjoy it!

©2008 PRINCIPLE WOODS, INC. Removal of copyright notice and copying are violations of Federal Law.

Answer Key — Answer Key — Answer Key **RIDING DUBS**

Reading Comprehension

After reading "Car Buying 101," choose the options that best answer questions 1–11.

1. What is the meaning of the word *consumer* as it is used in this sentence?
   As a future consumer, you can learn the basics about the car buying process now.

   A. someone who sells cars
   B. someone who works on cars
   C. someone who will buy a car
   D. someone who works in a car factory

2. Read these sentences.
   The contract may look scary to read, but you need to take the time to do that. The phrase "buyer beware" really does apply here.

   Based on these lines, what does the author mean by the phrase *buyer beware*?
   F. Buying a vehicle is an easy process that most people enjoy doing.
   G. One needs to be cautious and read the contract carefully prior to buying a vehicle.
   H. Car salespeople will not try to cheat you, so you can relax when it comes to signing the contract.
   I. Car dealerships should be cautious of their employees' safety and should know everything about a buy prior to selling a car.

3. From this article, the reader can tell that
   A. some people make costly mistakes during the car buying process.
   B. the rate of cars being sold is on the rise when compared to last year's sales.
   C. it is not important to research a vehicle prior to purchasing it from a car dealer.
   D. car buyers prefer to purchase sport utility vehicles over smaller four-door sedans.

4. According to the article, which of these is likely to occur?
   F. A car salesperson will earn commission based on the total price of a car purchase.
   G. Car dealerships will likely offer you a rebate if you purchase additional warranty and protective services.
   H. The average buyer is able to purchase a vehicle with cash and therefore will not need assistance with financing a car loan.
   I. Car dealerships will always offer the best deal, so you do not need to research the car buying process before you purchase a vehicle.

5. The author organize the article by
   A. listing the reasons why the reader should buy a car.
   B. comparing foreign cars to those made in the United States.
   C. providing a detailed account of a day in the life of a car salesperson.
   D. describing and then presenting the key events of the car buying process.

6. Which title best fits the article?
   F. Time to Sell a Car
   G. Where to Buy Cars
   H. The Best Bang for Your Buck
   I. The Ins and Outs of Leasing a Car

7. Why is it important to make a budget prior to buying a car?
   A. to ensure that the buyer can get car insurance
   B. so the buyer can purchase a car that is expensive
   C. so the buyer knows how much he/she can afford
   D. so the buyer can purchase additional equipment for the car

©2008 PRINCIPLE WOODS, INC. Removal of copyright notice and copying are violations of Federal Law.

Answer Key — Answer Key — Answer Key

Unit 5

8. What is the main advantage of buying a used car over a new car?
    F. The buyer gets a better warranty with a used car.
    G. The interest rates are better for used cars than for new cars.
    H. New cars have more manufacture defects than used cars do.
    I. One year after purchase, new cars are worth only half of the original price.

9. Which fact from the article provides the BEST evidence that a consumer should obtain financing prior to purchasing a vehicle?
    A. The buyer should look over the purchasing contract prior to signing it.
    B. The car salesperson's commission is based on the total price of the vehicle.
    C. Car dealerships will attempt to offer you financing from their provider of choice.
    D. Dealers mark up their interest rate to profit from the difference between the low rate and the higher rate.

10. People who read this article will learn how to
    F. apply for a car loan.
    G. get the best deal on a car.
    H. become a car salesperson.
    I. fix a car when a problem arises.

11. Based on the information provided in the article regarding BOTH commission and new cars, which of these conclusions is accurate?
    A. A car dealership would like to sell more used cars than new cars.
    B. Newer vehicles are easier for car dealerships to market than previously owned vehicles.
    C. A consumer can obtain a lower interest rate for buying a used car than for buying a new car.
    D. Given the same make and model, a car salesperson will likely receive more commission from the sale of a new car than from the sale of a used car.

Answer Key — Answer Key — Answer Key RIDING DUBS

Technical Writing Prompt

12. Imagine that it is time to buy your very first car. Explain to your parents that you are ready for a car and that you have done your research. Write down the steps you took to pick out the car you want to purchase and a proposal for how you will pay for it. Write a clear report for your parents, including facts from the article to show them that you are now an expert in the car buying process.

> Student answers may vary.
>
> The student should address the question to the best of his/her ability using the article and personal experience. The question is meant to prepare students to be active citizens who can accurately and effectively use written communication skills.
>
> Use the technical writing rubric to reference the criteria and determine the number of points to award.

Unit 5

Answer Key — Answer Key — Answer Key

Vocational Extension

HELP WANTED:
Salamento Automotive is looking for an automotive service technician to fill a part-time position. Candidates must have good knowledge of computer systems and basic mechanics, but recent high school graduates will be considered with on-the-job training available. To set up an interview, stop by the auto shop.

Since before Henry Ford introduced the Model T in 1908, mechanics have been busy. Things with motors are constantly breaking, so those with the know-how to repair, restore, and replace are in demand. Most things with motors require ongoing service that the average person can't do.

The job of a mechanic has changed since the 1900s as technology has become more complex. Mechanics used to need training and education mostly in mechanical engineering. In other words, they used their hands to fix engine problems. Although those skills are used some today, much of what a mechanic must learn to do now involves technology and computers.

Mechanics need technology skills and the ability to diagnose problems. In addition, having the basic skills of mechanical engineering is required. If you enjoy solving problems or fixing things that are broken, then perhaps mechanics is a field you would enjoy.

Training is the most important part of mechanical engineering. There are many options for getting experience. Many high schools offer programs such as Automotive Youth Education Service (AYES) that offer a great start. Many will then go on to take a full-time course that gives them basic knowledge and skills. Still others become apprentices and learn their skills by working under a mechanical expert. A select few go on to college and even to graduate school to get a degree in mechanical engineering. This allows them to work on complex machines such as airplanes.

Mechanics are important to society because almost everyone uses something with a motor daily. Not only do mechanics get to do what they love, but they help people with their problems every day. Mechanics are important to society because nearly everyone regularly uses something with a motor. Not only do mechanics get to do what they love—tinker, take apart, repair, and rebuild—but they help people with their problems every day.

Answer Key — Answer Key — Answer Key

Mechanic Career Options and Information

Job	Basic Description	Income
Automotive Air Conditioning Tech	Repairs and installs air conditioning	$14.71 median hourly wage
Automotive Body Repair Tech	Restores damaged motor vehicles	$15.71 median hourly wage
Automotive Glass Installer	Repairs and installs car window glass	$12.93 median hourly wage
Automotive Mechanic Supervisor	Manages and coordinates auto shop	$1,200- $4,500 monthly
Automotive Painter	Prepares and paints (spray) automobiles	$16.13 median hourly wage
Automotive Service Advisor	Works in customer service; prepares service order	$1,200- $4,500 monthly
Aviation Mechanic	Works on airframes, power plants, or repair	$40,000 yearly average
Brake Repairer	Adjusts, repairs, or replaces brake parts	$14.71 median hourly wage
Diesel Service Technician	Maintains and repairs diesel engines	$16.53 median hourly wage
Farm Equipment Mechanic	Services and repairs farm equipment	$13.03 median hourly wage
Front End Mechanic	Aligns and balances brakes; repairs steering	$14.71 median hourly wage
Heavy Equipment Mechanic	Maintains and repairs construction vehicles	$17.29 median hourly wage
Marine Mechanic	Maintains and repairs boat engines	$13.97 median hourly wage
Motorcycle Mechanic	Repairs and overhauls motorcycles	$25,100 yearly average
Railcar Repair Tech	Services and repairs railcars (trains, etc.)	$18.78 median hourly wage
Transmission Technician	Maintains and repairs vehicle transmissions	$14.71 median hourly wage
Tune-up Technician	Adjusts and replaces spark plugs and valves	$14.71 median hourly wage

©2008 PRINCIPLE WOODS, INC. Removal of copyright notice and copying are violations of Federal Law.

Unit 5 — Answer Key — Answer Key — Answer Key

Looking Forward

13. A mechanic plays an important role in society. If it were not for mechanics, many people would have a difficult time with their transportation and careers. Look at the list of Mechanic Career Options. If you were a mechanic, which field would you choose? Using personal experience and information from the article, explain why your chosen field would be best for you.

> Student answers may vary.
>
> The student should address the question to the best of his/her ability using the article and personal experience. The question is meant to encourage students to explore areas of interest for their future and begin to determine how they will prepare for a future career.
>
> Use the extended-response rubric to reference the criteria and determine the number of points to award.

Ethical Dilemma

14. You work as a mechanic in a busy repair shop near an interstate highway. A woman who is making a cross-country trip drives into the shop one afternoon and says she heard a strange noise from one of the tires. You determine that there is nothing wrong with any of her tires, but your boss instructs you to tell her that one of them is bad and must be replaced immediately. She apparently has the money to do this, but you know it isn't necessary. If you don't follow your boss's orders, you could lose your job. What do you do?

> Student answers may vary.
>
> The student should address the question to the best of his/her ability using background knowledge from the article as well as personal opinion and experience. The question is meant to encourage students to contemplate scenarios and make ethical decisions.
>
> Use the character education rubric to reference the criteria and determine the number of points to award.

©2008 PRINCIPLE WOODS, INC. Removal of copyright notice and copying are violations of Federal Law.

Answer Key — Answer Key — Answer Key

Unit Vocabulary Assessment

Matching
Match each word in Column I to its definition in Column II.

Column I

- **C** 1. amateur
- **A** 2. valet
- **E** 3. credibility
- **D** 4. depreciation
- **B** 5. luxury

Column II

a. a person who parks cars for customers
b. an object obtained for pleasure, not need
c. a person who is inexperienced
d. a loss in value
e. the quality of being believable

Multiple Choice
Choose the word that MOST NEARLY replaces the underlined word in each sentence.

6. Carson's public persona is very different from the way he acts in private.
   A. person
   B. picture
   C. reputation
   D. personality

7. When consumers spend money, it helps the economy.
   A. men
   B. women
   C. buyers
   D. businesses

8. It is our custom to get together every Friday evening.
   A. job
   B. routine
   C. customer
   D. interesting fact

9. The unique vase is in a very special place in our home.
   A. old
   B. strange
   C. unusual
   D. entertaining

Word Bank
- accessorize
- commission
- interest
- profit
- warranty

Fill in the Blank
Choose a word from the word bank to fill in the blank in the sentence below.

10. My decorator can **accessorize** any room in the house.
11. When you take out a loan, it's expected that you will pay **interest** to the bank.
12. The **profit** from the concert after expenses was very good.
13. Peter earned a **commission** of 5% on what he sold.
14. When the dryer broke, we were glad to have a **warranty**.

Answer Key — Answer Key — Answer Key

Unit 5

Authentic Assessment

Students will design their car of the future based on the unit "Riding Dubs." This activity combines the authentic components of research and creativity linked to the comprehension of a written text. Students should be given access to sources which detail the need for and examples of "green" cars.

Instructions for Car Design

1. **The need.** Explain to students that as environmental issues such as fuel worries and pollution concerns increase, there will be an ever-greater need to create cars that use alternative sources of fuel.

2. **Research.** Have students work in self-chosen or teacher-designed groups of four. Groups should research both the reasons for "going green" and current as well as projected ways in which the design of cars can reflect the green mentality.

3. **Design.** Groups will choose at least three design concepts for making their car green which can include fuel source, body design, mechanics, etc. Groups will then create a sketch of their car. After the sketch is approved by the teacher, groups will create a final design product.

4. **Reflection.** In addition to the group design, each member of the group will submit a reflection that includes answers to the following questions:

    a. What did you learn about green causes?

    b. Why did your group choose the particular design concepts?

    c. How will this car help the environment?

5. **Assessment.** Cooperative behaviors are a major factor in the assessment of this project. Inform students before they begin that they will be graded using the rubric below and that they must supply proof that they performed each of the required behaviors to a sufficient level. Once the designs are completed, have students complete a cooperative group rubric in order to self-assess the cooperative behaviors they exhibited during the project. Then have a teacher conference with each group and use the rubrics to assess cooperative behavior.

Resource List

GreenCar.com:
http://www.greencar.com/

greenercars.org:
http://www.greenercars.org/

Yahoo! Autos Green Center:
http://autos.yahoo.com/green_center/

Green Car Company:
http://www.thegreencarco.com/

Answer Key — Answer Key — Answer Key

Cooperative Learning Green Car Design Rubric

Instructions: Assess yourself in each of the areas below by circling the number that best reflects your participation in the cooperative learning assignment. On the lines below, list the specific ways you participated in each area.

1. You were active in researching green causes and the need for green cars.

    3- A lot   2- Some   1- Very little   0- Not at all

    Specific Activities: _____

    _____

2. You participated in determining which design concepts to incorporate.

    3- A lot   2- Some   1- Very little   0- Not at all

    Specific Activities: _____

    _____

3. You participated in planning the car design.

    3- A lot   2- Some   1- Very little   0- Not at all

    Specific Activities: _____

    _____

4. You participated in the sketch and/or final design product.

    3- A lot   2- Some   1- Very little   0- Not at all

    Specific Activities: _____

    _____

5. You worked collaboratively and successfully with your group.

    3- A lot   2- Some   1- Very little   0- Not at all

    Specific Activities: _____

    _____

The teacher will use student-completed rubrics and group conferences to assess each group's design and make goals for improvement in student cooperative learning.

Unit 6

THE RIGHT TO SUPPORT THEM

Reading Instructional Guide for High-Interest Article

BEFORE READING

Front-Loading Background Knowledge through Read Aloud/Think Aloud

Search the Internet for recent articles on supporting our troops and use them to model the effective habits of readers through a Read Aloud/Think Aloud.

Check out articles at the following websites to determine if they would be appropriate for your RATA:

- United Service Organizations. http://www.uso.org/.
- America Supports You: Our Military Men and Women. U.S. Department of Defense. http://www.americasupportsyou.mil/.

(Please keep in mind that it is the responsibility of the teacher to determine if articles from suggested sites are appropriate. The sites may have changed content since this publication. The publisher takes no responsibility for the current content of the site.)

Looking at the Words

Determining How the Word Sounds (Phonics)
Using the Syllable Guide and the Reading Instructional Guide Template found in the beginning of the book, follow the steps to help students learn how to break a word into manageable parts.

Determining What the Word Means (Vocabulary)

Words to Study	Breaking into Syllables	Short Definition
adrenaline	a-dren-a-line	(n.) a bodily hormone released in response to stress
advocate	ad-vo-cate	(n.) one who speaks or writes in support of something
criticize	crit-i-cize	(v.) to judge or find fault
legacy	leg-a-cy	(n.) something handed down
liberty	lib-er-ty	(n.) freedom
patriot	pa-tri-ot	(n.) a person who loves, supports, and defends his or her country
principle	prin-ci-ple	(n.) a belief or truth that forms the basis of other beliefs or truths
risky	risk-y	(adj.) involving danger
sacrifice	sac-ri-fice	(v.) to give up something for the greater value

©2008 PRINCIPLE WOODS, INC. Removal of copyright notice and copying are violations of Federal Law.

Answer Key — Answer Key — Answer Key

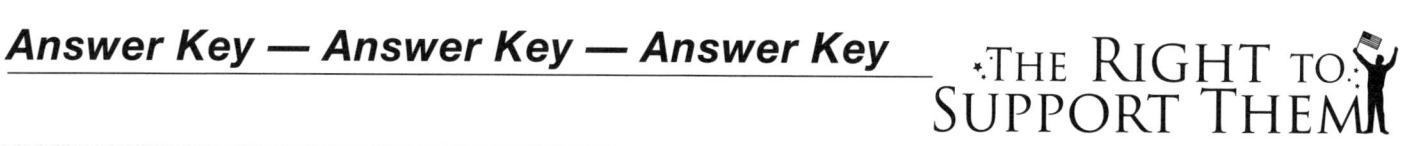

Activating Background Knowledge

Anticipation Guide
Have students mark each of the following statements True or False:

1. ____ Prior to Bob Hope's death, he provided inspirational support to our troops.
2. ____ Most Americans support our country's involvement in the Iraq war.
3. ____ Due to safety concerns, our government no longer allows celebrities to travel overseas to support our troops.
4. ____ The USO is as strong today as it was in the past.
5. ____ The goal of our military is to defend and protect our country's freedom.

Starter Questions
After completing the Anticipation Guide, have a group or class discussion with the students using the following questions:

1. What are the characteristics of a patriot?
2. What is the USO?
3. What is an advocate?
4. What is the main political difference between Matt Damon and Bruce Willis?
5. How do celebrities increase the morale of our troops who are overseas?

Make a prediction about what you think the article will be about.

DURING READING
Use the Reading Instructional Guide Template found in the front of the book.

AFTER READING

Discussion Starter Questions

1. Why do you think we have seen a decline in support for the war since 2003?
2. Should celebrities use their fame when supporting or opposing the war? Why? Why not?
3. How can staying informed help you form opinions and make responsible decisions regarding the war?
4. How can students in your school increase the morale of overseas troops?
5. Should movie producers continue making movies about war while soldiers are overseas defending our country? Why? Why not?

Teacher Reflection

Use the Reading Instructional Guide Template found in the front of the book.

THE RIGHT TO SUPPORT THEM

The Real Action Heroes

Pop-pop-pop! Machine-gun fire echoes through the night. Bright flashes of light and screaming rockets shower down upon them. America watches and roots them on, hopeful that they will escape again. On one screen you see Bruce Willis, star of *Live Free or Die Hard*. On the other, it is Matt Damon, star of *The Bourne Ultimatum*. Millions sit and watch the battles created by Hollywood, praying that their action heroes make it out alive.

Movies are fiction, but in real life Americans far away struggle to protect their own lives. Their stories aren't written in a script, and there is no director to yell "Cut!" when things don't work out right. Their wounds are real, not painted on. So is the adrenaline rushing through their bodies. These are the real members of the American military fighting wars against terrorism in Iraq and Afghanistan.

History will agree that these men and women are true American patriots. But what about the rest of us? What about entertainers who voice their opinions about the war in Iraq? What about those who ask whether America should be involved in these wars?

Code Name: Patriot

What is a patriot? Do patriots fire their rifles at enemies who threaten the freedom and principles our nation is built on? Or could a patriot be a person in America using his freedom of speech to protest our involvement in the war?

When the American military was sent to Iraq in 2003, most Americans stood behind the decision. But after several years, fewer people agree with our involvement in the war. Actors Bruce Willis and Matt Damon represent these opposing views.

Willis and Damon have starred in countless action films. In some, they have played war heroes. In real life, Bruce Willis has entertained the troops fighting in Iraq. He also supported President Bush's decision to invade Iraq. Matt Damon joins Willis in his support of the troops, but he doesn't think that the U.S. military should still be in Iraq four years later. However, he wants people to understand that he respects the troops and cares for their safety. Unlike many celebrities who have spoken out against the war, Damon actually traveled overseas in 2001 to show support for our troops.

So, of the two celebrities, who is the greater patriot? Bruce Willis, for being an advocate for the troops and the president they represent? Or Matt Damon, for supporting the troops but publicly criticizing a war that he believes is endangering the lives of his fellow Americans?

Lost Hope for Military Entertainment?

In past wars, many celebrities traveled to the countries where American troops were stationed. Comedian and entertainer Bob Hope led many United Service Organizations (USO) shows overseas. The purpose of these shows was to take a small taste of home to the troops. The performances were great for giving service members a break from the stress of war. Stars such as Marilyn Monroe gave the troops a reason to forget about the battles they were fighting.

Answer Key — Answer Key — Answer Key

But Bob Hope passed away several years ago, and his legacy was left to singer and entertainer Wayne Newton. Unfortunately, many of the soldiers aren't familiar with Mr. Newton. He has worked hard to find people to perform in Iraq. But it has been very difficult for the USO to build the same level of excitement that Bob Hope brought to the shows. In addition, Newton has had a tough time finding big-name celebrities who are willing to go to the war zone. Some of the biggest entertainers to make it over to Iraq through USO tours include Kid Rock, Jessica Simpson, Darryl Worley, Robin Williams, Drew Carey, Kelly Clarkson, 50 Cent, Al Franken, and Bruce Willis. Though these celebrities are appreciated, some troops still feel like they are being forgotten by their favorites back home.

Newton says that many celebrities won't travel to Iraq because they disagree with the reasons America is fighting the war. They are afraid that going will make it seem like they support the war. Others, such as comedians Robin Williams and Al Franken, are critics of the war itself, but have traveled to Iraq several times just to show support for the troops. They show that it is possible to disagree with the government but still be concerned about the safety of the troops.

Some entertainers won't go because they feel it is too dangerous. Comedian Al Franken recalls a time when he talked with actor Sylvester Stallone, who played aggressive action hero Johnny Rambo. Stallone said he didn't go to the war zone because he "heard it might be dangerous." Franken jokingly replied, "Weren't you Rambo?" Stallone reportedly answered, "Yeah, but I like my life."

Rapper 50 Cent realized how risky entertaining in Iraq could be. On the first day he was there, a soldier bluntly reminded him that he could die that day. 50 Cent later spoke of his respect for the U.S. military and the dangers they face each day during the war.

Support Even If You Don't Support

There are many different opinions about America's involvement in wars. Opinions are important to have, but they are only valuable if they are supported with facts. Therefore, it is important to become informed. You can watch the news, read the newspaper, and discuss your opinions with both peers and adults. This will help you know how to vote thoughtfully for the people who face the difficult job of deciding when to send troops to war.

Even if you don't agree with the reasons America is fighting a war, the troops and their families need your support. Consider the examples of those celebrities who support the troops, regardless of their opinions on the war. Our military members serve America to protect you and your liberty. They are following the orders they are given. They make sacrifices every day to help the world live with the same freedom that we enjoy.

Unit 6 — Answer Key — Answer Key — Answer Key

Reading Comprehension

After reading "The Right to Support Them," choose the options that best answer questions 1–14.

1. Read this sentence.
   Or could a patriot be a person in America using his freedom of speech to protest our involvement in the war?

   What is the meaning of the word *protest* as it is used in this sentence?
   A. cheer
   B. oppose
   C. provoke
   D. announce

2. Read this sentence.
   On the first day he was there, a soldier bluntly reminded him that he could die that day.

   What is the meaning of the word *bluntly* as it is used in the sentence?
   F. angrily
   G. happily
   H. timidly
   I. frankly

3. From this article, the reader can tell that
   A. actors Bruce Willis and Matt Damon are friends.
   B. troops do not enjoy having celebrities visit them overseas.
   C. the number of celebrities who visit our troops overseas has declined over the years.
   D. the number of people who go to a theater to watch a movie has increased over the years.

4. Bob Hope's greatest contribution to the armed forces was
   F. fighting in the Iraq war.
   G. financially supporting the troops.
   H. visiting the family members of those who were fighting overseas.
   I. providing entertainment to troops who were away from their families.

5. In the author's opinion,
   A. we should support the troops even if we don't approve of the war.
   B. fictional movies about war are more entertaining than most other movies.
   C. celebrities should not risk their lives by traveling overseas to visit the troops.
   D. celebrities should not publicly approve or disapprove of governmental policies.

6. The author organizes the article by
   F. listing the major events of the war in chronological order.
   G. raising the issue of supporting the military and providing varied opinions.
   H. describing various kinds of war movies that have been produced in recent years.
   I. providing the questions and answers from a recent interview with a top USO official.

7. Why does the author mention fictional movies about war?
   A. to entertain the reader
   B. to encourage the reader to support local movie theaters
   C. to persuade the reader to pursue a career in acting or film production
   D. to explain the difference between a war that is produced on camera and a war in reality

124

©2008 PRINCIPLE WOODS, INC. Removal of copyright notice and copying are violations of Federal Law.

Answer Key — Answer Key — Answer Key

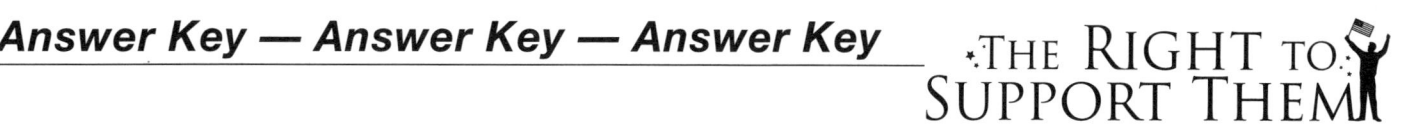

8. Which title best fits the article?
   F. Hopeless
   G. Hollywood Battles
   H. Striving to Strengthen Support
   I. Governmental Policies in Our Country

9. What is the tone of this article?
   A. sad
   B. angry
   C. opinionated
   D. disinterested

10. Why do some celebrities decline to visit Iraq?
    F. They believe their safety is in jeopardy.
    G. They do not want to endure the long flight.
    H. Their hectic schedules will not allow them to travel.
    I. They worry about being exposed to illnesses while there.

11. The major difference between Bob Hope's USO and Wayne Newton's USO is that
    A. Wayne Newton is more famous than Bob Hope was.
    B. Wayne Newton has worked harder than Bob Hope did in promoting the USO.
    C. Bob Hope was able to attract more talent for performances than Wayne Newton can today.
    D. Bob Hope focused on attracting musical celebrities, while Wayne Newton employs movie actors and actresses.

12. Which statement about the USO is LEAST accurate?
    F. It is as strong today as it was prior to Bob Hope's death.
    G. The troops enjoy receiving visits from famous celebrities and watching them perform.
    H. The goal of the USO is to increase the morale of those troops who are based overseas.
    I. The USO has more difficulty than before with getting celebrities to become a part of their program.

13. Which quotation from the article provides the BEST evidence of the author's argument that the troops should be supported?
    A. Rapper 50 Cent realized how risky entertaining in Iraq could be.
    B. There are many different opinions about America's involvement in wars.
    C. They make sacrifices every day to help the world live with the same freedom that we enjoy.
    D. This will help you know how to vote thoughtfully for the people who face the difficult job of deciding when to send troops to war.

14. Which statement is correct according to the article?
    F. Opinions should be supported with facts.
    G. Facts are always more important that opinions.
    H. One should never discuss opinions with friends.
    I. The news should not influence a person's opinion.

Unit 6 — *Answer Key — Answer Key — Answer Key*

Reading Strategy

Directions: Words have been selected from the article for you to connect with meaning. Use the information from the article to help you create sentences that connect the words. Be as specific as you can. Draw lines between the words and create five new sentences. By making connections among words, you will be practicing activating background knowledge, inferencing, and connecting. An example is shown below.

Celebrities   Opinions   Patriots

Respect   Sacrifices   Entertainers

Stress   Terrorism   Criticize

Liberty   Adrenaline   Dangerous

The vocabulary words are not necessarily difficult, but this activity will allow the opportunity for students to use context and play with words and meanings.

#	Word	Word	Sentence
1	Entertainers	Patriots	Although **entertainers** aren't all in favor of having troops in Iraq, those who are willing to travel overseas to entertain and support the troops can be considered **patriots**.
2	Terrorism	Adrenaline	When I see soldiers on TV fighting the war against **terrorism**, I know that my **adrenaline** must be rising when I feel my pulse increasing and my hands becoming sweaty.
3	Stress	Terrorism	Entertainers give the soldiers some relief from the **stress** of fighting in the war on **terrorism**.
4			
5			
6			

©2008 PRINCIPLE WOODS, INC. Removal of copyright notice and copying are violations of Federal Law.

Answer Key — Answer Key — Answer Key

Interpreting the Data

PART I

How does President Bush's approval rating during his presidency compare to that of Congress during the same time period?

Refer to Figure 1 to answer questions 15–20.

Figure 1. Approval ratings of President Bush and Congress

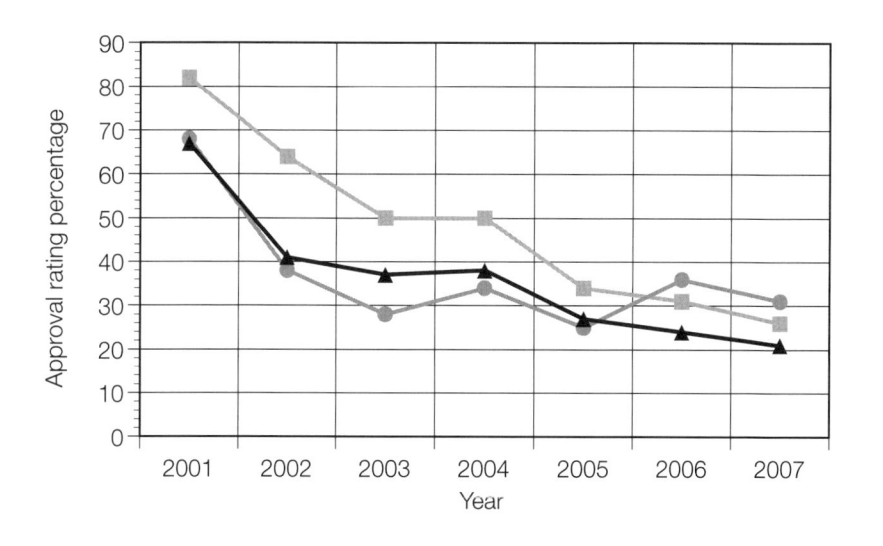

15. About what percentage of people approved of President Bush when he was re-elected in 2004?

50

16. About what percentage of people approved of President Bush after the attack on the Twin Towers in 2001?

82

17. What was the approximate difference in 2001 between the approval rating of President Bush and that of Democrats in Congress? (Answer in percentage points.)

15 percentage points

18. In what year was there a dramatic shift to a greater approval of Democrats in Congress after four years of Republicans having a higher approval rating?

2006

Answer Key — Answer Key — Answer Key
Unit 6

19. Based on Figure 1, describe the general trend of the public's approval of President Bush and their approval of the Republicans and Democrats in Congress between 2001 and 2007. Who began with the highest approval rating? Who ended with the highest approval rating? What does this trend show?

ANALYZE
COMPREHEND
EVALUATE

Student answers could contain facts such as the following:

The public's approval of President Bush and of both Democrats and Republicans in Congress steadily declined in the years between 2001 and 2007. President Bush began with the highest approval rating, at 82%. Democrats ended with the highest approval rating, at 31%. This trend demonstrates that the public's approval of government leaders decreased over the years.

Use the extended-response rubric to reference the criteria required for an acceptable answer and to determine the points to award.

20. Former President George H.W. Bush enjoyed his highest approval rating at the beginning of the Persian Gulf War. Approval ratings of both President Bush and Congress were the highest in 2001, the time of the terrorist attacks known as 9/11. Why do you think this was the case?

ANALYZE
EVALUATE
EXPLAIN

Student answers could contain facts such as the following:

In times of tragedy, American citizens tend to rally behind their government leaders. They may feel greater patriotism when faced with the possibility or reality of war, and they may put their trust in their government when faced with uncertain enemies.

Use the short-response rubric to reference the criteria required for an acceptable answer and to determine the points to award.

Answer Key — Answer Key — Answer Key

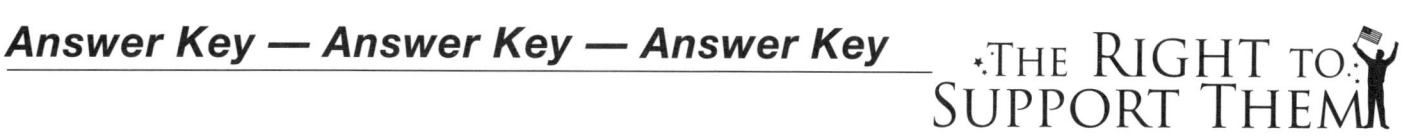

THE RIGHT TO SUPPORT THEM

PART II

How does the number of soldier casualties in the Iraq War compare to the number of casualties in other wars the United States has participated in?

Answer questions 21–25 by filling in the pie chart and the key in Figure 2.

Table 1. U.S. casualties of war (battle deaths)

War	U.S. casualties	% of total U.S. casualties
Iraq War (2003–present*)	3,287	0.51
Persian Gulf War (1990–1991)	148	0.02
Vietnam War (1964–1975)	47,355	7.37
Korean War (1950–1953)	33,746	5.25
World War II (1941–1945)	291,557	45.36
World War I (1917–1918)	53,402	8.31
Spanish-American War (1898–1902)	385	0.06
Civil War (1861–1865)	212,938	33.12
Total U.S. casualties	**642,818**	**100.00**

*Note: Iraq War number is based on "hostile" death statistics available as of March 29, 2008.

Figure 2. U.S. casualties of war

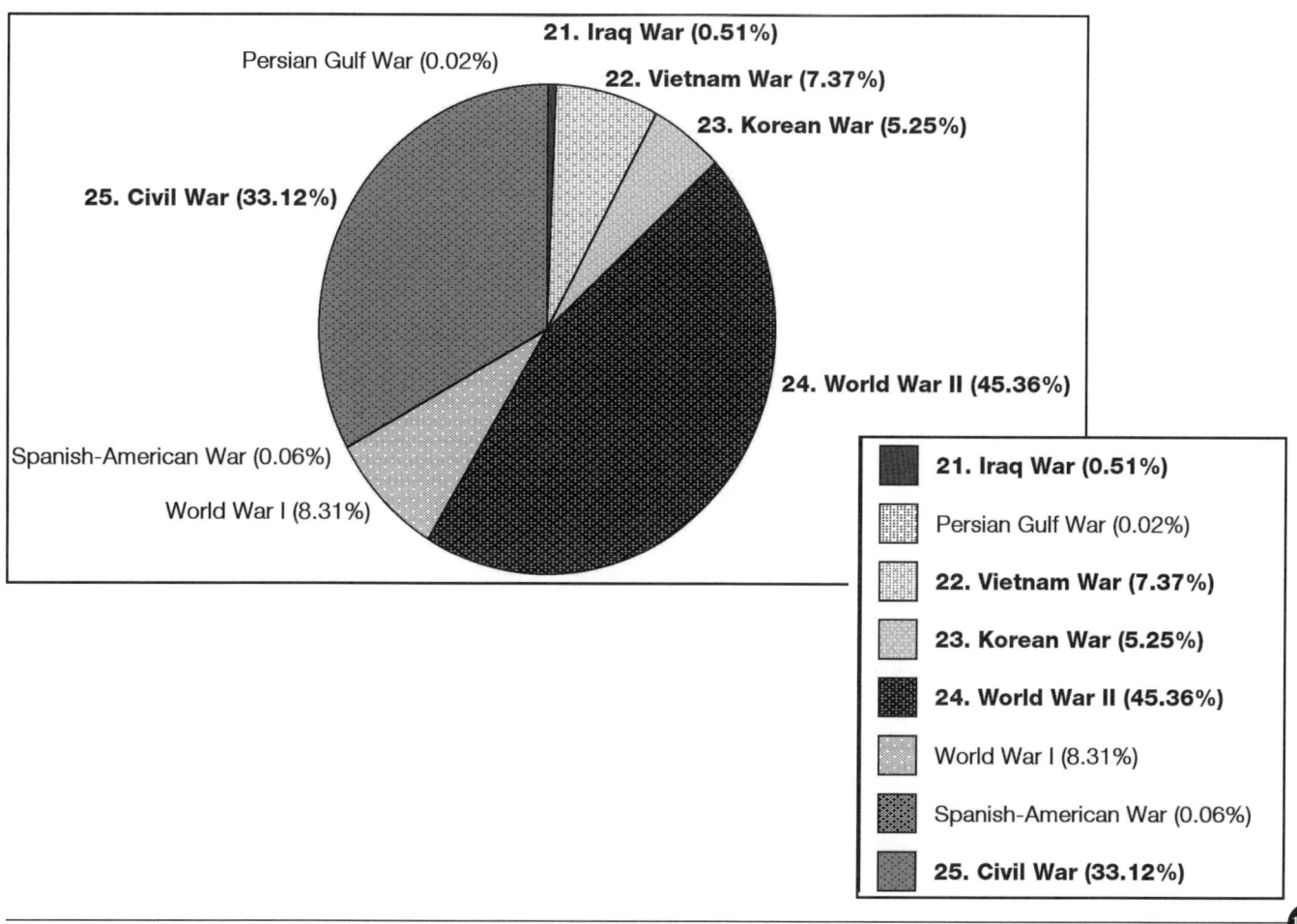

Pie chart segments:
- 21. Iraq War (0.51%)
- Persian Gulf War (0.02%)
- 22. Vietnam War (7.37%)
- 23. Korean War (5.25%)
- 24. World War II (45.36%)
- World War I (8.31%)
- Spanish-American War (0.06%)
- 25. Civil War (33.12%)

Key:
- 21. Iraq War (0.51%)
- Persian Gulf War (0.02%)
- 22. Vietnam War (7.37%)
- 23. Korean War (5.25%)
- 24. World War II (45.36%)
- World War I (8.31%)
- Spanish-American War (0.06%)
- 25. Civil War (33.12%)

Unit 6 — Answer Key — Answer Key — Answer Key

Reflect and Respond

26. The majority of military members who have fought in our country's wars have not been much older than you are right now. Use what you've learned from this unit to develop your own thoughts on war and joining the military. Then use the space below for a free-write that expresses your ideas. Here are some questions you may choose to consider while putting your thoughts on paper:
    - Is war necessary? Is it unavoidable when different cultures want to live together on the same earth?
    - If you were president of the United States, what are three situations in which you could justify going to war with another nation?
    - If you were a soldier fighting in a war and a friend of yours protested the war, would you still consider that person your friend?
    - If you were the leader of a small country and had to create a budget for your country, would you spend more money on your military or on your schools? Explain your answer.

> Student answers may vary, but students should address each part of the question. The question is meant to elicit strong classroom conversation about character. Students should be able to demonstrate their opinions about the subject of war and their ability to use facts learned from this unit to make decisions as responsible citizens.
>
> Use the character education rubric to reference the criteria and number of points to award.

Answer Key — Answer Key — Answer Key

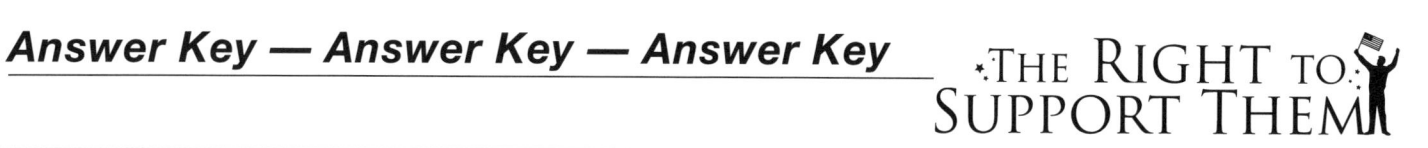

THE RIGHT TO SUPPORT THEM

Reading Instructional Guide for Technical Extension

BEFORE READING

Looking at the Words

Determining How the Word Sounds (Phonics)
Technical texts often necessitate the use of multisyllabic words that are unfamiliar to students. Use the Syllable Guide to help students decode any words they might have trouble reading.

Determining What the Word Means (Vocabulary)

Words to Study	Breaking into Syllables	Short Definition
continuous	con-tin-u-ous	(adj.) uninterrupted
issue	is-sue	(n.) a point of discussion
minority	mi-nor-i-ty	(n.) a small group of citizens
perspective	per-spec-tive	(n.) point of view
relatively	rel-a-tive-ly	(adv.) in comparison with something else
vital	vi-tal	(adj.) necessary

Activating Background Knowledge

Graphic Organizer
Either individually or in groups, students may brainstorm about the pros and cons of our media sources, recalling anything previously learned and any prior experience with the subject. Next, encourage students to see the relationships between their ideas by having them complete the following table to demonstrate what they already know about the methods we use to stay informed regarding the news.

Media Source	Pros	Cons
Television		
Internet		
Blogs		
Radio		
Newspaper		

Unit 6

Answer Key — Answer Key — Answer Key

Starter Questions
After completing the Graphic Organizer, generate a group or class discussion to come up with questions about the subject, a prediction about the article, and at least one learning goal. The first question has been provided for you.

Question: Why do so many more people get their news from the Internet than from other media sources?

Question: _____

Prediction: _____

Goal: _____

DURING READING
Use the Reading Instructional Guide Template found in the front of the book.

AFTER READING
After reading, you may teach reading strategy use by giving students opportunities to do the following:
- Review, paraphrase, and summarize
- Participate in main-idea discussions by describing the information in their own words
- Reflect on concept maps and generate additional discussion starter questions based on the mappings
- Participate in small-group discussions using discussion starter questions

Discussion Starter Questions

The first question has been provided for you.

1. How do you think technological advancements influence the way our society obtains news and updates?

2. _____

3. _____

Answer Key — Answer Key — Answer Key

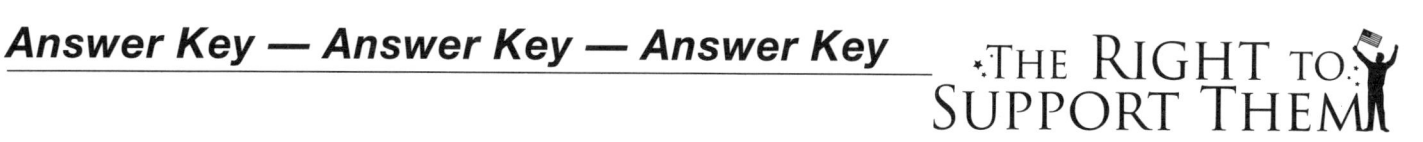

Technical Extension

THE INFORMATION HIGHWAY

Because we live in a democracy, it is important for all citizens to be informed. This is especially true in a year of a presidential vote. This is so we can make the best possible use of our right to vote. Without informed citizens, elections can be determined by a minority of the population. But everyone must still obey the laws that are decided by those who vote.

So, where do Americans get most of their information? Various media sources report every day on the issues and the candidates. About 9.7 million people read one or more daily newspapers to gather the facts. This method gives them the opportunity to read the news at any time of the day. They can carry the paper with them wherever they go, and they can re-read sections as often as they choose.

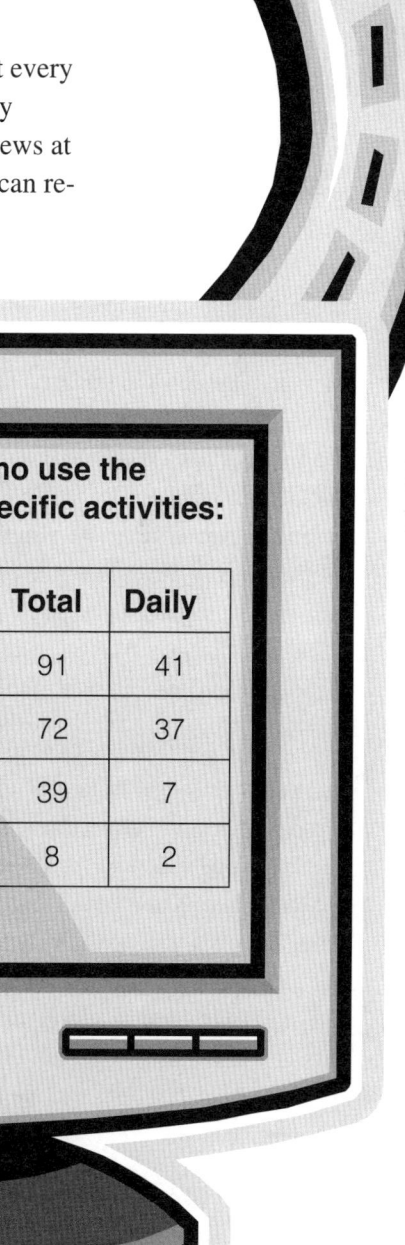

Percentage of Americans who use the Internet for the following specific activities:

Activity	Total	Daily
Use search engine to find info	91	41
Get news	72	37
Read blog	39	7
Write blog	8	2

Television also provides millions of people with their daily dose of news. In 1980 Ted Turner created CNN, the first channel to broadcast news 24 hours a day. Today there are many news stations that run around the clock. Networks also offer daily news, including "breaking news" whenever something important happens during the day. Nearly all households in our country now have at least one television, and many people prefer one station or newscaster. But it is still important to listen to the views of many different people. This helps develop a well-rounded understanding of the issues.

Today about 72% of Americans read the news over the Internet, with 54% of those saying that they use this information to learn about political candidates and issues. Many newspapers offer online versions, while some companies provide information strictly over the Internet. The news is updated continuously, so it is more current than what you will find in newspapers. The Internet also gives readers the chance to quickly read and compare many sources. But reading the news online is limited to those with Internet access. Many people can't afford to buy their own computer or to pay to get online. Many cities now provide free Internet access in public libraries in order to make it more available.

A relatively new source of information on the Internet is provided by those who write web logs, or blogs. A blog is an online diary or journal where anyone can post his or her own opinions and thoughts. While 39% of Americans read blogs, only 8% create their own, which means that a small percentage of Internet users have the potential to influence a large number of readers. This is another reason for all of us to become informed about issues, and we need to use many different sources.

Radio is an additional source of information. Political talk radio shows are especially popular during election years. The interactive aspect of calling in to discuss an issue with the host appeals to many people. It also allows the listeners to hear many differing opinions and discussions on those perspectives. Listening to talk radio, of course, requires having the equipment and having it where you can use it. Many people listen in their cars as well as in their offices.

In reality, most of us use more than one of these methods to get the facts. We watch and listen as we go through our days. We gather the information that is vital to making our decisions. A democracy like ours is a government "of the people" and "for the people," and those people include you and me. It's our responsibility to make the best decisions we can. We all have to live with the results.

Answer Key — Answer Key — Answer Key

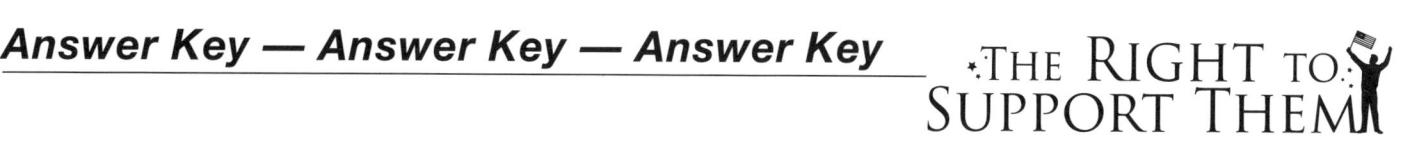

Reading Comprehension

After reading "The Information Highway," choose the options that best answer questions 1–11.

1. Read this sentence.
   Without informed citizens, elections can be determined by a minority of the population.

   What is the meaning of the word *citizens* as it is used in this sentence?
   A. voters
   B. illegal immigrants
   C. a national newspaper
   D. the people of a country or state

2. Read this sentence.
   Today there are many news stations that run around the clock.

   What is the meaning of the phrase *around the clock* as it is used in the sentence?
   F. limited news
   G. all day long
   H. in different time zones
   I. a different time for each newscast

3. Which of the following statements is supported by the information in the text box?
   A. More people use the Internet to get the news on a daily basis than on a monthly basis.
   B. Most Americans would rather use the Internet to get information than to interact with others.
   C. The Internet will be a more informative source for Americans when more people create web logs, or blogs.
   D. More Americans used the Internet to get news about a campaign and its issues in one day than in an entire month.

4. According to the article, most people who read the news on the Internet use that information to
   F. support their own beliefs.
   G. learn about political candidates and issues.
   H. persuade others to support particular candidates.
   I. write letters to their local newspaper about the candidates.

5. The author organizes this article by
   A. giving statistics for all media sources.
   B. describing the disadvantages of each media source.
   C. describing various media sources and their advantages and disadvantages.
   D. listing the most important media sources in order of usage by the American public.

6. What is the main idea of the third paragraph?
   F. Many viewers form a bond with one station or newscaster.
   G. Ted Turner created CNN in 1980 in order to broadcast news 24 hours per day.
   H. Today there are hundreds of television stations available to us through cable and satellite outlets.
   I. Since the majority of Americans now own at least one television, millions of people stay informed by watching the news on TV.

Answer Key — Answer Key — Answer Key
Unit 6

7. According to the article, many cities provide free access to the Internet in their libraries because
   A. they can no longer afford to buy books for the libraries.
   B. they need to attract more customers to their library systems.
   C. many people cannot afford to pay for a computer or access to the Internet.
   D. the school budgets in many cities do not include computers or access to the Internet.

8. The author states that an advantage of obtaining news from the Internet rather than other media sources is that
   F. it is portable.
   G. the reading level is better for most people.
   H. fewer people have radios in their homes today.
   I. the news is updated frequently throughout the day and is therefore more current.

9. Which statement provides the BEST evidence that few people want to keep their own online diary?
   A. 8% of Americans create their own blogs.
   B. 39% of Americans read others' blogs daily.
   C. 72% of Americans read the news over the Internet.
   D. 12% of Americans participate in online discussions.

10. Which statement from the article BEST supports the idea that the media is important in a democracy, especially during election years?
    F. In reality, most of us use more than one of these methods to get the facts.
    G. Without informed citizens, elections can be determined by a minority of the population.
    H. The interactive aspect of calling in to discuss an issue with the host appeals to many people.
    I. A small percentage of Internet users have the potential to influence large numbers of readers and possible voters.

11. Based on the article and the text box, which conclusion is MOST accurate?
    A. Americans should use the Internet more during election years.
    B. Most Americans just use one media source with which they are comfortable.
    C. Americans have a responsibility to be informed about issues that affect everyone, no matter which media sources they use.
    D. Since most Americans don't have computers, it doesn't matter how many use the Internet to learn about the candidates and issues during an election year.

Answer Key — Answer Key — Answer Key

Technical Writing Prompt

12. You are a college student and an active member of a political organization of young voters. After reading "The Information Highway," decide which information source you believe is the most reliable for getting information about political candidates. Write a clear and concise recommendation to the other voters in your group about which source to rely on for valid, reliable information. Use facts from the article to educate the young voters and support your recommendation.

Student answers may vary.

The student should address the question to the best of his/her ability using the article and personal experience. The question is meant to prepare students to be active citizens who can accurately and effectively use written communication skills.

Use the technical writing rubric to reference the criteria and determine the number of points to award.

Unit 6

Answer Key — Answer Key — Answer Key

Vocational Extension

HELP WANTED:

Major political party seeks college graduate to work as a contact between the party and the campaigns of the candidates. Duties include administrative tasks as well as coordinating fundraising efforts and tracking political data. Person chosen will also manage the activities of outside consultants, such as advertising firms and pollsters. A degree in political science or government is desirable. This entry-level position starts at $40,000 based on education and work experience, but the potential exists for salaries of up $75,000 after a period of time. If you want to be in the middle of a political campaign, this is the job for you!

Have you ever turned on the television or opened a newspaper during a political election year? You have probably been amazed at the amount of information reported and discussed for months before even one vote is cast on Election Day.

How do candidates make political decisions about what to focus on? How do they decide how to advertise? It's the job of the political analyst to help the candidates. Polls are taken every day, asking people questions about their preferences on issues. Then the analyst interprets the results. The amount of data collected, analyzed, and reported is stunning. However, the polls help the candidates to be informed.

A political analyst's responsibilities might include some of the following:

- Researching public opinion
- Collecting data
- Presenting findings and conclusions
- Conducting public opinion surveys and interpreting results
- Writing articles to inform the public
- Presenting information on television and radio

Sometimes data can be read differently. It might show information that is confusing. What do we do then? It's not the job of the political analyst to tell each of us what to think. His or her job is to give people the information they need to form their own positions. This gives people in a democracy the ability to think for themselves.

If being the person behind the scenes sounds interesting, you could begin now by joining the student government at your school. As elections happen, you might create polls that will help the candidates and those voting. In college you'll learn more about using technology to create, administer, and interpret data from all over the country, or even the world. Communication skills are also important for this job. A career as a political analyst is an exciting one that comes with many rewards. Above all is the satisfaction of knowing that you played an important role in the democratic process.

Answer Key — Answer Key — Answer Key

THE RIGHT TO SUPPORT THEM

Looking Forward

13. One of the jobs of a political analyst is to seek the public's opinion on different topics. Think of a question and create a simple poll to survey your peers about their opinions on that question. Interpret the data to create a conclusion. How did the majority of those who were surveyed vote? What was the minority opinion? Using your experience and information from the article, write a brief report to illustrate your findings to the class.

Looking Forward

Student answers may vary.

The student should address the question to the best of his/her ability using the article and personal experience. The question is meant to encourage students to explore areas of interest for their future and begin to determine how they will prepare for a future career.

Use the extended-response rubric to reference the criteria and determine the number of points to award.

Ethical Dilemma

14. You are the political analyst for a presidential candidate. The election is only two months away, and you are preparing information for the last presidential debate. After giving the candidate the data that you have collected on a major issue, the candidate's assistant asks you to make a slight change to some of the figures in order to better support the candidate's stand. You are certain the candidate is the most qualified to be president, and the change is minor. Will you do it? If not, how will you handle the situation?

Ethical Dilemma

Student answers may vary.

The student should address the question to the best of his/her ability using background knowledge from the article as well as personal opinion and experience. The question is meant to encourage students to contemplate scenarios and make ethical decisions.

Use the character education rubric to reference the criteria and number of points to award.

©2008 PRINCIPLE WOODS, INC. Removal of copyright notice and copying are violations of Federal Law.

Unit 6 — Answer Key — Answer Key — Answer Key

Unit Vocabulary Assessment

Matching
Match each word in Column I to its definition in Column II.

Column I
- **A** 1. legacy
- **C** 2. issue
- **B** 3. sacrifice
- **D** 4. adrenaline
- **E** 5. continuous

Column II
- a. something handed down
- b. to give up something for greater value
- c. a point of discussion
- d. a bodily hormone released in stress
- e. uninterrupted

Multiple Choice
Choose the word that MOST NEARLY replaces the underlined word in each sentence.

6. Putting her whole life on hold for the campaign was a risky move for her career.
   - A. easy
   - B. criticized
   - **C. dangerous**
   - D. unnecessary

7. It is vital that we all show support for the troops.
   - A. true
   - B. incorrect
   - **C. necessary**
   - D. unnecessary

8. One of the most important principles that America stands for is liberty.
   - A. needs
   - B. prizes
   - **C. beliefs**
   - D. principals

Word Bank
- advocate
- criticize
- liberty
- minority
- patriot
- perspective
- relatively

Fill in the Blank
Choose a word from the word bank to fill in the blank in the sentence below.

9. One who has been held a prisoner of war can be called a true **patriot**.
10. As a supporter of wildlife, Owen became an **advocate** for the cause.
11. It was a **relatively** warm day, compared to the usual harsh weather.
12. She gained an entirely new **perspective** on life while visiting Africa.
13. The forefathers believe in life, **liberty**, and the pursuit of happiness.
14. Only a **minority** of the class, not even half, did the homework.
15. Please don't **criticize** me just because you disagree with what I say.

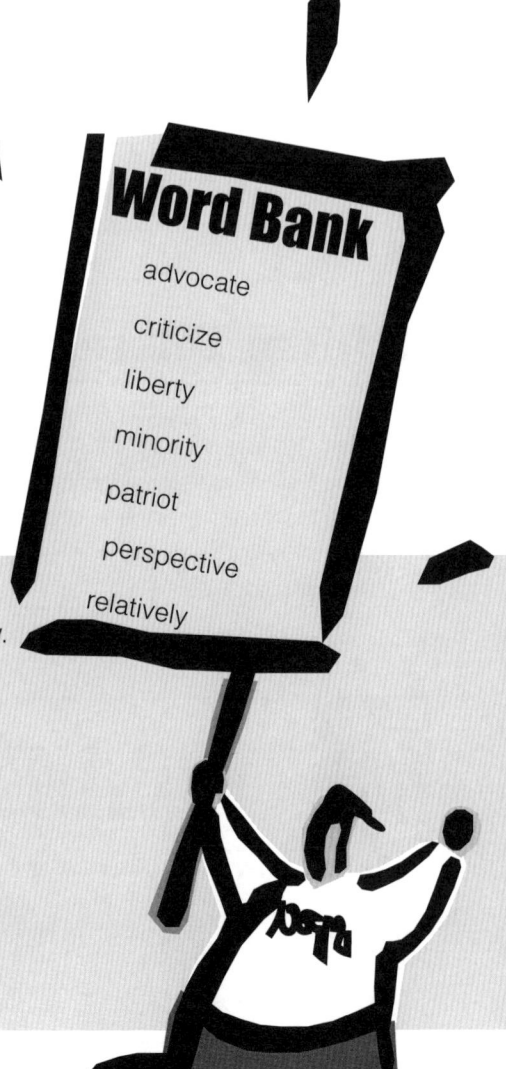

Answer Key — Answer Key — Answer Key

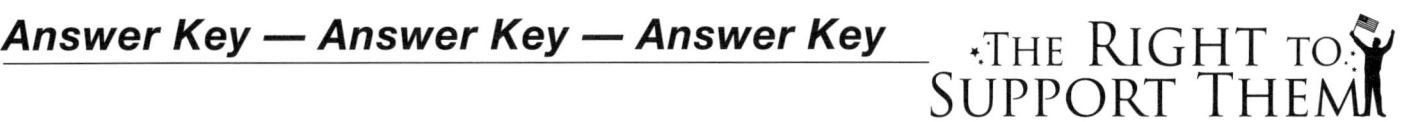

Authentic Assessment

Students will complete a technology research project based on the unit "The Right to Support Them." This activity combines the authentic components of research, scientific exploration, and writing linked to the comprehension of a written text. The teacher should provide basic guidance on how to look up online data and how to interpret that data. The Interpreting the Data section of this unit may provide a starting point for discussion.

Instructions for Technology Research Project

1. **Question.** Have students write a research question about the possible relationship between the number of fatalities in Iraq and the American public's opinion on the war between 2003 and 2007. The question should ask whether there is a relationship between the two variables

2. **Hypothesis.** Have students write a hypothesis addressing whether they think there will be a correlation between the two variables (fatalities and public opinion).

3. **Data collection.** Instruct students to collect data from websites that address their research question. Websites cited in the resource list below may be used as a starting point. Students should collect and record data for troop fatalities between 2003 and 2007 and public opinion of the war over those same years.

4. **Data analysis.** Ask students to analyze the data they collect. Following are some questions they might answer:

    a. What was public opinion on the war when it began?

    b. How did public opinion change over time?

    c. Did the fatality rate go up or down?

    d. Which year saw the most fatalities?

    e. Do the two seem to be related?

5. **Conclusion.** Have students write a conclusion statement that discusses the trends of both variables and the possible relationships between the two.

6. **Assessment.** Assess the research project using the rubric on the following page.

Resource List

World Public Opinion:
http://www.worldpublicopinion.org/

Polling Report:
http://www.pollingreport.com/index.html

Iraq Coalition Casualty Count:
http://icasualties.org/oif/

U.S. Casualties in Iraq:
http://www.globalsecurity.org/military/ops/iraq_casualties.html

Answer Key — Answer Key — Answer Key

Unit 6

Technology Research Rubric

Requirement	8–10 Points	4–7 Points	0–3 Points	Points Earned
Research Question and Hypothesis	The student writes a clearly stated research question and hypothesis with correctly identified variables.	The student writes a research question and hypothesis that is somewhat unclear.	The student does not write a research question or hypothesis.	
Technology Use	The student uses appropriate technology to collect data and complete the assignment.	The student uses somewhat appropriate technology to collect data and complete the assignment.	The student does not use appropriate technology to collect data or does not complete the assignment.	
Data Collection and Analysis	The student collects a proper amount of data and correctly interprets it.	The student collects some data and attempts to correctly interpret it.	The student does not collect data or interprets it completely incorrectly.	
Conclusion Statement	The student writes a clearly stated conclusion based on the data collected.	The student writes a conclusion statement that is somewhat unclear and/or not entirely based on the data collected.	The student does not write a conclusion statement or writes a statement that is not based on data.	

©2008 PRINCIPLE WOODS, INC. Removal of copyright notice and copying are violations of Federal Law.

Unit 7

A MOMENT 2 LOSE

Reading Instructional Guide for High-Interest Article

BEFORE READING

Front-Loading Background Knowledge through Read Aloud/Think Aloud

Search the Internet for recent articles on social networking sites and use them to model the effective habits of readers through a Read Aloud/Think Aloud.

Check out articles at the following websites to determine if they would be appropriate for your RATA:
- Irvine, Martha/Associated Press. "Social Network Users Overlook Privacy Pitfalls." *USA Today*. April 28, 2008. www.usatoday.com/tech/news/internetprivacy/2008-04-28-social-network-privacy_N.htm.
- Israel, Betsy. "The Overconnecteds." *New York Times*. November 5, 2006. http://www.nytimes.com/2006/11/05/education/edlife/connect.html.

(Please keep in mind that it is the responsibility of the teacher to determine if articles from suggested sites are appropriate. The sites may have changed content since this publication. The publisher takes no responsibility for the current content of the site.)

Looking at the Words

Determining How the Word Sounds (Phonics)
Using the Syllable Guide and the Reading Instructional Guide Template found in the beginning of the book, follow the steps to help students learn how to break a word into manageable parts.

Determining What the Word Means (Vocabulary)

Words to Study	Breaking into Syllables	Short Definition
casually	ca-su-al-ly	(adv.) in a relaxed manner; naturally
disappointment	dis-ap-point-ment	(n.) a feeling of dissatisfaction when expectations are not met
occasional	oc-ca-sion-al	(adj.) occurring now and then
permission	per-mis-sion	(n.) approval to do something
potential	po-ten-tial	(n.) possibility
reputation	rep-u-ta-tion	(n.) the general opinion the public has of a person
uncomfortable	un-com-fort-a-ble	(adj.) not relaxed; uneasy

Activating Background Knowledge

Anticipation Guide
Mark each of the following statements True or False:

1. ____ It takes a long time to damage a reputation.

2. ____ Only high-profile people can be damaged by having inappropriate pictures online.

Unit 7

Answer Key — Answer Key — Answer Key

3. ____ Online social networking sites can hinder someone's reputation.

4. ____ Online sites are losing popularity.

5. ____ It is easy to erase information and pictures once they have been posted online.

Starter Questions
After completing the Anticipation Guide, have a group or class discussion with the students using the following questions:

1. Who is Matt Leinart?

2. How did the Internet hurt Matt Leinart's reputation?

3. What are social networking sites?

4. What is blogging?

5. Can anyone online see someone's Facebook page or blog?

Make a prediction about what you think the article will be about.

DURING READING
Use the Reading Instructional Guide Template found in the front of the book.

AFTER READING

Discussion Starter Questions

1. Why do you think online communities have increased in popularity?

2. Should potential employers be allowed to use the Internet as a way to screen applicants?

3. Why do you think people post inappropriate pictures and information online when they know it could hurt their reputation?

4. Do you think Matt Leinart should have faced more serious consequences for the photos online? Why or why not?

5. What advice would you give to a friend who wants to create an online blog or social networking site?

Teacher Reflection

Use the Reading Instructional Guide Template found in the front of the book.

A LIFETIME to BUILD, a MOMENT to LOSE

Deidra had been a good student. She was president of her junior class and a member of the Spanish Honor Society. She played soccer and kept up her grades. Deidra spent three weeks last summer in Central America fixing up old school buildings. She spent one Saturday a month volunteering at the food pantry. She was well-liked by her friends. Deidra was proud of all she had accomplished so far.

After school one week, Deidra was thrilled to get permission from her parents to attend a party. She didn't know the person throwing the party very well but thought that it sounded like fun. When she got to the party, it was much wilder than she expected. She felt uncomfortable by the way some people were acting. She thought about leaving, but her ride was nowhere to be found. Someone handed her a drink. Even though she'd never tried alcohol, she held it casually. She didn't want to stick out, so she took occasional sips. She eventually found a few friends and began talking and laughing. She had fun once she was in her comfort zone.

When Deidra returned to school on Monday, her faculty advisor called her into his office. He showed her another student's Facebook page on his computer. Her heart pounded when she saw herself on the screen. She was sipping from the drink that she had held throughout the party. Someone had taken her picture with a cell phone. She was forced to resign as class president and was suspended from school for underage drinking. Her parents were notified. Worse yet, she had just begun applying to colleges. Not only would she have to explain her suspension, but the photos were online for anyone to see.

One former beauty queen knows all too well what a few photos on the Internet can do. This young woman was fired after inappropriate photos of her showed up online. The pictures were taken over five years before they were made public. However, the pageant organization decided that she could no longer represent them. The first runner-up replaced her in the national pageant. In a statement, the beauty queen said that the photos didn't represent who she was as a person. Sadly, whether the pictures were representative of her or not, the price she paid was high.

Young NFL quarterback Matt Leinart recently landed himself in a similar situation. He called his coach early one Monday morning to let him know about several pictures that would be in the press. The racy photos showed Leinart partying at his home and drinking alcohol with girls who appeared to be underage. Coach Whisenhunt gave Leinart

It Could Happen to You: True Stories

- A college applicant was turned down because he posted negative comments about college officials.

- Swimmers were kicked off the team for talking badly about their coaches online.

- A student was suspended because of online photos.

- Police showed up at a party with underage drinking after seeing the online invitations.

- A job applicant was denied after the potential employer Googled him and didn't like what he saw.

- An intern was fired when his boss saw on his Facebook profile that he described his job as getting paid to IM and talk to his friends.

some credit for recognizing his mistake and notifying the coach. But he also expressed disappointment in the events. The coach pointed out that as a former Heisman Trophy winner, Leinart is especially interesting to the media. Leinart didn't suffer strong consequences this time. But it isn't always so easy. Publicity like this could damage both his reputation and his career.

It isn't just high-profile people who can be hurt by content on the Internet. Social networking sites are an easy way to keep in touch with friends. Unfortunately, they can quickly ruin anyone's reputation. There are several sites to choose from—Facebook, Xanga, LiveJournal, and MySpace, to name a few. Blogging, a kind of online journal writing, has become another popular pastime. It offers the opportunity for people to share their daily events, thoughts, and photos. But once these blogs are released into cyberspace, they are open for public view.

Most teens don't think anything of posting their unedited thoughts online. They vent about their teachers, their parents, and even each other. They post pictures of all their life happenings. Whether they like it or not, their friends might not be the only ones looking at their sites. Because of the nature of the Internet, almost anyone can gain access to what is posted online. And the Internet is unique because once something is posted, it is nearly impossible to erase. Everything has the potential to become a permanent record of a person's life.

Many college admissions officials and potential employers routinely search online to get better insight into the people they are considering for admission or a job. In fact, one study found that as many as 75% of employers use the Internet as part of the process they use to screen applicants. Although networking sites can be fun, it's important to carefully consider what information you would want someone deciding your future to see. Pictures and comments you make that are posted on other people's websites and pages can cause problems too. An Internet search can pull up any page with your name on it. You can ask your friends to delete information about you that you don't like. If the information is posted by someone you don't know or someone trying to hurt your reputation, contact the networking site to ask them to take the information down. Many sites will do so when what is posted violates their terms of service.

When used carefully, blogs and social networking sites can be fun. Just keep in mind that everything posted can be seen by anyone. That way, inappropriate comments and photos won't hurt you later. It takes a lifetime to build a reputation, but only a moment to lose it.

Answer Key — Answer Key — Answer Key   **A MOMENT 2 LOSE**

Reading Comprehension

After reading "A Lifetime to Build, a Moment to Lose," choose the options that best answer questions 1–14.

1. Read these sentences.
   She eventually found a few friends and began talking and laughing. She had fun once she was in her comfort zone.

   What is the meaning of the phrase *comfort zone* as it is used in this sentence?
   A. a social situation
   B. the weather in an environment
   C. environment where a person feels comfortable
   D. when a person is able to maintain a normal temperature

2. Read this sentence.
   She was forced to resign as class president and was suspended from school for underage drinking.

   What is the meaning of the word *suspended* as it is used in this sentence?
   F. supported
   G. counseled
   H. postponed permanently
   I. excluded for a period of time

3. According to the article, why do many companies use the Internet before hiring an applicant?
   A. to find additional applicants
   B. to learn more about the applicant's lifestyle
   C. to research the salary of the same job at other companies
   D. to look for additional training and education for an applicant

4. What is the purpose of blogging?
   F. to easily research various topics
   G. to share opinions and thoughts with others online
   H. to allow people who have recently moved into a new city to meet others
   I. to encourage people to use the computer rather than cell phones to communicate

5. With which statement would the author of the passage most likely agree?
   A. The Internet is a safe place to post personal information.
   B. Online networking sites provide a great resource for someone to meet people
   C. Be careful about what you post on the Internet because it is open to public view.
   D. Employers should use the Internet when deciding whether they should hire an applicant.

6. The author organizes the article by
   F. explaining how to post photos on the Internet.
   G. providing the history of the Internet in chronological order.
   H. listing the reasons why the reader should open an online networking account.
   I. providing examples and key information about the consequences of posting some information online.

©2008 PRINCIPLE WOODS, INC. Removal of copyright notice and copying are violations of Federal Law.

Unit 7 — Answer Key

7. Why does the author mention deleting information from the Internet?
   - **A. to help the reader protect his or her reputation**
   - B. to encourage the reader to put more information and photos online
   - C. to prevent the reader from putting photos or information online that may hurt others
   - D. to explain that information cannot be deleted from the Internet once it is posted online

8. Which title best fits the article?
   - F. Online Networking
   - G. Internet Instruction
   - H. Promoting a Lifestyle
   - **I. Reputation in Jeopardy**

9. Why did Leinart tell his coach about the photos prior to the coach viewing them?
   - A. to encourage the coach to view the photos
   - B. to resign from his position on the football team
   - **C. to warn the coach that the photos were being released**
   - D. to get his instructions for removing the photos from the Internet

10. According to the passage, posting photos and information online is dangerous because
    - **F. anyone can view the information.**
    - G. posting photos can become an expensive hobby.
    - H. a computer can contract viruses from downloaded pictures.
    - I. spending too much time on the Internet can cause one's grades to fall.

11. What was the major difference between the situations involving the beauty queen and Matt Leinart?
    - A. The beauty queen was more apologetic for her behavior than Leinart.
    - B. Leinart was able to delete his photos, while the beauty queen was not.
    - **C. The beauty queen lost her title, but Leinart was able to keep his job.**
    - D. Leinart's photos were taken five years ago, but the beauty queen's photos were recent.

12. How does the author organize the first two paragraphs of the passage?
    - **F. by using a fictitious story to explain a realistic situation**
    - G. by presenting ways someone can create a safe online social network
    - H. by providing interviews with people who have been harmed by online photos
    - I. by encouraging the reader to remove inappropriate information from the Internet

13. According to the text box,
    - **A. a person's education and career can be affected by online photos.**
    - B. blogging is an enjoyable pastime enjoyed by many high school students.
    - C. a student fought back and was not suspended from school for a personal blog.
    - D. it is unlawful for companies to use the Internet to screen applicants prior to hiring.

14. Based on the information about the beauty queen and Leinart, which of these conclusions is accurate?
    - F. The online photos will not hinder their careers.
    - G. Neither Leinart nor the beauty queen appears to have regret about the online photos that surfaced.
    - H. Both Leinart and the beauty queen will continue to engage in behaviors that put them at risk for indecent photos.
    - **I. Both Leinart and the beauty queen would likely discourage others from posting photos online that might hurt someone's reputation.**

©2008 PRINCIPLE WOODS, INC. Removal of copyright notice and copying are violations of Federal Law.

Answer Key — Answer Key — Answer Key   **A MOMENT 2 LOSE**

Reading Strategy

Directions: Using information from the article, briefly summarize what went wrong for the high school student, the beauty queen, and the NFL player. Include each individual's actions and the consequences he or she faced.

SUM IT UP!

HIGH SCHOOL STUDENT

> She went to a party where underage drinking was going on. She held a drink. Someone took a picture of her and posted it on Facebook. She was suspended from school and was forced to resign as class president.

BEAUTY QUEEN

> Inappropriate photos of her ended up online five years after they were taken. She was fired from her position as state beauty queen. She was replaced in the national beauty pageant.

NFL PLAYER

> Photos showing him drinking and partying with young girls surfaced online for everyone to see. He had to face a disappointed coach and bad publicity.

After looking at your summaries, what is one practical lesson you can learn from these experiences that will help you protect your own reputation?

> **Answers may vary.** Students may conclude that anyone could easily spread information about their behavior, so they should not do anything that they wouldn't want the public or someone in their future to see.

©2008 PRINCIPLE WOODS, INC. Removal of copyright notice and copying are violations of Federal Law.

Unit 7

Answer Key — Answer Key — Answer Key

Interpreting the Data

Do teens need to be educated on the ways technology can hurt their reputations?

Use Figure 1 to answer questions 15–17.

Figure 1. Percentage of teens who use the Internet and online journal/blog

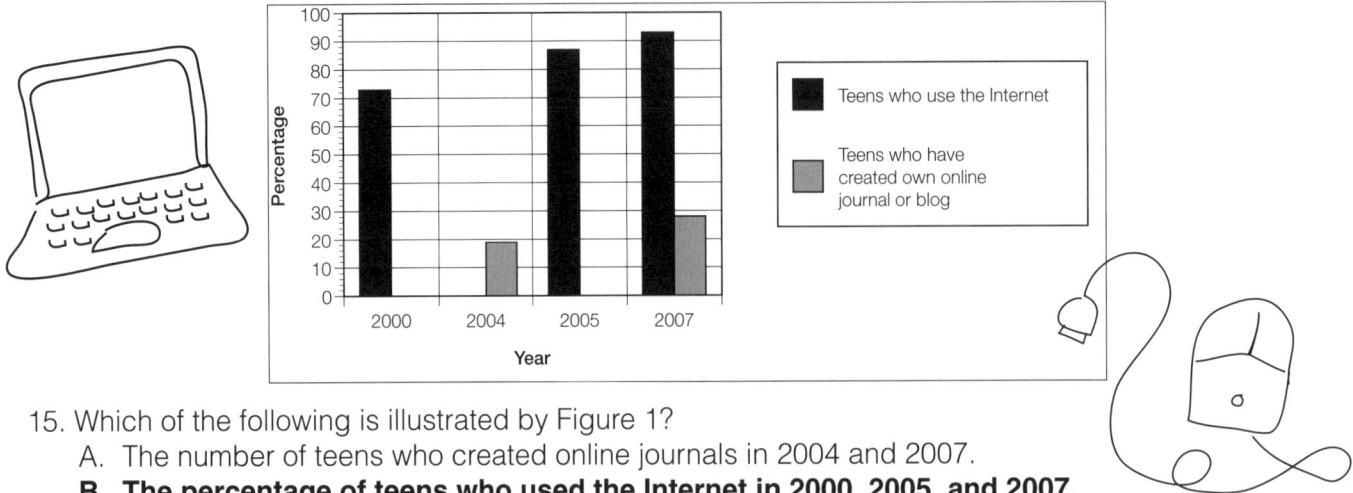

15. Which of the following is illustrated by Figure 1?
    A. The number of teens who created online journals in 2004 and 2007.
    B. The percentage of teens who used the Internet in 2000, 2005, and 2007.
    C. The percentage of teens using the Internet that created blogs from 2004 to 2007.
    D. The number of teens who used the Internet and online journals from 2000 to 2007.

16. Which of the following statements is correct based on Figure 1?
    A. Internet use among teens increased nearly 20% between 2000 and 2007.
    B. The percentage of teens using the Internet went from above 70% in 2000 to below 20% in 2004.
    C. The percentage of teens who created their own blogs jumped from about 19% in 2004 to about 85% in 2005.
    D. Teen Internet use has increased over the last seven years, while the use of online journals has decreased.

17. Mark the following statements as T (true) or F (false) based on information in Figure 1.
    a. __T__ Just over 90% of teens used the Internet in 2007.
    b. __F__ Just over 90% of Internet users in 2007 were teens.
    c. __F__ Just over 90% of teens used the Internet to create their own blogs in 2007.
    d. __F__ In 2007, the number of teens who created online journals increased from just under 30% to just over 90%.

Figure 2. Online teens, social network sites, and false information

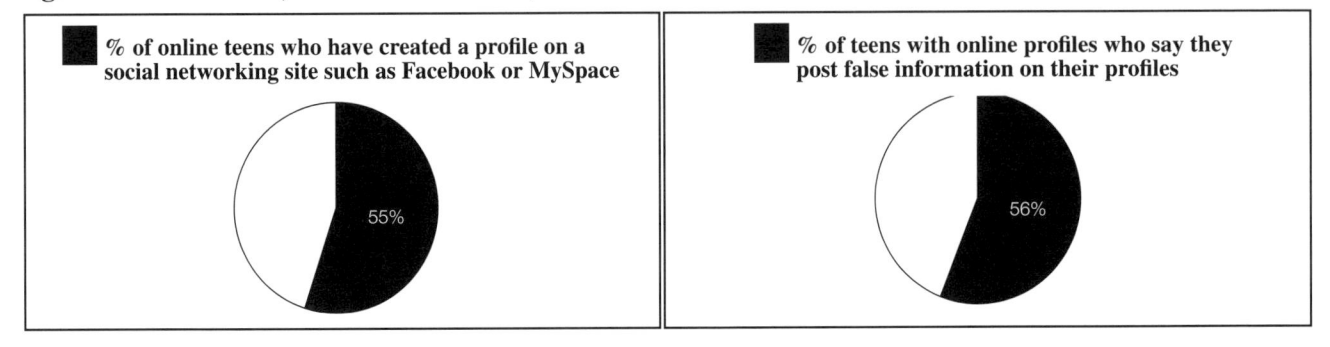

% of online teens who have created a profile on a social networking site such as Facebook or MySpace — 55%

% of teens with online profiles who say they post false information on their profiles — 56%

Answer Key — Answer Key — Answer Key

A MOMENT 2 LOSE

18. Study Figure 2 and explain how these statistics could be alarming to teens who are concerned about their own image being ruined by what others might read about them online.

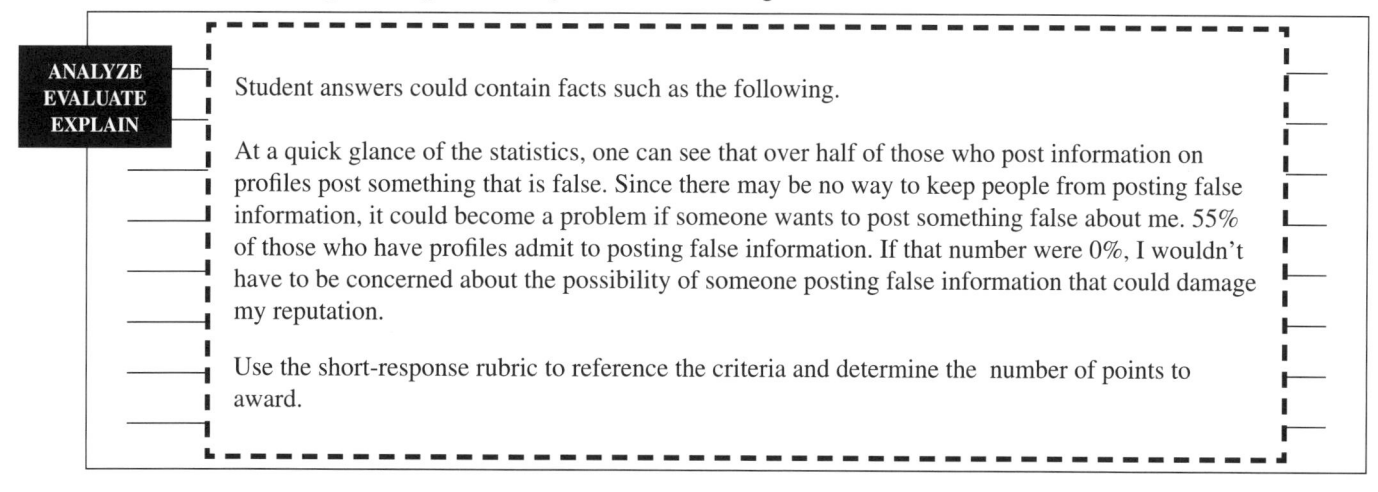

ANALYZE EVALUATE EXPLAIN

Student answers could contain facts such as the following.

At a quick glance of the statistics, one can see that over half of those who post information on profiles post something that is false. Since there may be no way to keep people from posting false information, it could become a problem if someone wants to post something false about me. 55% of those who have profiles admit to posting false information. If that number were 0%, I wouldn't have to be concerned about the possibility of someone posting false information that could damage my reputation.

Use the short-response rubric to reference the criteria and determine the number of points to award.

19. Based on the information from Figures 1 and 2, determine how many teens in a group of 100 probably post something false on an online profile. Complete your work in the box below.

If you don't need assistance, complete your work below:	If you need assistance, follow the steps below:
100 students X 93% = 93 93 students X 55% = 51 students 51 students X 56% = **29 students**	1. **Statistic: 93% of teens use the Internet.** What is 93% of 100 teens? 2. **Statistic: 55% of online teens have created a profile on social networking sites.** What is 55% of your answer for question 1? 3. **Statistic: 56% of teens with online profiles say they post false information.** What is 56% of your answer for question 2? _____ This is your final answer.

Figure 3. Percentage of teens who use blogs, by gender and age group

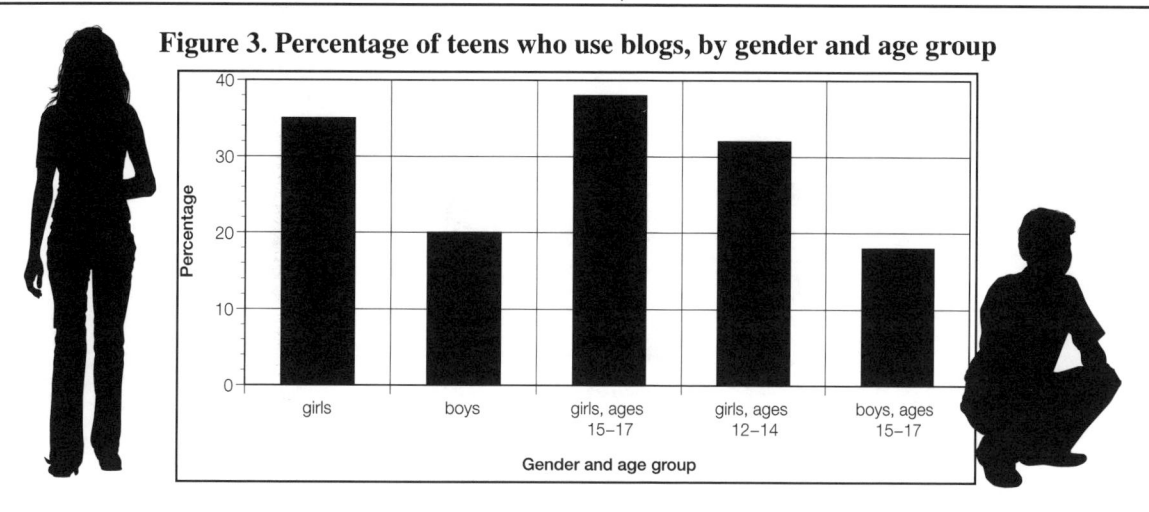

20. Based on Figure 3, which gender is leading the charge in the use of blogs as a social tool?

    A. boys   **B. girls**

©2008 PRINCIPLE WOODS, INC. Removal of copyright notice and copying are violations of Federal Law.

Unit 7

Answer Key — Answer Key — Answer Key

21. Explain how Figure 3 might lead you to believe that this trend will continue in the future.

> A larger percentage of girls ages 12–14 are blogging compared to the percentage of boys ages 15–17, which means that a larger percentage of girls will probably still be out-blogging boys in the future.

Figure 4. Percentage of people who upload photos online, by gender and age group

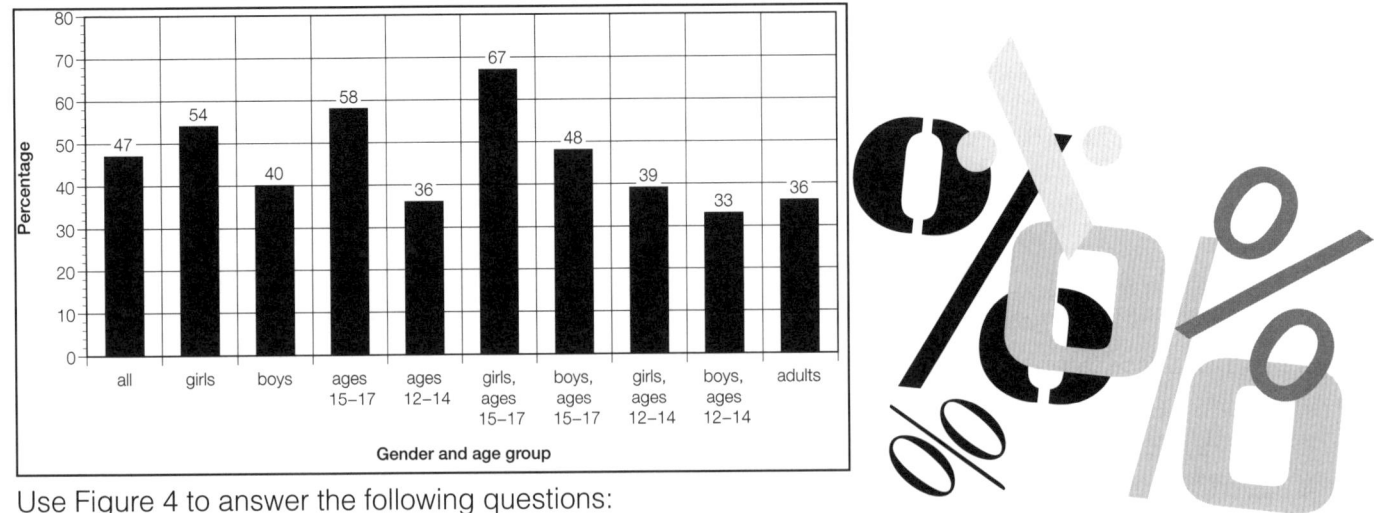

Use Figure 4 to answer the following questions:

22. How do teens compare to adults in the percentage that upload photos online?

   A larger percentage of teens upload photos online than adults.

23. How do girls compare to boys in the percentage that upload photos online?

   A larger percentage of girls upload photos online than boys.

24. How do girls ages 12–14 compare to boys ages 15–17 in the percentage that upload photos online?

   11% less girls ages 12–14 upload photos than boys ages 15–17.

Figure 5. Percentage of teens who regularly restrict access to photos they post online

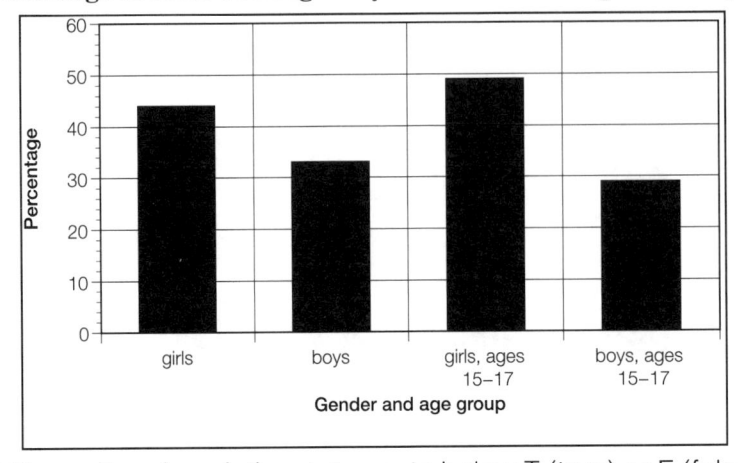

25. Study Figure 4 and Figure 5 and mark the statements below T (true) or F (false).

   a. __F__ Boys seem to be more careful than girls with the photos they post online.

   b. __F__ A larger percentage of boys ages 15 to 17 post photos than girls ages 15 to 17.

   c. __T__ Girls appear to be more concerned about being safe with photos they post online.

Answer Key — Answer Key — Answer Key   A MOMENT 2 LOSE

26. Based on the article and the data in this unit, should teens be educated on the dangers that technology can pose to their reputations? Use statistics and details to support your answer.

ANALYZE EVALUATE EXPLAIN

Student answers could contain facts such as the following.

Teens must be educated on the dangers that technology use poses to their reputations. Internet use and the creation of online journals/blogs are on the rise, which means that teens are more and more capable of using technology to gossip and share information about people. The fact that 56% of teens with online profiles admit to posting false information shows that teens cannot assume that teens are truthful in what they post online about others. Teens should be educated about the damage they can do by posting information about others and about how easy it is for private information or photos to be spread for almost anyone to see. Now, more than ever before, teens must learn to monitor how they act in public.

Use the extended-response rubric to reference the criteria and determine the number of points to award.

Reflect and Respond

27. What lessons could you teach elementary age students about the dangers of technology use? Think about the Internet, social networking sites, the use of digital cameras, the use of camera phones, the ability to text message, and other technology in your life that may be dangerous if used inappropriately. Consider also the fact that your actions in public (or private) may be recorded and shared with almost anyone. Create an outline below for a speech you might give to a fifth-grade class on the impact of technology on your private life.

Reflect & Respond

Answers may vary, but students should address each part of the question. The question is meant to elicit strong classroom conversation about character. Students should be able to make text-to-self connections based on the situations illustrated in this unit. They should then use those connections to write the outline they could use to teach a lesson about the importance of being careful with what they post online and about monitoring their behavior in public because people now have the ability to share our behavior with anyone.

Use the character education rubric to reference the criteria and number of points to award.

©2008 PRINCIPLE WOODS, INC. Removal of copyright notice and copying are violations of Federal Law.

Unit 7

Answer Key — Answer Key — Answer Key

Reading Instructional Guide for Technical Extension

BEFORE READING

Looking at the Words

Determining How the Word Sounds (Phonics)
Technical texts often necessitate the use of multisyllabic words that are unfamiliar to students. Use the Syllable Guide to help students decode any words they might have trouble reading.

Determining What the Word Means (Vocabulary)

Words to Study	Breaking into Syllables	Short Definition
amendment	a-mend-ment	(n.) a change made by an addition
assume	as-sume	(v.) to presume or take for granted
boundary	bound-a-ry	(n.) something that sets a limit
intrusion	in-tru-sion	(n.) a trespassing on something (as a right)
privacy	pri-va-cy	(n.) the state of being free from intrusion
restriction	re-stric-tion	(n.) the act of confining something

Activating Background Knowledge

Graphic Organizer
Either individually or in groups, students may brainstorm about privacy, recalling anything previously learned and any prior experience with the subject. Next, encourage students to see the relationships between their ideas by having them complete the star diagram to demonstrate what they already know about privacy: the definition, statistics, pros, cons, and other important information.

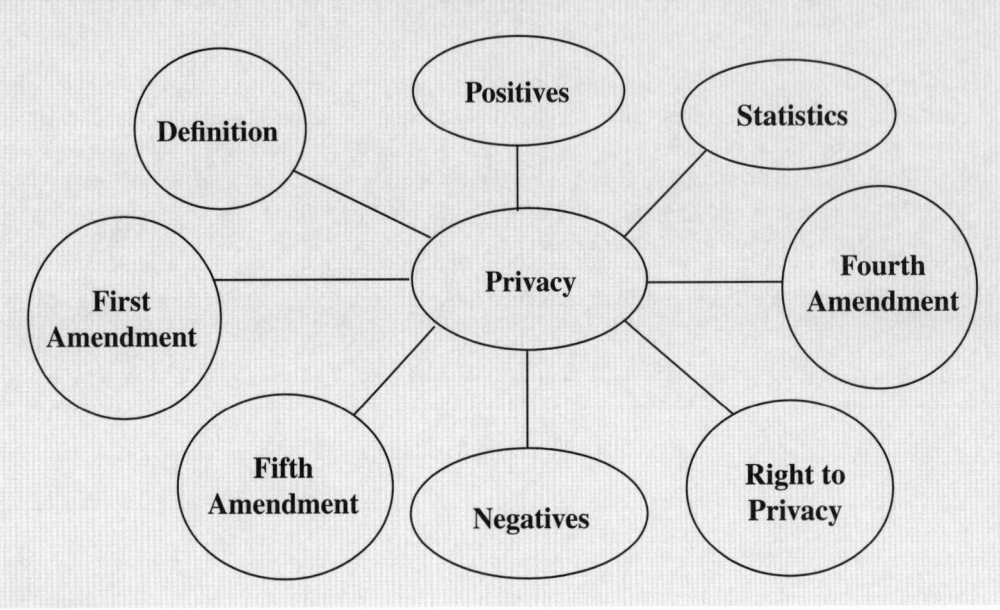

Star diagram with "Privacy" in the center, connected to: Definition, Positives, Statistics, First Amendment, Fourth Amendment, Fifth Amendment, Negatives, Right to Privacy.

©2008 PRINCIPLE WOODS, INC. Removal of copyright notice are violations of Federal Law.

Answer Key — Answer Key — Answer Key   A MOMENT 2 LOSE

Starter Questions
After completing the Graphic Organizer, generate a group or class discussion to come up with questions about the subject, a prediction about the article, and at least one learning goal. The first question has been provided for you.

Question: What is the purpose of the Fifth Amendment?

Question: _____

Prediction: _____

Goal: _____

DURING READING
Use the Reading Instructional Guide Template found in the front of the book.

AFTER READING
After reading, you may teach reading strategy use by giving students opportunities to do the following:
- Review, paraphrase, and summarize
- Participate in main-idea discussions by describing the information in their own words
- Reflect on concept maps and generate additional discussion starter questions based on the mappings
- Participate in small-group discussions using discussion starter questions

Discussion Starter Questions

The first question has been provided for you.

1. Do you think the government has the right to limit our privacy to ensure that our safety is protected? Why or why not?

2. _____

3. _____

Unit 7
Technical Extension

BIG BROTHER AND THE RIGHT TO PRIVACY

Who is Big Brother, and is he really watching us? In 1948 English author George Orwell wrote a book called *Nineteen Eighty-Four* in which citizens were watched by the government all the time. The figure that saw everything everyone did was called "Big Brother." Orwell viewed the right to privacy as crucial. He believed that if the government knew the details of peoples' private lives, the results could be terrible. He said it was a threat to freedom.

Our 21st-century technology can make our lives more entertaining. We talk on our cell phones and use them to take pictures and video. Then we access the Internet and send those images to others. We send text messages. We sit at our computers and post web logs, called "blogs." Social Internet sites like MySpace and Facebook keep us in touch with friends who live right next door or across the world. It is an exciting time in history.

However, there is a downside to this technology. Our right to privacy can be invaded easily. Cyberspace has no boundaries, at least not yet. Cell phones and computers send our thoughts and images out for anyone to find. Do you assume that your friends will respect your privacy in photos from last night's party? Do you want strangers to see what you do in all situations?

What exactly *is* our "right to privacy"? Surprisingly, the term doesn't even appear in our Constitution. But the United States Supreme Court has used some of the amendments to the Constitution to talk about privacy. These protect us from the government's intrusion into our personal business:

- The First Amendment gives us freedom of speech. We can give our opinions about the government without fear of getting into trouble.

- The Fourth Amendment gives us the right to be with other people without the government's approval. It also protects us from "unreasonable" search by police.

- The Fifth Amendment protects our privacy because it states that we cannot be forced to make things about ourselves public. It also says that we have the right to "due process," which means that the police and the government can't do whatever they want with us. They have to follow the rules too.

Privacy is defined simply as the right to be left alone. However, who we are often determines how the right is applied. Celebrities might expect that their photos will be taken without their permission. But "regular" people like you and me expect more privacy. The problem today is that technology is pushing the boundaries of who hears our conversations and who sees what we write. Pictures that we take and send to our friends could end up being seen by strangers. We never know exactly where these pictures are being sent or who is viewing them.

Answer Key — Answer Key — Answer Key **A MOMENT 2 LOSE**

On one hand, our personal business is available because we put it out there. Some people might be surprised to know that we also leave a "trail" on the Internet when we look at sites. People can track this trail without our permission. Also, lists of our cell phone calls can be bought by anyone with the time or money.

Most countries have not decided how they can deal with the privacy issue. Who should be given the power to control all of this information? The terrorist bombings on 9/11 have made many Americans more willing to give up some privacy so that future terror attacks can be prevented. Other people believe that once we give up these rights, we will never get them back. After all, it sounds a bit like Big Brother, doesn't it?

This is a difficult question in a democracy like ours. We want our privacy respected, but we don't want restrictions placed on how we use our technology. We want to be safe, but we want to keep the right to privacy as described by the amendments. One thing is certain at this point: others can see our words and images. Even if there isn't really a Big Brother, we have to behave as if everyone else is watching.

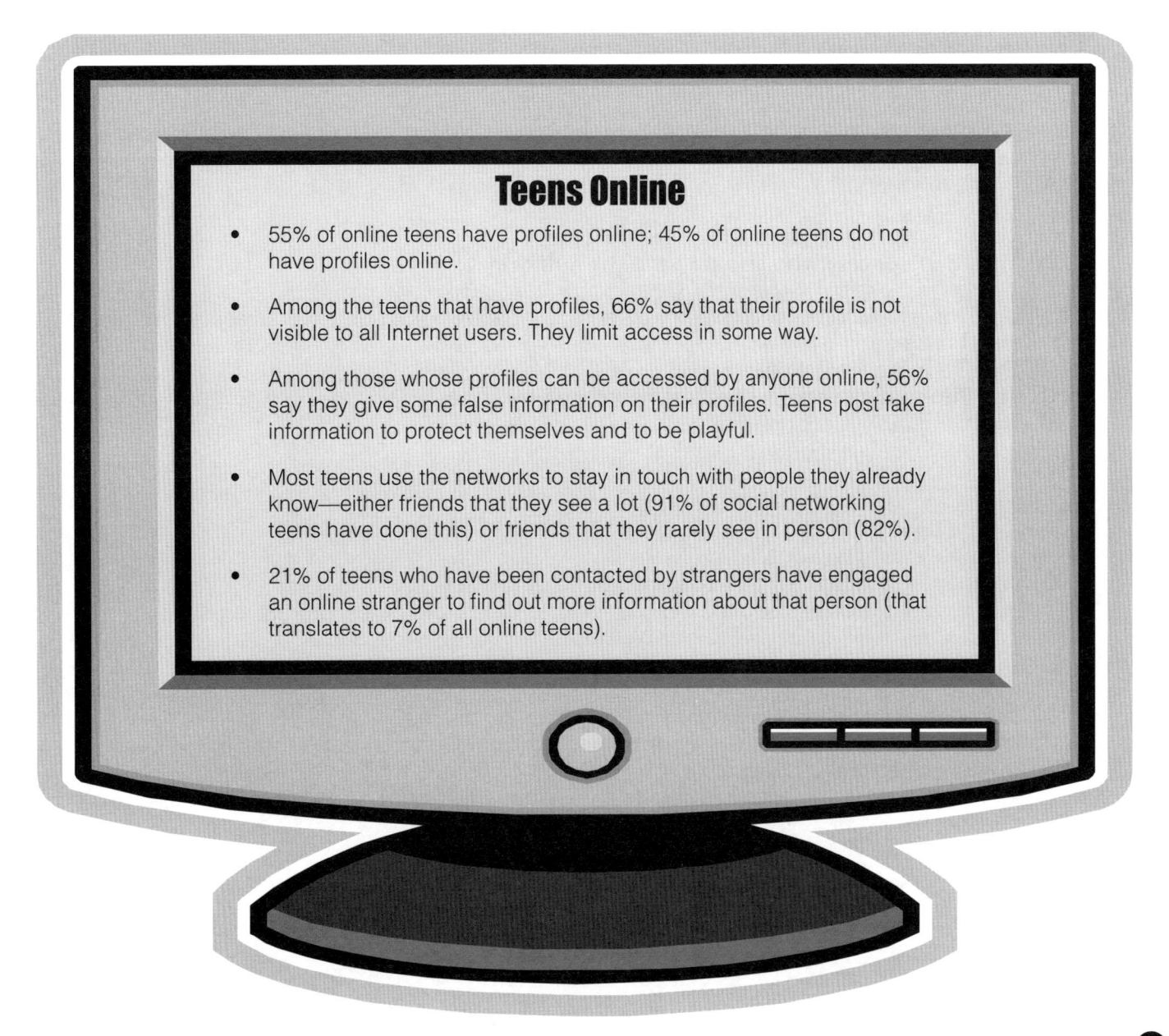

Teens Online

- 55% of online teens have profiles online; 45% of online teens do not have profiles online.

- Among the teens that have profiles, 66% say that their profile is not visible to all Internet users. They limit access in some way.

- Among those whose profiles can be accessed by anyone online, 56% say they give some false information on their profiles. Teens post fake information to protect themselves and to be playful.

- Most teens use the networks to stay in touch with people they already know—either friends that they see a lot (91% of social networking teens have done this) or friends that they rarely see in person (82%).

- 21% of teens who have been contacted by strangers have engaged an online stranger to find out more information about that person (that translates to 7% of all online teens).

©2008 PRINCIPLE WOODS, INC. Removal of copyright notice and copying are violations of Federal Law.

Unit 7 — *Answer Key — Answer Key — Answer Key*

Reading Comprehension

After reading "Big Brother and the Right to Privacy," choose the options that best answer questions 1–11.

1. Read this sentence.
   Orwell viewed the right to privacy as crucial.

   What is the meaning of the word *crucial* as it is used in this sentence?
   A. useless
   B. important
   C. endangered
   D. without value

2. According to the information provided about the Fourth Amendment, what does the word *unreasonable* mean in the phrase *unreasonable search*?
   F. unnecessary
   G. without witnesses
   H. interference by police
   I. without a good reason

3. According to this article, why haven't most countries dealt with the issue of the right to privacy in the use of technology and information?
   A. It isn't important.
   B. The citizens don't care about it.
   C. Most countries don't have a lot of technology.
   D. They can't decide who should have the authority to control it.

4. What do we have to assume today when we send information using our cell phones, the Internet, and other technology?
   F. The information might not arrive.
   G. The information is being seen or heard by everyone.
   H. The information is changed or deleted after it is read.
   I. The information will be used against us at some point.

5. The author uses the image of Big Brother to
   A. describe the Internet.
   B. explain Orwell's book.
   C. compare the image with current invasions of privacy.
   D. help the reader understand the three amendments that deal with our right to privacy.

6. What is the main idea of the paragraph that begins with "On one hand…"?
   F. Most of us don't care about our privacy.
   G. The government cannot invade our privacy over the Internet.
   H. We like to communicate using our technology, but we often don't think about our privacy when we're doing it.
   I. The concept of a "Big Brother" watching us and reading all of our messages is not possible due to the amendments discussed in the article.

©2008 PRINCIPLE WOODS, INC. Removal of copyright notice and copying are violations of Federal Law.

Answer Key — Answer Key — Answer Key   A MOMENT 2 LOSE

7. According to this article, why is there the possibility of abuse of our information on social sites like MySpace and Facebook?
   - **A. It can be passed on to others without our knowledge or permission.**
   - B. The owner of a space has no way to control who views a particular space.
   - C. The sender has no way of knowing that it is received by the person they hoped to send it to.
   - D. The information can be changed by the person receiving it, and then it cannot be deleted without permission.

8. The Fourth and Fifth Amendments are similar in that
   - F. both mention freedom of the press.
   - G. both provide protection from search and seizure.
   - H. both protect our right to practice our religion without interference.
   - **I. both deal with our freedoms as related to the police or other government officials.**

9. According to this article, which statement about our "right to privacy" is MOST accurate?
   - A. Internet sites provide adequate protection.
   - **B. It is not mentioned in the U.S. Constitution.**
   - C. The right to privacy is protected only in the First Amendment.
   - D. Most countries have found that it is the government's role to protect its citizens' right to privacy.

10. People who read this article will learn that
    - **F. "privacy" is defined as the right to be left alone.**
    - G. the U.S. Constitution provides for our right to privacy.
    - H. there is no way to track all of the Internet sites we visit.
    - I. George Orwell argued that government must be more involved in our lives.

11. Based on information in the article and the text box, which of these conclusions is MOST accurate?
    - **A. Many teens do understand the issue of protecting their privacy online.**
    - B. The majority of teens who use social networking sites post complete profile.
    - C. Nearly two-thirds of teens use social networking sites keep in touch with their friends.
    - D. Most teens don't realize that no one is protecting them from being contacted by strangers.

Want to be my friend?

©2008 PRINCIPLE WOODS, INC. Removal of copyright notice and copying are violations of Federal Law.

Unit 7 — Answer Key — Answer Key — Answer Key

Technical Writing Prompt

12. After reading the article, write your own privacy policy to give to your friends explaining the way you would like them to respect and protect your privacy. Use bullet points within your policy to list concise rules for your friends to follow. Should your friends be able to take pictures of you without your permission and post them on MySpace or Facebook? If you send them a text message, what should be kept confidential? How do they know what to share and what not to share? Use specific examples and write concisely so that your friends will clearly understand your privacy policy statement.

Technical Writing

Student answers may vary.

The student should address the question to the best of his/her ability using the article and personal experience. The question is meant to prepare students to be active citizens who can accurately and effectively use written communication skills.

Use the technical writing rubric to reference the criteria and determine the number of points to award.

Vocational Extension

HELP WANTED:
Small law firm seeks attorney. Applicants must have juris doctorate degree from an accredited law school and must have passed bar exam. Five years of courtroom experience preferred. Submit resume in person at 124 Oak St.

Attorneys play a critical role in the legal system in our country. Their job is to act as an advocate for their clients. An advocate represents the interests of another person or group of people, like a business. In this way, their clients are protected in the best way possible within the laws of the country and state.

Educational requirements for attorneys are challenging. They must first receive a four-year undergraduate degree. This is followed by three years of law school. Once they have been awarded a juris doctorate degree at the end of law school, they take a test known as the bar exam. If they want to practice law in more than one state, they must pass this exam in each state.

Those who receive their law degree and pass the bar exam have many types of opportunities within the field of law. Most of these opportunities fall within four broad groups of practice:

- Private practice: Law firms range from one- or two-person offices to large groups of attorneys. Many small firms focus on a specialized area of the law, like personal injury, immigration, family, or criminal law. Larger firms usually have lawyers that cover various areas of law.
- Public interest: These attorneys focus on specific causes or services. They file lawsuits that deal with public policy, such as the environment.
- Government: These lawyers might work for a district attorney's office or a public defender's office. The federal government also uses lawyers in various departments like the Department of Justice.
- Corporations: Businesses always have a need for attorneys who will represent the company in things like labor and employment issues. Companies also need help with mergers with other businesses and with laws that affect how they do business in other states and countries.

There are various types of lawyers within these broad categories. There is a specialty for just about everyone! Young people who are interested in becoming lawyers should talk with lawyers in local law firms or an advisor at a local law school. They can learn more about the profession and specialties. A summer job in a law firm would be a great opportunity to get an inside look at the day-to-day activities of attorneys.

Do you think you might have what it takes to be a lawyer? Problem-solving skills and the ability to "think on your feet" are important. People who practice law must also understand how the law applies in many situations. They have to be organized and able to work with a wide variety of people. Sometimes lawyers work on teams, so they must work well with others. Attorneys also work very long hours.

There is a wide range of salaries for attorneys too. Generally, lawyers in large firms in major cities make the most, while public defenders and district attorneys earn less. Starting salaries for lawyers joining a large law firm can range from $111,750 to $137,000, but beginning salaries for district attorneys currently range from about $35,000 to $55,000. In 2004 the U.S. Department of Labor reported that the median salary for all lawyers was $94,930.

As we can see, lawyers play an important role in our world. We are affected by hundreds of laws every day, even when we are not aware of them. Attorneys are there when we need a helping hand.

Unit 7 — *Answer Key — Answer Key — Answer Key*

Looking forward

13. A lawyer advocates for people to ensure that their interests are protected. Which one of the four main groups of practice do you think would best suit your interests and talents? Why do you think you could best serve people in this kind of practice? What strengths would you bring to this field? Use personal experience and information from the article in your answer.

> Student answers may vary.
>
> The student should address the question to the best of his/her ability using the article and personal experience. The question is meant to encourage students to explore areas of interest for their future and begin to determine how they will prepare for a future career.
>
> Use the extended-response rubric to reference the criteria and determine the number of points to award.

Ethical Dilemma

14. You are an attorney and own a small law firm. A disabled person hires you to represent her so that she can receive full disability benefits from the government. During your meetings with her, you discover that her disabilities are not as severe as she wants everyone to believe. Your firm needs as many clients as possible to stay in business. What do you say to your client?

> Student answers may vary.
>
> The student should address the question to the best of his/her ability using background knowledge from the article as well as personal opinion and experience. The question is meant to encourage students to contemplate scenarios and make ethical decisions.
>
> Use the character education rubric to reference the criteria and number of points to award.

©2008 PRINCIPLE WOODS, INC. Removal of copyright notice and copying are violations of Federal Law.

Answer Key — Answer Key — Answer Key   A MOMENT 2 LOSE

Unit Vocabulary Assessment

Matching
Match each word in Column I to its definition in Column II.

Column I
- **B** 1. restriction
- **C** 2. privacy
- **A** 3. occasional
- **E** 4. boundary
- **D** 5. permission

Column II
a. occurring now and then
b. the act of confining something
c. being free from intrusion
d. approval to do something
e. something that sets a limit

Multiple Choice
Choose the word that MOST NEARLY replaces the underlined word in each sentence.

6. The First <u>Amendment</u> to the constitution guarantees freedom of speech.
    A. right
    B. change
    C. memory
    D. America

7. He has the <u>potential</u> to be a great player.
    A. skills
    B. potent
    C. pressure
    D. possibility

8. Public displays of affection make me very <u>uncomfortable</u>.
    A. under
    B. angry
    C. uneasy
    D. relaxed

9. She <u>casually</u> baked the birthday cake without even following a recipe.
    A. formally
    B. naturally
    C. necessarily
    D. consciously

Word Bank
- assume
- disappointment
- intrusion
- reputation

Fill in the Blank
Choose a word from the word bank to fill in the blank in the sentence below.

10. Her **reputation** as a good person comes from her charitable works.

11. The kids experienced great **disappointment** when their grandparents couldn't come for the weekend.

12. The **intrusion** made me feel uneasy in my own house.

13. Don't **assume** that we'll always be ready to go.

Unit 7 — Answer Key — Answer Key — Answer Key

Authentic Assessment

Students will participate in a constructed response based on the unit "A Moment to Lose."

Instructions for a Constructed Response

1. **Choice of subject.** Following is a list of people in history who lost or were in danger of losing their good reputation after stories surfaced about their actions: Michael Vick (football player), Tonya Harding (figure skater), Barry Bonds (baseball player), Martha Stewart (business celebrity), Lil' Kim (artist), Richard Nixon (politician), Gary Hart (politician), Marion Jones (track star), Roger Clemens (baseball player), Fuzzy Zoeller (golfer).

2. **Research.** Select one person from the list to study. Then research that person and his or her major accomplishments or contributions. Depending on the person chosen, you may use Internet sources, encyclopedias, books, or other periodicals to do your research. You will turn in notes that answer the following questions:

    Person of Study

    a. Who is the person?

    b. When and where did he/she live?

    c. What was his/her background?

    d. What did he/she do or believe that was unique?

    e. What happened to hurt his/her reputation?

    f. Was he/she able to overcome the hurt reputation?

3. **Constructed response.** After you complete your research, write an extended response to the following question: Michael Iapoce said, "Reputation is character minus what you've been caught doing." What do you think this quotation would mean to the person you chose to research? What would this person say about the connections between actions, character, and reputation? Offer specific examples explaining your answer. This response is worth 40 points.

4. **Assessment.** Your constructed response will be assessed using the rubric on the following page.

©2008 PRINCIPLE WOODS, INC. Removal of copyright notice and copying are violations of Federal Law.

Answer Key — Answer Key — Answer Key   A MOMENT 2 LOSE

Rubric for Constructed Response

31-40 points	The response correctly interprets the meaning of the quotation in the context of the person the student chose. The student's answer is correct, complete, and addresses all aspects of the prompt. The response uses information from well-documented research for support. Any additional information provided by the student is related to the assigned task and acts as a support for his/her response.
21-30 points	The response correctly interprets the meaning of the quotation in the context of the person the student chose. The student's answer is correct and addresses most aspects of the assigned task. The student provides detail and support, but it is not complete or from well-documented research.
11-20 points	The response correctly interprets the meaning of the quotation in the context of the person the student chose. The student's answer is correct; however, it is generalized and not specific enough. The student is missing specific details and support research that would prove his/her full understanding of the assigned task.
1-10 point	The response shows very little understanding of what is being asked in the assigned task and does not correctly interpret the meaning of the quotation in the context of the person the student chose. The answer is incomplete, has many things wrong with it, or addresses very little of the question.
0 points	The answer is completely incorrect, has nothing to do with the assigned task, or no answer is provided.

©2008 PRINCIPLE WOODS, INC. Removal of copyright notice and copying are violations of Federal Law.

Unit 8

Journey of the Tiger

Reading Instructional Guide for High-Interest Article

BEFORE READING

Front-Loading Background Knowledge through Read Aloud/Think Aloud

Search the Internet for recent articles on Tiger Woods and use them to model the effective habits of readers through a Read-Aloud-Think-Aloud.

Check out articles at the following websites to determine if they would be appropriate for your RATA:

- Litsky, Frank. "Earl Woods, 74, Father of Tiger Woods, Dies." *New York Times*. May 4, 2006. http://www.nytimes.com/2006/05/04/sports/golf/04woods.html/.

- Tiger Woods Foundation. http://www.tigerwoodsfoundation.org.

(Please keep in mind that it is the responsibility of the teacher to determine if articles from suggested sites are appropriate. The sites may have changed content since this publication. The publisher takes no responsibility for the current content of the site.)

Looking at the Words

Determining How the Word Sounds (Phonics)
Using the Syllable Guide and the Reading Instructional Guide Template found in the beginning of the book, follow the steps to help students learn how to break a word into manageable parts.

Determining What the Word Means (Vocabulary)

Words to Study	Breaking into Syllables	Short Definition
amateur	am-a-teur	(n.) an athlete who does not compete professionally for money
endorsement	en-dorse-ment	(n.) a promotional agreement
multiracial	mul-ti-ra-cial	(adj.) representing more than one race
obstacle	ob-sta-cle	(n.) something that stops progress
subliminal	sub-lim-i-nal	(adj.) producing a reaction even though one is not aware
tremendous	tre-men-dous	(adj.) great in size

Activating Background Knowledge

Anticipation Guide
Have students mark each of the following statements True or False:

1. ____ Tiger Woods comes from a diverse background.
2. ____ Tiger Woods has won over 82 tournaments in his career.

Answer Key — Answer Key — Answer Key Journey of the Tiger

3. _____ Tiger became a professional golfer at the age of 18.
4. _____ Tiger Woods has been called "one of the best golfers in history."
5. _____ Tiger's name came from the Chinese zodiac calendar.

Starter Questions
After completing the Anticipation Guide, have a group or class discussion with the students using the following questions:

1. How did Tiger Woods's father help his career?

2. What was the birth name given to Tiger Woods?

3. Name some companies that have publicly endorsed Tiger Woods.

4. What are the names of some major golf tournaments Tiger has won?

5. What are some charities that Tiger Woods supports?

Make a prediction about what you think the article will be about.

DURING READING
Use the Reading Instructional Guide Template found in the front of the book.

AFTER READING

Discussion Starter Questions

1. What racial barriers do you think Tiger's father feared Tiger would face if he practiced at a country club?

2. How do you think the subliminal tapes increased Tiger's performance?

3. If you were given the opportunity to help a charity, which charity would you support? How would you assist the charity?

4. If you could interview Tiger Woods, what questions would you ask him?

5. Do you think Tiger Woods is a strong role model for our youth? Why or why not?

Teacher Reflection

Use the Reading Instructional Guide Template found in the front of the book.

Journey of the Tiger

His real name is Eldrick, but most people call him "Tiger." He is known as one of the most successful golfers of all time. At age 32, he is one of the most respected and well-known names in sports. When he was just 2 years old, he putted against Bob Hope on *The Mike Douglas Show*. That was just the beginning. However, the road Tiger traveled to become a world-class golfer was not without obstacles.

Though Tiger's talent was noticed at a young age, the golf community was not fully open to multiracial members. Many people think of Tiger Woods as African-American golfer. But, his family tree is actually more complicated. Tiger's diverse family makes him one-quarter Chinese, one-quarter Thai, one-quarter African-American, one-eighth Native American, and one-eighth Dutch. Because of racial issues during Tiger's childhood, his father knew that his son would not be allowed to practice at local country clubs. So Tiger spent hours in his garage watching his dad putt, later imitating him on public golf courses.

Tiger's golf game got better and better as time went on. As he improved, his dad began challenging him more. He used subliminal tapes to improve Tiger's mental toughness. He also used "psychological warfare." While Tiger was swinging, his father would cough, yell, scream, jump, run, or throw something to distract him. The more distractions Tiger learned to ignore, the better his concentration. And the better his concentration, the better his game. At age 5, he appeared in *Golf Digest* and on ABC's *That's Incredible*. He went on to win the Optimist International Junior Golf Championship six times by the time he was 15. At age 15, he became the youngest U.S. Junior Amateur Champion in golf history. He competed in his first Professional Golf Association (PGA) event, the Nissan Los Angeles Open. At age 19, he competed in his first Masters event and was the only amateur to make the cut.

Through his determination, Tiger Woods went on to fame. In 1996, at the age of 20, he became a professional golfer.

Answer Key — Answer Key — Answer Key Journey of the Tiger

He immediately earned endorsements from Nike and Titleist that were worth about $60 million. Since then, he has won over 65 tournaments on the PGA Tour. He even won the 2008 U.S. Open with a torn ligament and a stress fracture. Because of his inspirational story, he is credited with opening up the golf community.

In 2006 Tiger Woods was the highest paid athlete in the United States. He had about $100 million in endorsement deals. His talent and public appeal prompted *Golf Digest* to predict that Tiger will be the first billionaire athlete by 2010. All of these wins have made Tiger a very rich man. Tiger has used his wealth as an opportunity to do good things, especially for young people.

In 1996 Tiger and his father, Earl, founded the Tiger Woods Foundation. This organization seeks to promote golf and other activities for disadvantaged youth. It is estimated that the foundation has reached over 10 million children through youth clinics and the Tiger Woods Learning Center. The Learning Center is a solar-powered building that provides character education as well as free tutoring. The Center also includes a 23-acre golf teaching facility on the same golf course where Tiger played as a high school student. To raise money for the Tiger Woods Foundation, Tiger has started an annual concert called Tiger Jam. He donates part of the money made to other charities, such as the Boys and Girls Club of Las Vegas and the Center for Independent Living.

Though he has won 14 major championships and over 80 tournaments so far in his lifetime, Tiger Woods always gives back to his community. Tiger has made a tremendous impact on our country through his unselfish giving. Through the example of his own life, Tiger inspires today's youth to overcome obstacles and make a difference in the world. By pushing himself to be his best and reaching out to help others do the same, Tiger Woods has shown that a little boy with a big dream can go a long way.

In Chinese mythology, the tiger is admired. Tigers represent royalty and courage. Tigers have a mark on the forehead that resembles the Chinese character for king. The tiger is also one of the 12 animals used in the Chinese cycle of years. Those born in the year of the tiger are said to be strong and competitive leaders. The tiger represents the drive to achieve.

"Tiger" was a nickname given to Tiger Woods by his father in honor of his friend, a Vietnamese soldier. Tiger Woods was born just before the year of the tiger, but he shows many "tiger" traits. On the golf course, Tiger is fearless and competes with his whole heart. In fact, many magazines call Tiger the "King of Golf." Tiger Woods is as distinguishable on a golf course as a tiger in the jungle.

Unit 8 — Answer Key — Answer Key — Answer Key

Reading Comprehension

After reading "Journey of the Tiger," choose the options that best answer questions 1–14.

1. Read this sentence.
   He used subliminal tapes to improve Tiger's mental toughness.

   What is the meaning of the word *subliminal* as it is used on the sentence?
   - A. dubbed
   - B. hindered
   - C. superficial
   - **D. unconscious**

2. Read this sentence.
   Though Tiger's talent was noticed at a young age, the golf community was not fully open to multiracial members.

   This sentence means that
   - F. Some people believe Tiger had an unfair advantage due to his multicultural family.
   - **G. Due to his diverse background, the community was not ready to accept Tiger's abilities.**
   - H. When he was younger, critics felt that Tiger should not be permitted to play golf due to his age.
   - I. The golf community welcomed Tiger and was in awe over his diverse heritage and physical ability.

3. From the article, the reader can tell that
   - A. Tiger was a pleasant and entertaining toddler.
   - B. Tiger's parents always fed him nutritious meals.
   - C. Tiger's neighbors were amazed by his golfing ability.
   - **D. Tiger's talent was noticeable enough to draw attention at a young age.**

4. What change did Tiger's father make during practices to improve Tiger's performance?
   - F. Tiger practiced for only a few hours each day to reserve his energy.
   - **G. He used distractions while Tiger was practicing to improve concentration.**
   - H. Practices were closed to spectators and media to allow Tiger to focus on his game.
   - I. Tiger continually practiced with competitors to better prepare himself for competition.

5. What aspect of Tiger's career does the author seem to admire the most?
   - A. his determination to perform his best when competing
   - **B. his perseverance and ability to win championships as an amateur**
   - C. his dedication to becoming the world's richest golfer at such a young age
   - D. his respect toward his father for instilling the desire to keep practicing and to enjoy a victory when it happens

6. The author organizes the article by
   - F. presenting a timeline of Tiger Woods's life.
   - **G. describing how Tiger Woods rose to fame and the honors he has won.**
   - H. providing a flashback of Tiger's early career through his father's eyes.
   - I. comparing the accomplishments of Tiger Woods to other famous golfers.

Answer Key — Answer Key — Answer Key   Journey of the Tiger

7. What was the author's purpose in writing this article?
    A. to encourage others to play golf
    B. to persuade others to give to charity
    C. to prove that golf is an entertaining sport that everyone should watch
    D. to show how a superior golfer finds time to give back to his community

8. What is the main idea of the first paragraph?
    F. Tiger did not begin playing golf until he was in middle school.
    G. Tiger enjoys appearing on television shows and magazine covers.
    H. Tiger is an exceptional golfer who began his career at a young age.
    I. Meeting celebrities such as Bob Hope has been the highlight of Tiger's career.

9. Which word BEST describes the role Tiger's father played in his career?
    A. upset
    B. supportive
    C. disenchanted
    D. disapproving

10. According to the passage, Tiger has been able to increase interest in golf because
    F. he talks to the fans while he is playing.
    G. he has held many clinics to teach others about golf.
    H. his personal story and triumphs are watched by many fans.
    I. he tells jokes while he is playing golf and therefore entertains the fans.

11. What is true of BOTH the Boys and Girls Club of Las Vegas and the Center for Independent Living?
    A. Both organizations sponsor Tiger Woods.
    B. Both assist elderly people who have difficulty with daily skills.
    C. Both receive monetary donations from Tiger Woods's charity events.
    D. Both provide after-school and summer enrichment for struggling students.

12. Which statement about Tiger Woods is the LEAST accurate?
    F. Tiger has won over 82 tournaments.
    G. In 2006 Tiger was the highest paid athlete.
    H. Tiger was the birth name given to Tiger Woods.
    I. At age 15, he became the youngest U.S. Junior Amateur Champion in golf history.

13. Based on information in the text box, Tiger Woods resembles the tiger in the Chinese zodiac in that
    A. he is the strong, competitive King of Golf.
    B. he was born during the Year of the Tiger in the zodiac calendar.
    C. his father named him after the tiger symbol in the Chinese zodiac calendar.
    D. he uses the Chinese zodiac calendar to plan all of the major events in his life.

14. According to the article, what is the main reason that Tiger Woods is an inspiration to others?
    F. Tiger and his father were able to enjoy golf together.
    G. His determination and charity inspire others to achieve goals.
    H. His celebrity status and television appearances inspire others to learn to play golf.
    I. At a young age, Tiger was able to travel to many different cities while playing golf.

©2008 PRINCIPLE WOODS, INC. Removal of copyright notice and copying are violations of Federal Law.

Unit 8

Answer Key — Answer Key — Answer Key

Reading Strategy

Directions: Use facts from the article to fill in a timeline to discover how Tiger Woods created his own destiny.

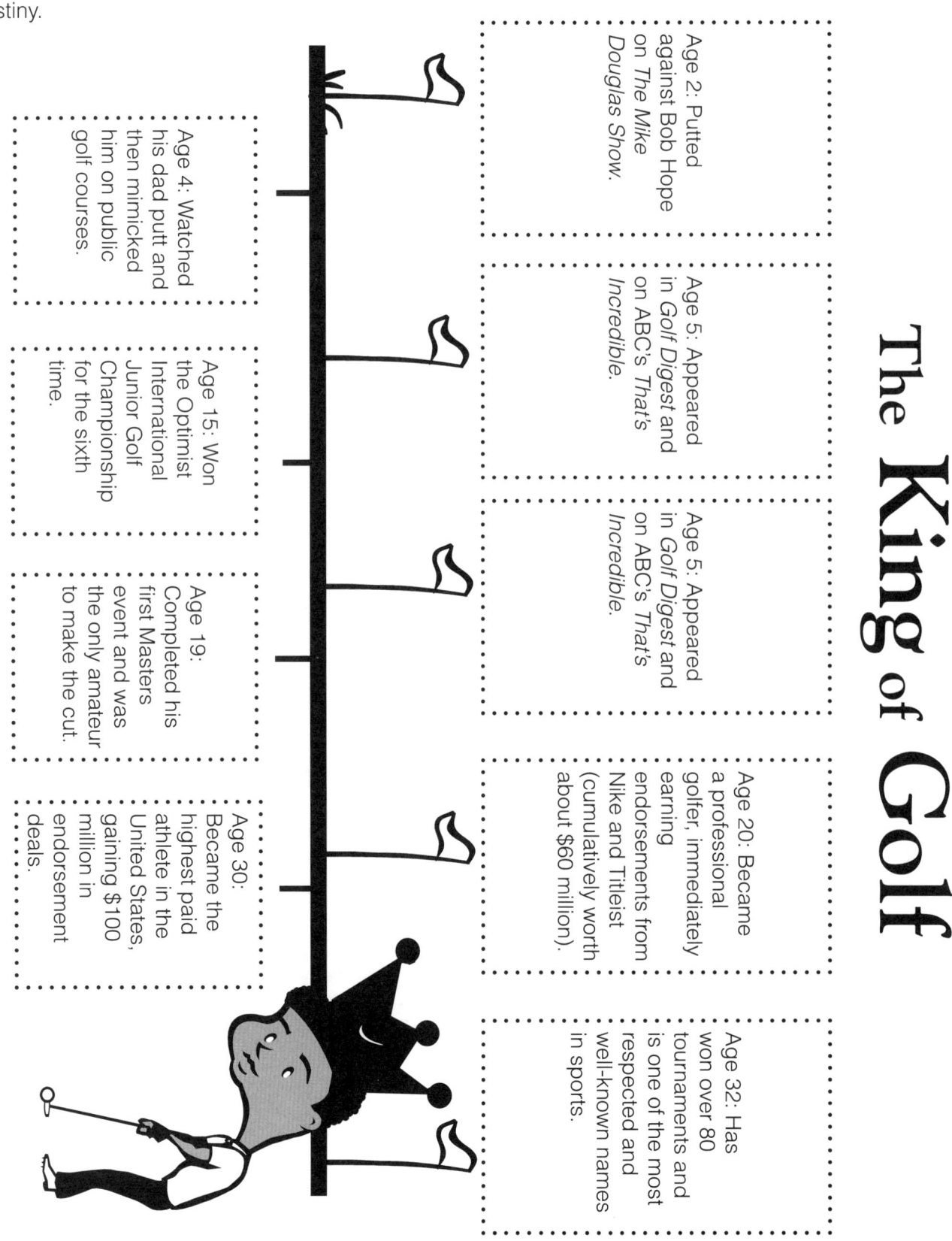

The King of Golf

Age 2: Putted against Bob Hope on *The Mike Douglas Show*.

Age 4: Watched his dad putt and then mimicked him on public golf courses.

Age 5: Appeared in *Golf Digest* and on ABC's *That's Incredible*.

Age 15: Won the Optimist International Junior Golf Championship for the sixth time.

Age 5: Appeared in *Golf Digest* and on ABC's *That's Incredible*.

Age 19: Completed his first Masters event and was the only amateur to make the cut.

Age 20: Became a professional golfer, immediately earning endorsements from Nike and Titleist (cumulatively worth about $60 million).

Age 30: Became the highest paid athlete in the United States, gaining $100 million in endorsement deals.

Age 32: Has won over 80 tournaments and is one of the most respected and well-known names in sports.

172
©2008 PRINCIPLE WOODS, INC. Removal of copyright notice and copying are violations of Federal Law.

Answer Key — Answer Key — Answer Key

Journey of the Tiger

Interpreting the Data

PART I

How do income and expenses compare when working with a fictional charity budget?

Fill in Table 1 to complete questions 15–16.

Table 1. 2006 Budget for Caring for Kids yearly income

Income sources	Projected income	Actual income
Fundraisers	$4,000	$3,600
Private donations	$1,500	$1,500
Investments	$700	$600
Auction	$1,300	$1,300
Other	$0	$130
Subtotals	**15.** $7,500	**16.** $7,130

Fill in Table 2 to complete questions 17–22.

Table 2. 2006 Budget for Caring for Kids yearly expenses

Expense items	Projected cost	Actual cost	Difference
Program implementation	$3,000	$3,100	**17.** $100
Program supplies	$1,200	$1,350	**18.** $150
Program manager	$1,200	$1,200	$0
Rent and utilities	$1,000	$1,000	$0
Fundraising costs	$350	$300	**19.** +$50
Miscellaneous expenses	$100	$0	+$100
Subtotals	**20.** $6,850	**21.** $6,950	**22.** $100

Fill in Table 3 to complete questions 23–24.

Table 3. 2006 Budget for Caring for Kids projected balance vs. actual balance

Projected balance (projected income minus expenses)	**23.**	$650
Actual balance (actual income minus expenses)	**24.**	$180

©2008 PRINCIPLE WOODS, INC. Removal of copyright notice and copying are violations of Federal Law.

Unit 8 — **Answer Key — Answer Key — Answer Key**

25. Why is it important that the actual balance after subtracting expenses from income is a positive number? What could be done with the money in the balance?

> **ANALYZE EVALUATE EXPLAIN**
>
> Student answers could contain facts such as the following:
>
> It is important that the actual balance be positive because that means that the charity is not spending more than it has budgeted for expenses. If a charity is overspending, it has less potential to benefit the community. The money in the balance could be donated to another charity, used to help more people in Caring for Kids, or invested and put away for next year or the next event.
>
> Use the short-response rubric to reference the criteria required for an acceptable answer and to determine the points to award.

PART II

How do you create a charity budget? (Students may complete this section individually or in groups.)

26. Create a charity. Decide what cause the charity will support and how that will be accomplished. List the details in the following box.

> **THINK EVALUATE EXPLAIN**
>
> Students should write a complete response to the question.
>
> Use the short-response rubric to reference the criteria required for an acceptable answer and to determine the points to award.

27. Now create a projected budget for the charity, including projected income and projected expenses.

Yearly income sources	Projected income
Subtotal	

Answer Key — Answer Key — Answer Key Journey of the Tiger

Yearly expense items	Projected cost
Subtotal	

28. What percentage of your projected income is the projected cost? _____

29. What are steps your charity can take to make sure that there is a positive balance?

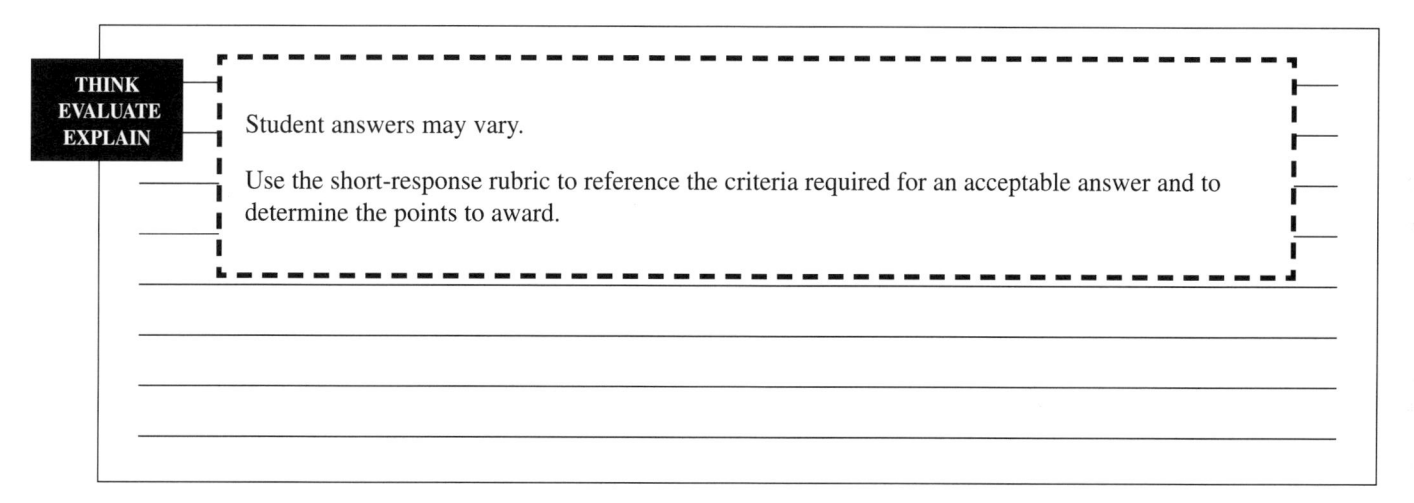

THINK EVALUATE EXPLAIN

Student answers may vary.

Use the short-response rubric to reference the criteria required for an acceptable answer and to determine the points to award.

Reflect and Respond

30. If you could start a charity for any cause, what would it be? Explain who or what your charity would be for, what you would do, and why the cause is important to you.

Reflect & Respond

Answers may vary, but students should address each part of the question. The question is meant to elicit strong classroom conversation about character. Students should be able to demonstrate an ability to think beyond themselves and plan activities to benefit others in their community.

Use the character education rubric to reference the criteria and number of points to award.

©2008 PRINCIPLE WOODS, INC. Removal of copyright notice and copying are violations of Federal Law.

Unit 8 — **Answer Key — Answer Key — Answer Key**

Reading Instructional Guide for Technical Extension

BEFORE READING

Looking at the Words

Determining How the Word Sounds (Phonics)
Technical texts often necessitate the use of multisyllabic words that are unfamiliar to students. Use the Syllable Guide to help students decode any words they might have trouble reading.

Determining What the Word Means (Vocabulary)

Words to Study	Breaking into Syllables	Short Definition
cardiovascular	car-di-o-vas-cu-lar	(adj.) having to do with the heart or blood vessels
elite	e-lite	(adj.) best or most skilled
endurance	en-dur-ance	(n.) the ability to last
regimen	reg-i-men	(n.) a course of intensive physical training
stability	sta-bil-i-ty	(n.) the quality of being firm; strength

Activating Background Knowledge

Graphic Organizer
Either individually or in groups, students may brainstorm about how athletes train for a match or event, recalling anything previously learned and any prior experience with the subject. Next, encourage students to see the relationships between their ideas by having them complete a four-square chart to demonstrate what they already know about the specific muscles and parts of the body that various athletes need to train.

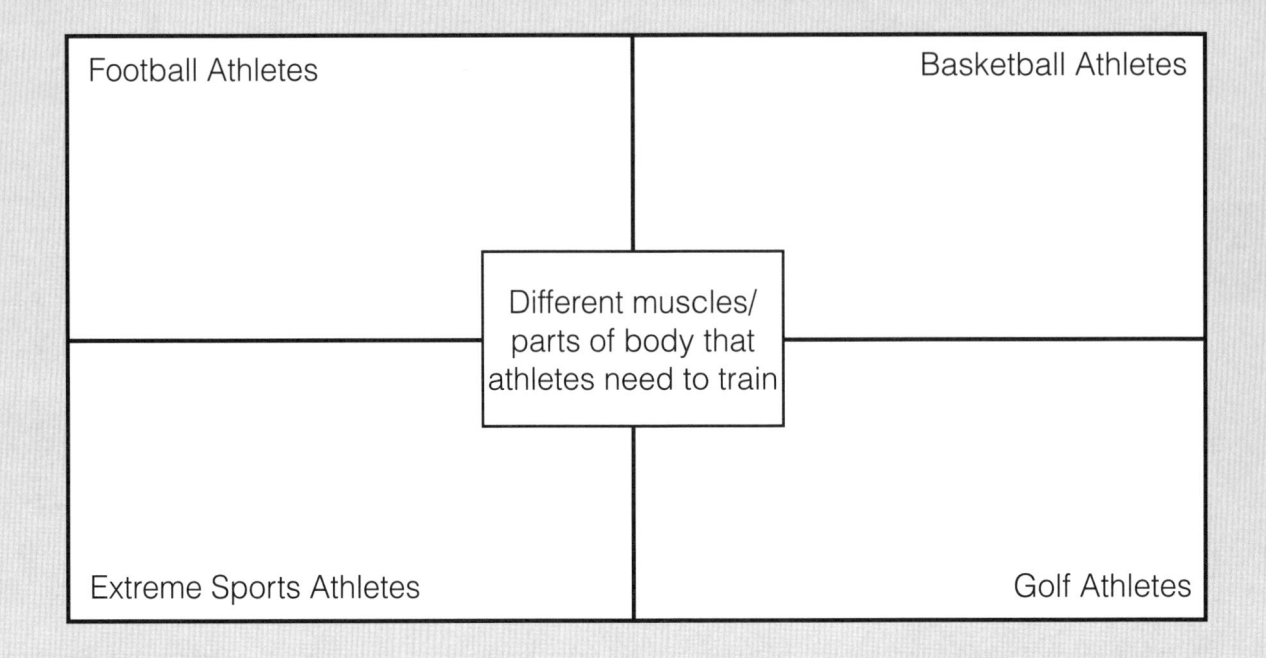

Football Athletes	Basketball Athletes
	Different muscles/ parts of body that athletes need to train
Extreme Sports Athletes	Golf Athletes

176

©2008 PRINCIPLE WOODS, INC. Removal of copyright notice and copying are violations of Federal Law.

Answer Key — Answer Key — Answer Key Journey of the Tiger

Starter Questions

After completing the Graphic Organizer, generate a group or class discussion to come up with questions about the subject, a prediction about the article, and at least one learning goal. The first question has been provided for you.

Question: Why is it important for professional athletes to train prior to competing in an event?

Question: _____

Prediction: _____

Goal: _____

DURING READING

Use the Reading Instructional Guide Template found in the front of the book.

AFTER READING

After reading, you may teach reading strategy use by giving students opportunities to do the following:
- Review, paraphrase, and summarize
- Participate in main-idea discussions by describing the information in their own words
- Reflect on concept maps and generate additional discussion starter questions based on the mappings
- Participate in small-group discussions using discussion starter questions

Discussion Starter Questions

The first question has been provided for you.

1. Which of the exercise methods mentioned in this article do you prefer? Why?

2. _____

3. _____

Unit 8

Technical Extension

Training to Perfection

Training to be an elite athlete is probably very different than you might imagine. Fans usually see only the excitement of competition. They don't see all the hours these athletes spend training their bodies. Tiger Woods and others at the top of their sports dedicate their lives to trying to win.

Getting ready to compete at the highest level of any sport means more than showing up at the gym every day. Athletes like Tiger Woods must commit to a training program that is ongoing. They train both their bodies and their minds. Athletes must practice to prepare for distractions such as noise and pressure. They hope to perform even better during an actual match since those distractions probably won't happen then. They also learn to rely on their training to take over during a competition. You might hear this described by athletes as being "in the zone."

In training their bodies, athletes must build up flexibility, balance, muscle strength, and endurance. According to Sean Cochran, a golf fitness instructor, any training program for a sport must include preventing injury. In golf this means that training must develop the body to the golf swing. Golfers train in a way that keeps the lower back and shoulders injury-free.

Football players train differently than golfers because different parts of the body are used. Sometimes unusual exercises can add unexpected results. Quinn Early, a former football player, found that the martial art called tai chi worked well with his regular training program. He believed that tai chi added relaxation to the more forceful football workout. The result was a more focused performance with better results during a game.

Many other football players have added classes like ballet, yoga, karate, or Pilates to their workouts. Although the players might face some good-natured teasing, they report that these activities improve their reflexes and flexibility.

Extreme sports trainers face a different challenge. Skateboarders, in-line skaters, surfers, and snowboarders are usually not comfortable with the rigid traditional programs. Their sports demand coordination and balance, so their trainers concentrate on developing a good cardiovascular base. They then build in exercises to push the athletes past their normal competition times while training. This produces better results during competition.

Extreme sports athletes have to understand plyometrics too. These exercises are free body movements like jumping high off the ground. They are done without weights or machines to train the muscles that help with quick movements. Trainers add these movements into the training regimen one or two times a week. They also make sure that they are done correctly to prevent injuries.

Professional basketball players are on the court for most of the year now, with very little off-season. Their training programs make sure the players stay healthy and free from injury. This means a training program that includes warm-ups, strength training, plyometrics, and prehabilitation. Rehabilitation is a special set of exercises to repair an injured athlete. Prehabilitation is a way of reducing injuries before they happen. For example, most injuries in basketball are ankle sprains. Adding stability exercises for the ankle in workouts can help strengthen that area of the body.

Most athletes don't like to practice. Many question why they can't perfect their skills during competition. But if an athlete wants to improve, it's important to practice without the pressure of winning. During an actual game, an athlete's training takes over, and he or she performs at an unconscious level. During practice, the athlete can concentrate on a specific move that isn't getting the desired results. The player can also get feedback from the coach, who spends time watching the athlete's performances. Then the player can concentrate on making changes and practicing the move until he or she can do it without thinking.

Athletes at the elite level in any sport must make a commitment to be the best they can be. Whether the sport is golf, football, basketball, or skateboarding, practice makes not only perfect, but permanent.

Exercise Vocabulary

Pilates. Exercise that focuses on core strength. Pilates exercises emphasize breathing and alignment of the spine.

Anaerobic. The anaerobic energy system produces energy without oxygen. The purpose of anaerobic conditioning is to improve the body's ability to tolerate oxygen debt.

Plyometrics. Exercise without weights or machines. A free body movement exercise system emphasizing calisthenics and repeated movements.

Calisthenics. Gymnastic exercises designed to develop physical health and vigor, usually performed with little or no special apparatus.

Rehabilitation. The process of restoring to a condition of good health and the ability to work.

Prehabilitation. Exercises done to maintain good health; done before there is an injury.

Unit 8

Answer Key — Answer Key — Answer Key

Reading Comprehension

After reading "Training to Perfection," choose the options that best answer questions 1–11.

1. Read this sentence.
   Training to be an elite athlete is probably very different than you might imagine.

   What is the meaning of the word *elite* as it is used in this sentence?
   A. amateur
   B. professional
   C. best or most skilled
   D. participating only at the community level

2. Read this sentence.
   You might hear this described by athletes as being "in the zone."

   What is the meaning of the phrase *in the zone* as it is used in this sentence?
   F. nearing the finish line
   G. training for all possible events or scenarios
   H. allowing training to take over during a game
   I. having the correct zoning for the playing field

3. According to this article, why do extreme sports trainers face challenges that other trainers might not have?
   A. They are not as qualified as trainers in other sports.
   B. Athletes who participate in extreme sports don't like to train in the usual ways.
   C. There are not many trainers who are qualified to work with extreme sports athletes.
   D. Extreme sports athletes are never in one place long enough for the trainers to et a schedule.

4. Golf fitness trainer Sean Cochran believes that
   F. athletes in any sport must train their bodies to prevent injury.
   G. elite golfers place more demands on their bodies than athletes in any other sport.
   H. most athletes don't need to develop all parts of their bodies in a training program.
   I. a cross-specific training program is necessary only in the highly skilled game of golf.

5. The author organizes the article by
   A. using the concept of "practice makes permanent."
   B. discussing the training demands of several sports.
   C. using golf and its challenges as the main topic of the article.
   D. comparing a football training program with that of extreme sports.

6. What is the main idea of this article?
   F. Most athletes don't like to practice.
   G. Proper techniques can be taught and are used to prevent injuries.
   H. Athletes involved in golf, basketball, football, and extreme sports all use the same training programs.
   I. Top athletes commit their lives to training their bodies and their minds, which includes a consistent training regimen of practice as well as game-day performance.

7. According to this article, why do athletes practice with unusual noise or distractions?
   A. to learn to rely on unconscious movements to win games
   B. to develop anger that will increase the determination to win
   C. to make sure the athlete is ready for unusual distractions during competition
   D. to learn to stay focused on the practice rather than on what they are going to eat for dinner that night

©2008 PRINCIPLE WOODS, INC. Removal of copyright notice and copying are violations of Federal Law.

Answer Key — Answer Key — Answer Key   Journey of the Tiger

8. The training of golfers and football players is different in that
   - **F. they focus on different parts of the body.**
   - G. golfers have better flexibility than football players.
   - H. football players develop more endurance than golfers.
   - I. golf practice takes much less concentration than football practice.

9. What does the author use to support the statement about the importance of prehabilition in basketball?
   - A. The author believes that rehabilitation doesn't work.
   - B. Prehabilitation helps the athlete develop proper shooting skills.
   - C. Coaches support the use of prehabilitation techniques over all other training systems.
   - **D. The author discusses how basketball trainers work to improve basketball players' ankle strength in order to prevent injuries.**

10. People who read this article will learn how
    - **F. athletes in a variety of sports train for success.**
    - G. cross-specific training exercises build muscle strength and flexibility.
    - H. pogos, rocket jumps, squat jumps, and tuck jumps are used in skateboarding.
    - I. anaerobic exercises build muscle fibers that are required for explosive performance.

11. Based on the information in this article, what does "practice makes not only perfect, but permanent" mean?
    - A. Performance is determined only by practice.
    - B. Conscious movements are learned during game situations.
    - C. Trainers must make athletes work harder during practice than they do during competition.
    - **D. What an athlete learns by performing a move over and over during practice takes over on game day.**

Unit 8

Answer Key — Answer Key — Answer Key

Technical Writing Prompt

12. You are a high school coach who has had unique success in producing winning athletes. You are preparing a PowerPoint presentation for a coaching seminar on the importance of both physical and mental training for athletic success. Design two PowerPoint pages outlining the key steps players must take to physically train and to mentally train for an event. Title your pages, use bullet points, and keep your pages brief so they will be easy for the audience to read during your oral presentation. You may choose to write for coaches of a particular sport or for coaches representing various sports.

Technical Writing

Student answers may vary.

The student should address the question to the best of his/her ability using the article and personal experience. The question is meant to prepare students to be active citizens who can accurately and effectively use written communication skills.

Use the technical writing rubric to reference the criteria and determine the number of points to award.

Answer Key — Answer Key — Answer Key   Journey of the Tiger

Vocational Extension

HELP WANTED:

Exclusive private golf course is seeking young players to train as caddies for their customers. Applicants must know the rules of the game and be willing to caddy under all weather conditions. Apprenticeship program through the Professional Caddies Association is available after a probationary period of three months. If you love golf and would like to join an elite group of professional caddies, call the club manager, Daniel Anderson, at 886-7845.

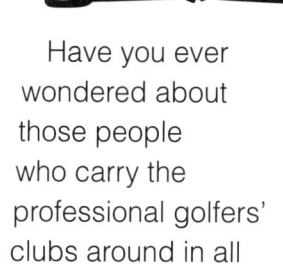

Have you ever wondered about those people who carry the professional golfers' clubs around in all weather? You might be surprised to learn that caddies are usually golfers themselves. However, some people who play golf can't or don't want to become professional golfers. An alternative is to caddy for someone else. Caddies are still able to play a lot of golf in their free time. They can do this while also building a respected career. Caddies are an important part of the golf team because they allow golfers to focus on their swings and getting the ball where it needs to be. The caddy takes care of everything else.

There isn't any one path to becoming a caddy on elite tours like the Professional Golf Association (PGA) Tour. A good way for those interested in this career is to caddy at a local golf club. This allows future caddies to form networks of people who can help them break into the field at the national level. Another way is to join online communities and other groups of golf professionals.

One way for a caddy to get work is to show up at a tournament on Monday and hope that one of the golfers needs a caddy. There are usually over a hundred golfers starting a tournament, and they all need caddies. Most golfers bring their own caddy, but some might need one at the last minute. Even if a caddy isn't needed, the networking opportunities while hanging around the golf course could be helpful in finding work in the future.

The Professional Caddies Association (PCA) offers an apprenticeship program to teach caddies all the "tricks of the trade." The course is the beginning of a three-level program. It includes topics such as the history of the game, teamwork, caddy signals, rules, and course management. Caddies then go on to the PCA Worldwide Graduate Program. The purpose of this stage is to put caddies on courses to practice what they have learned. The final part of "caddy school" is the PCA Worldwide Master Program where caddies will learn from Master Caddies how to be the best in their field.

Unit 8

Answer Key — Answer Key — Answer Key

The caddy's job includes things like cleaning the player's clubs, checking elevations, and estimating yardage and wind direction. The caddy also suggests which club to use, rakes bunkers, replaces divots, and carries the golf bag. A caddy knows all the rules of the game and must use them correctly. Any mistake made by the caddy could bring a penalty to the player.

So, what is a caddy paid? A caddy at a club or resort is paid by the player, usually between $25 and $50 a round. A caddy on the professional tour is paid by the player too. This payment is usually a weekly wage plus a percentage (usually 5%–10%) of the player's winnings. Tour caddies have to pay their own expenses, like hotel rooms and transportation to and from the tournaments. One of the best caddies in the world, Steve Williams, caddies for Tiger Woods. He made about $1.27 million in 2006. This is a career that can allow a golfer to perfect the game and make some money at the same time!

Answer Key — Answer Key — Answer Key   Journey of the Tiger

Looking Forward

13. In order to be a caddy on a professional golf tour, you must have experience and training. The article illustrates many ways someone can acquire the skills needed to be a successful caddy. Being sure to include both personal experience and information presented in the article, explain what steps you would take to become an accomplished caddy. Would you like to caddy at a resort, or do you have aspirations of becoming a caddy on a professional tour?

> Student answers may vary.
>
> The student should address the question to the best of his/her ability using the article and personal experience. The question is meant to encourage students to explore areas of interest for their future and begin to determine how they will prepare for a future career.
>
> Use the extended-response rubric to reference the criteria and determine the number of points to award.

Ethical Dilemma

14. You are a caddy for a professional golfer, and your player is in first place going into the final round of a major tournament. On the 17th hole, his ball slices, and the two of you find it in the rough behind a tree. It will be nearly impossible for the player to hit the ball without adding a stroke to his score. That one stroke might cost him the lead, and your earnings will drop right along with his. After you go to get a club from the player's bag, you see that the player has decided to move the ball as allowed in the rules. After the hole is completed, however, the player doesn't add the stroke to his score as required by the rules. What do you do? What are your choices?

> Student answers may vary.
>
> The student should address the question to the best of his/her ability using background knowledge from the article as well as personal opinion and experience. The question is meant to encourage students to contemplate scenarios and make ethical decisions.
>
> Use the character education rubric to reference the criteria and number of points to award.

Answer Key — Answer Key — Answer Key

Unit 8

Unit Vocabulary Assessment

Matching
Match each word in Column I to its definition in Column II.

Column I
- __B__ 1. cardiovascular
- __D__ 2. stability
- __A__ 3. multiracial
- __C__ 4. endurance

Column II
- a. representing more than one race
- b. having to do with the heart
- c. the ability to last
- d. strength

Multiple Choice
Choose the word that MOST NEARLY replaces the underlined word in each sentence.

5. One of the <u>elite</u> swimmers she has coached is an Olympic medalist.
   - **A. best**
   - B. worst
   - C. popular
   - D. elevated

6. The athlete's <u>endorsement</u> of the basketball shoes tripled the company's sales.
   - A. use
   - B. viewing
   - **C. promotion**
   - D. entertainment

7. The response to his hit single has been <u>tremendous</u> and supportive.
   - **A. huge**
   - B. sublime
   - C. emotional
   - D. overpowering

Word Bank
amateur
obstacle
regimen
subliminal

Fill in the Blank
Choose a word from the word bank to fill in the blank in the sentence below.

8. The movie theater used **subliminal** messages to advertise their snack bar.

9. The **amateur** athlete isn't allowed to make money from her competitions.

10. Harry's knee injury has been an **obstacle** to his marathon training.

11. To train for the season, I follow a strict **regimen** of aerobics and weightlifting.

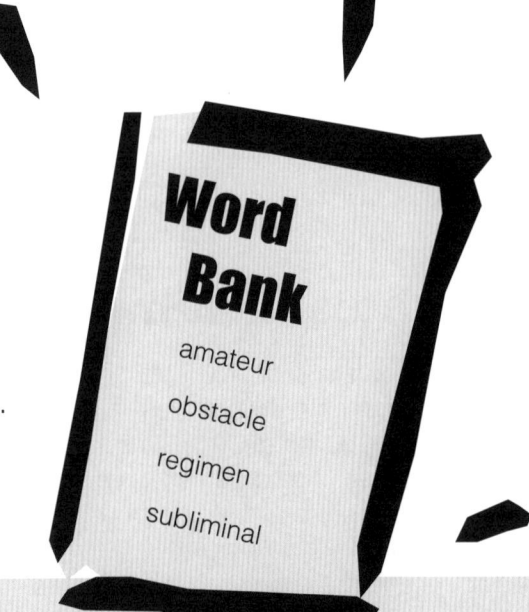

©2008 PRINCIPLE WOODS, INC. Removal of copyright notice and copying are violations of Federal Law.

Authentic Assessment

Students will create an advertising promotion based on the unit "Journey of the Tiger." This activity combines the authentic components of research, writing, and creativity linked to the comprehension of a written text.

Instructions for Advertising Promotion

1. **Samples.** Students should find or be provided with as many advertising promotions as possible that feature athletes. These might include television commercials, magazine or newspaper ads, radio commercials, billboards, etc.

2. **Planning.** Students will form cooperative groups and choose the following for teacher approval:

    a. The "company" for which the promotion is being done (ex. Nike)

    b. The product being advertised (can be a "real" product or student-invented)

    c. The athlete being featured

    d. The type of advertisement (commercial, magazine ad, etc.)

3. **Budget.** Students should then create a simple budget for their advertisement, including the cost of making the commercial/ad (including payment to the athlete) and the amount of money the company is expected to make from the advertisement. Groups may use the article as a basis for their budget or do their own research to determine a realistic budget.

4. **Design.** After creating these basic elements of their advertising campaign, each group should begin the design portion of the product. Each group must produce a complete advertisement, including the text and audio/video if applicable. Students should put thought into the connection between their athlete and the product, and they may create a slogan for their advertisement.

5. **Presentation.** Groups should present their live, taped, or printed ads to the class and then discuss the impact an athlete can have on the advertising for a company. The discussion should include their personal experience as well as information from the article and their own research.

6. **Assessment.** Assess the promotion using the rubric on the following page.

Unit 8 — Answer Key — Answer Key — Answer Key

Advertisement Rubric

Requirement	8–10 Points	4–7 Points	0–3 Points	Points Earned
Cooperative Groups	The students work well together to complete the project.	The students generally worked well together, with minor setbacks.	The students did not work well together to complete the project.	
Budget	The group completed a simple budget based on information from the article or separate research.	The group completed most of a budget, but had little article or research support.	The group did not complete a budget or used no article or research support.	
Advertisement	The group produced well-constructed live, taped, or print advertisement.	The group produced a live, taped, or print advertisement that was generally complete.	The group did not produce a live, taped, or print advertisement, or there were missing elements.	
Reflection	The students participated in a class discussion using support from the article and/or research.	The students participated in a class discussion but used little support.	The students did not participate in a class discussion.	

©2008 PRINCIPLE WOODS, INC. Removal of copyright notice and copying are violations of Federal Law.

— Unit 9 —

Above the *Influence*

Reading Instructional Guide for High-Interest Article

BEFORE READING

Front-Loading Background Knowledge through Read Aloud/Think Aloud

Search the Internet for recent articles on driving under the influence and use them to model the effective habits of readers through a Read Aloud/Think Aloud.

Check out articles at the following websites to determine if they would be appropriate for your RATA:
- Students Against Destructive Decisions. http://www.sadd.org/.
- Insurance Information Institute. "Drunk Driving: The Topic." http://www.iii.org/media/hottopics/insurance/drunk/.

(Please keep in mind that it is the responsibility of the teacher to determine if articles from suggested sites are appropriate. The sites may have changed content since this publication. The publisher takes no responsibility for the current content of the site.)

Looking at the Words

Determining How the Word Sounds (Phonics)
Using the Syllable Guide and the Reading Instructional Guide Template found in the beginning of the book, follow the steps to help students learn how to break a word into manageable parts.

Determining What the Word Means (Vocabulary)

Words to Study	Breaking into Syllables	Short Definition
apparent	ap-par-ent	(adj.) easily seen or understood
humble	hum-ble	(adj.) not proud or boasting
incident	in-ci-dent	(n.) an individual event
influence	in-flu-ence	(n.) the power to produce an effect (v.) to encourage a thought or action
notable	not-a-ble	(adj.) important or unique
rehabilitation	re-ha-bil-i-ta-tion	(n.) the process of restoring a condition of health
victim	vic-tim	(n.) a person who is hurt

Activating Background Knowledge

Anticipation Guide
Have students mark each of the following statements True or False:

1. ____ Recently it appears that there is a rise in celebrities being charged with DUI.
2. ____ Lindsay Lohan's first stay in rehabilitation proved to be successful.

©2008 PRINCIPLE WOODS, INC. Removal of copyright notice and copying are violations of Federal Law.

Unit 9
Answer Key — Answer Key — Answer Key

3. _____ Entertainment celebrities are the only celebrities who fall victim to DUI.

4. _____ Baseball player Josh Hancock was killed while driving under the influence.

5. _____ In addition to serving jail time, an individual can receive a suspended driver's license as a result of a DUI.

Starter Questions

After completing the Anticipation Guide, have a group or class discussion with the students using the following questions:

1. What is DUI?

2. What are some examples of substances that may impact your driving ability?

3. What are the consequences of a formal DUI charge?

4. How can testing positive for a controlled substance affect an athlete's career?

5. What programs exist to assist people who have difficulty controlling their alcohol consumption and/or drug use?

Make a prediction about what you think the article will be about.

DURING READING

Use the Reading Instructional Guide Template found in the front of the book.

AFTER READING

Discussion Starter Questions

1. Should celebrities make more of a conscious effort to abide by the law since they are continually in the public eye and are admired by many?

2. Why do you think many people, including celebrities, decide to get behind the wheel after using alcohol or drugs?

3. Should the places that provide and sell alcohol be held more accountable for ensuring that their patrons drink responsibly?

4. When they commit crimes, should celebrities receive more lenient punishments than others who do not have celebrity status? Why or why not?

5. How do you think the celebrities mentioned in this article should go about changing their lives?

Teacher Reflection

Use the Reading Instructional Guide Template found in the front of the book.

Above the Influence

An All-Too-Familiar Story

It seems that she has it all: a successful career, worldwide fame, and unlimited money. We watch her life and imagine that she is above the problems of the "regular" world. And then one day, unexpectedly, it all comes crashing down. We see in the news that she was arrested for DUI, or driving under the influence of alcohol or drugs. Despite her reputation for wild behavior, no one expected America's sweetheart to fall so hard, so fast.

Does this sound like a script from a movie? Or maybe it sounds familiar or common among young celebrities today. Although individual stories may vary, many celebrities have fallen victim to similar events. In fact, one website called 2006 "The Year of the Celebrity DUI." This problem happens so often that it leads some to question what kind of example these celebrities are setting. How are celebrities influencing the average young person who hears about them in the news day in and day out? You may already be thinking of several famous young people whose lives have played out like the situation above.

Fallen Pop Princesses

One of the most notable princesses of popular culture who has recently been associated with drug and alcohol abuse is Lindsay Lohan. After years of media rumors, this young woman recently hit a personal low. Lindsay Lohan's lifestyle of partying finally caught up with her. First, Lindsay crashed her Mercedes Benz into a tree and fled the scene. When police questioned her, they determined that her alcohol level was above the legal limit. And this arrest occurred before Lindsay even reached the legal drinking age of 21. She spent six weeks in a rehabilitation center and wore an alcohol-monitoring ankle bracelet when she left. This was supposed to prove that she could stay sober. Unfortunately, her efforts were unsuccessful. Shortly after she left, Lindsay was involved in another road incident. This time it was an argument with the family of a former employee. After this incident, she was charged with driving under the influence, reckless driving, and being under the influence of cocaine. She pleaded guilty to these charges and received a sentence of 1 day in jail, 10 days of community service, and 36 months of probation. In addition, she was sentenced to pay hundreds of dollars in fines and complete an alcohol education program for 18 months.

Celebutantes Off the Wagon

Paris Hilton and Nicole Richie are two young women who are famous for being famous. They made headlines in 2006 and 2007 for DUI arrests and their punishments. Paris Hilton served 23 days in jail after being found guilty of driving on a suspended license while on probation for a DUI. Nicole Richie was arrested for driving the wrong way on an interstate, which violated her probation for an earlier heroin charge. She was sentenced to four days behind bars, but served only 82 minutes because of overcrowding in the Los Angeles jail.

Some have accused the California judges of giving celebrities like Paris, Nicole, and Lindsay light sentences. Some think that because they are role models they should be held to a higher standard of behavior. However, legal experts have said that the punishments received by these young celebrities are what any normal person would have received. Unfortunately, the first DUI arrest wasn't enough to prevent these celebrities from making bad choices with alcohol and drugs again. In almost every case, the

Unit 9

celebrity chose to get back behind the wheel while under the influence, placing her life and the lives of everyone on the road in danger.

Entertainer Taking Responsibility

In the endless line of celebrities with drunken driving charges, one recent example has readily taken responsibility. Kiefer Sutherland, star of TV's *24*, is no stranger to DUI trouble. In several incidents dating all the way back to 1994, Sutherland has made poor decisions to drive while intoxicated. After his latest arrest, he was sentenced to 30 days in jail along with 18 days from a 2004 DUI arrest. Saying that he was disappointed in himself, Sutherland chose to quietly serve all 48 days in a suburban jail. He was also concerned about his coworkers on *24*. He offered to serve more time in order to work around the production schedule of the show, therefore protecting his coworkers' salaries. Reports about his time state that he was humble, uncomplaining, and hardworking. He did daily laundry duty to pass his days and had few visitors. Hopefully, his 48 days served will prevent him from ever driving while intoxicated again.

Athletic Tragedy

Entertainment celebrities aren't the only ones to drink or do drugs and drive. Recently, Tampa Bay Buccaneers player David Boston was fired because of this behavior. The illegal drug GHB was found in his system after he was found unconscious in his car. This mistake caused the wide receiver to lose his job and quite a bit of money.

Nothing can compare, however, to the consequences faced by Josh Hancock. Hancock was a former relief pitcher for the St. Louis Cardinals. After pitching three innings during a game against the Chicago Cubs, he made a fatal decision. He got in his car with a blood alcohol level that was almost twice the legal limit. While talking on his cell phone and still under the influence of alcohol, he crashed his SUV into the back of a tow truck. The truck was stopped on the side of the road, and Hancock was killed instantly. Police later also found marijuana and drug supplies in his car. Because he was a professional athlete, Hancock's death brings a great deal of attention to the issue of driving under the influence. Players are held to a high level of responsibility both on and off the field. Sadly, Hancock clearly didn't live up to that responsibility. However, this tragedy can teach us an important lesson about the dangers and consequences of driving under the influence.

Celebrity Influence

Celebrities are the most well-known examples of those affected by drug and alcohol abuse. But this issue isn't limited to famous people. It affects people from all walks of life. Many young people are influenced by the lives of celebrities. Rather than follow the pattern of those celebrities who hurt themselves and others, we can focus on living more responsibly. And instead of making headlines for DUI arrests, perhaps more celebrities could be using their public influence to lead the way to safer lives.

Possible DUI Penalties

- Suspension of driver's license
- Probation
- Community service
- Fines
- Seizure of vehicle
- Drug and alcohol classes
- Increased automobile insurance rates
- Jail time
- Liability for injury or property damage

Answer Key — Answer Key — Answer Key

ABOVE the Influence

Reading Comprehension

After reading "Above the Influence," choose the options that best answer questions 1–14.

1. Read this sentence.
   Shortly after being released, Lindsay was involved in another road incident.

   What is the meaning of the word *incident* as it is used in the sentence?
   A. trip
   B. episode
   C. accident
   D. disagreement

2. Read this sentence.
   And instead of making headlines for DUI arrests, perhaps more celebrities could be using their public influence to lead the way to safer lives.

   What is the meaning of the word *influence* as it is used in the sentence?
   F. power
   G. manners
   H. character
   I. manipulation

3. From this article, the reader can tell that
   A. the lifestyles that celebrities lead do not influence young teenage girls.
   B. public opinion of the celebrities is not affected by their personal mishaps.
   C. celebrities have an easy time balancing their stardom with their social lives.
   D. there appears to be a recent increase in the number of celebrities that drive under the influence.

4. According to the article, which of these is likely to occur?
   F. The youth in our society will continue to be influenced by celebrities.
   G. Celebrities will continue to engage in behaviors that involve driving under the influence.
   H. Professional athletic organizations will impose mandatory drug and alcohol education for their athletes.
   I. The government will begin to create tougher punishments for celebrities who are arrested for driving under the influence.

5. In the author's opinion,
   A. a celebrity's public image is not affected by social behavior.
   B. the judicial system appears to give celebrities tougher sentences for DUIs.
   C. the media should leave celebrities alone and allow them to live their own lives.
   D. some of the punishments received by celebrities did not prevent their behavior from happening again.

6. The author organizes the article by
   F. listing the reasons why someone should not drive under the influence.
   G. describing the problem of celebrity DUI and presenting popular examples.
   H. providing a personal account of one famous celebrity's struggle with substance abuse.
   I. comparing the treatment options available for celebrities who have a problem with substance addiction.

©2008 PRINCIPLE WOODS, INC. Removal of copyright notice and copying are violations of Federal Law.

Unit 9 — Answer Key — Answer Key — Answer Key

7. Why does the author mention athletes such as David Boston and Josh Hancock?
   A. to introduce the reader to famous athletes
   B. to explain the rules of professional football and baseball
   C. to entertain the reader by adding information about athletes
   D. to prove that entertainment celebrities are not the only ones who drive under the influence

8. If the article were published in a newspaper, which would be the most informative headline?
   F. An Athlete's Anguish
   G. Celebrating Celebrities
   H. Celebrities Under Influence
   I. Driving Conditions in America

9. Based on her actions as described in this article, which two words BEST describe Lindsay Lohan's apparent attitude toward driving under the influence after her first arrest?
   A. remorseful and reckless
   B. remorseful and cautious
   C. unremorseful and reckless
   D. unremorseful and cautious

10. According to the passage, the death of Josh Hancock has affected society most by
    F. proving that driving under the influence can have fatal consequences.
    G. hindering the Chicago Cubs' chances of winning the World Series that year.
    H. showing that sport utility vehicles (SUVs) need more safety regulations to prevent fatalities.
    I. illustrating how talking on a cell phone can distract drivers and negatively impact their ability to drive a car.

11. What is true of BOTH Paris Hilton and Nicole Richie?
    A. Their careers have suffered because of wrong choices.
    B. They served the same jail sentence for driving under the influence.
    C. They served brief jail sentences for driving under the influence or other related charges.
    D. They travel around the country speaking to society's youth about the dangers of driving under the influence.

12. Which sentence from the article provides the BEST evidence that celebrity DUIs are on the rise?
    F. In fact, one website called 2006 "The Year of the Celebrity DUI."
    G. Since they are role models for countless young people, many believe that they should act the part.
    H. Entertainment celebrities aren't the only ones to make the unfortunate decision to drink or do drugs and drive.
    I. While celebrities are the most visible examples of those affected by drug and alcohol abuse, this issue affects people from all walks of life

13. According to the text box, which of these is NOT a penalty for DUI?
    A. a fine
    B. jail time
    C. mandatory curfew
    D. alcohol or drug classes

14. Based on the information provided about Lohan, Hilton, and Richie, which of these conclusions is accurate?
    F. Lohan, Hilton, and Richie were not penalized for their wrongdoing.
    G. Lohan, Hilton, and Richie received lesser penalties because of their fame.
    H. The court was stricter on the celebrities because of their influence on society.
    I. The court gave the celebrities the same penalties they would give non-celebrities.

Answer Key — Answer Key — Answer Key

ABOVE the Influence

Reading Strategy

Directions: Use the two graphic organizers below to help categorize information from the article. The graphic organizers look different, but each one will help you organize information to compare and contrast. The Athletic Tragedy graphic organizer asks you to use prior knowledge to compare someone you are already familiar with to the two athletes from the article.

Celebutantes Off the Wagon Chart

Paris Hilton	Similarities	Nicole Richie
- drove on a suspended license while on probation for DUI - served 23 days in jail	- celebrity - young - arrested more than once - behavior involved alcohol and drugs - role model for teenagers - put lives at risk	- arrested for DUI while on probation for drug charge - sentenced to 4 days behind bars but served only 82 minutes

Athletic Tragedy Complex Venn Diagram

Use this graphic organizer to compare and contrast three items. Use the outsides of the ovals to write facts specific to the indicated person and the overlapping parts of the ovals to write facts that the athletes share. In the very center, write two things that all three athletes have in common. Use the article to find information on David Boston and Josh Hancock. Then think of an athlete that you already know well enough to compare with David and Josh.

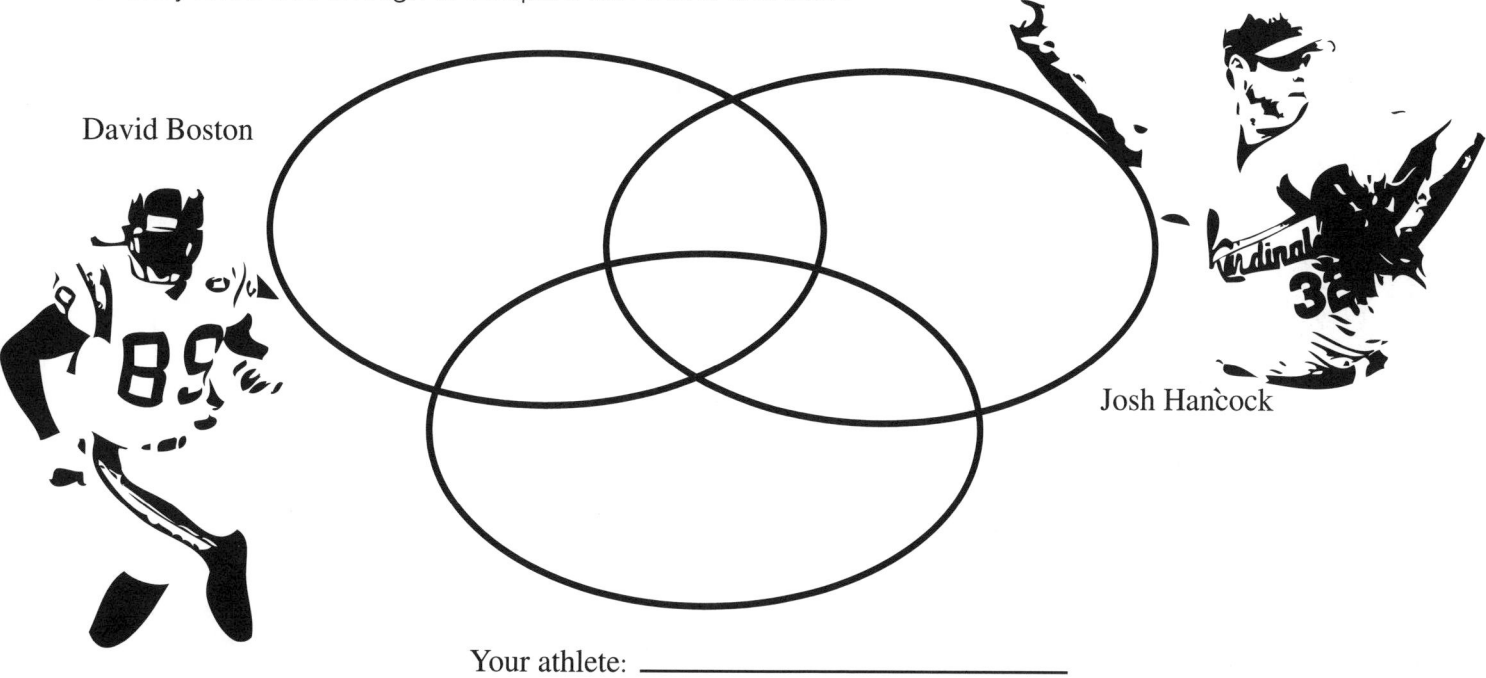

David Boston

Josh Hancock

Your athlete: _____

©2008 PRINCIPLE WOODS, INC. Removal of copyright notice and copying are violations of Federal Law.

Unit 9

Answer Key — Answer Key — Answer Key

Interpreting the Data

PART I

How effective has MADD been?

Mothers Against Drunk Driving (MADD) is an organization that was started in 1980 by the mother of a girl in California who was killed by a drunk driver. MADD now has chapters (small groups) all over the United States. They have worked hard over the last two and a half decades to get tougher drunk driving laws passed.

In this section, you will determine how effective the work of MADD has been. Figure 1 shows the number of people killed in all car accidents per hour and the number of people killed in alcohol-related car accidents per hour from 1982 to 2004.

Figure 1. Car accident deaths per hour in the United States

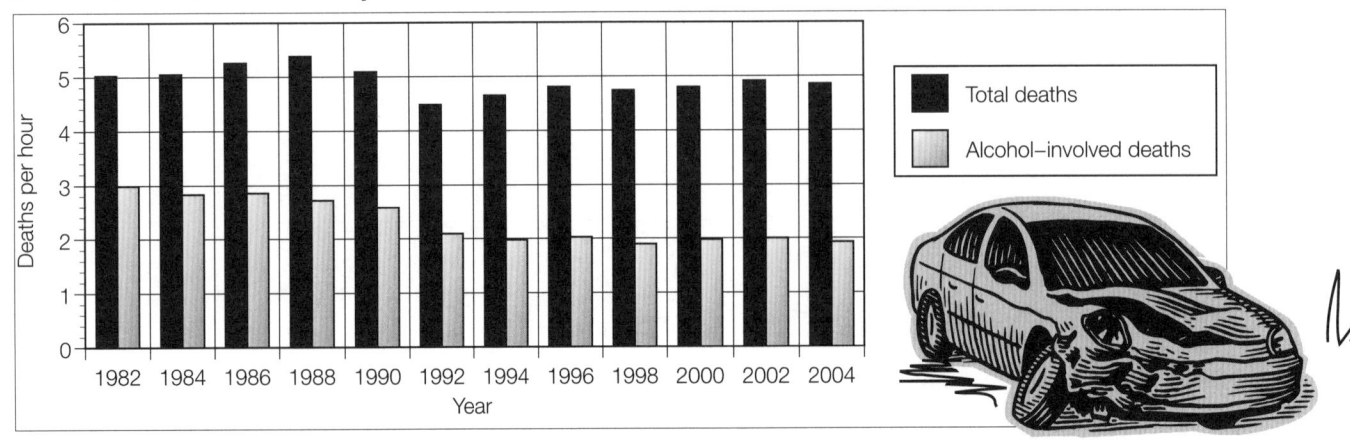

15. Based on the 2004 number, about how many people have been killed in the United States as a result of alcohol-involved accidents during the time that you have been in this class today?

    2   (Answer assumes a one-hour class period.)

16. Statistically speaking, does it appear that the work of Mothers Against Drunk Driving has been effective in decreasing the number of alcohol-involved car accident deaths as compared to the total number of car accident deaths since 1980? Use data to explain your answer.

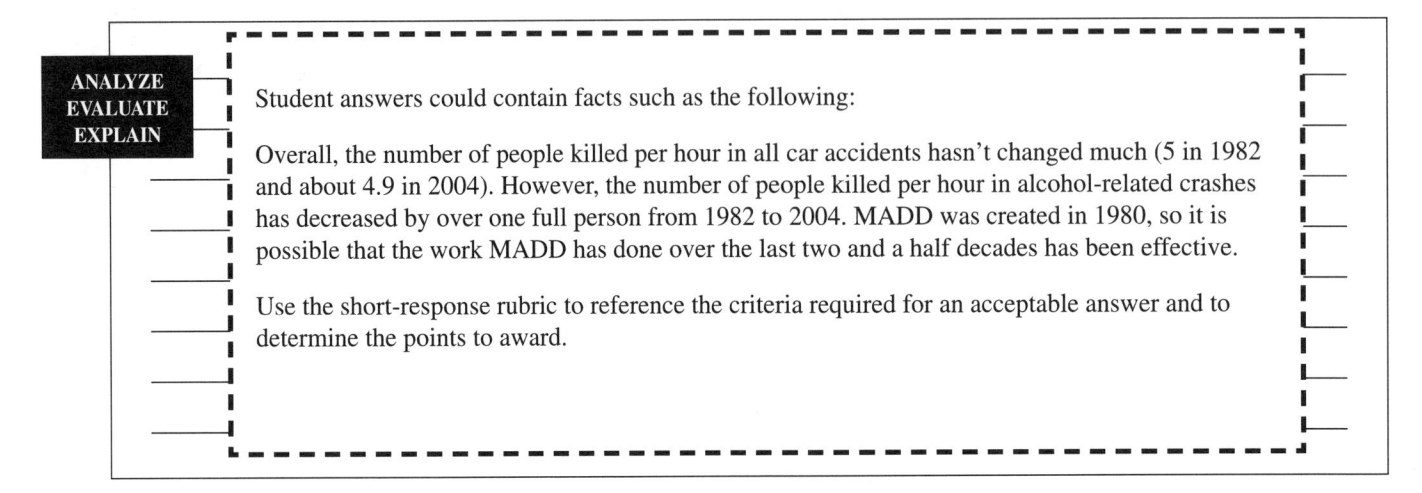

ANALYZE EVALUATE EXPLAIN

Student answers could contain facts such as the following:

Overall, the number of people killed per hour in all car accidents hasn't changed much (5 in 1982 and about 4.9 in 2004). However, the number of people killed per hour in alcohol-related crashes has decreased by over one full person from 1982 to 2004. MADD was created in 1980, so it is possible that the work MADD has done over the last two and a half decades has been effective.

Use the short-response rubric to reference the criteria required for an acceptable answer and to determine the points to award.

Answer Key — Answer Key — Answer Key

ABOVE the Influence

PART II

Can tougher enforcement of DUI laws save lives?

Driving Under the Influence (DUI) is the legal term for the crime of driving a motor vehicle while under the influence of alcohol or drugs. Use the information in Table 1 to help you interpret the data in Figures 2 and 3 concerning the percentage of alcohol-related accidents resulting in death and the number of DUI arrests in 2005. Then use the data to answer questions 22–25 to help you determine whether states with stricter enforcement of DUI laws have fewer car-accident deaths related to alcohol.

Table 1. Three groups of states leading the U.S. with different DUI statistics in 2005

Group 1	California, Texas, Florida, Pennsylvania, Illinois	Group of states with the **highest number** of car-accident deaths related to alcohol.
Group 2	Hawaii, Rhode Island, Montana, Delaware, Alaska	Group of states with the **highest percentage** of car-accident deaths related to alcohol.
Group 3	Utah, Iowa, Nebraska, Idaho, Georgia, Kentucky	Group of states with the **lowest percentage** of car accident deaths related to alcohol.

Figure 2. Percentage of alcohol-related car accidents resulting in death (2005)

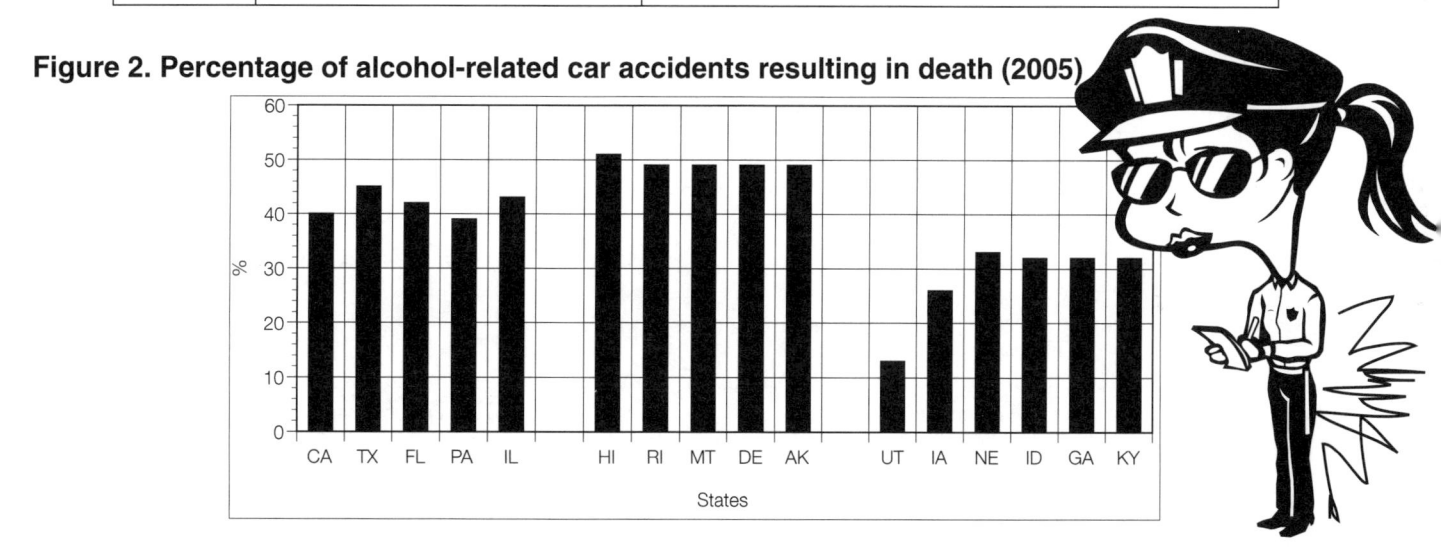

Figure 3. DUI arrests per 1,000 people (2005)

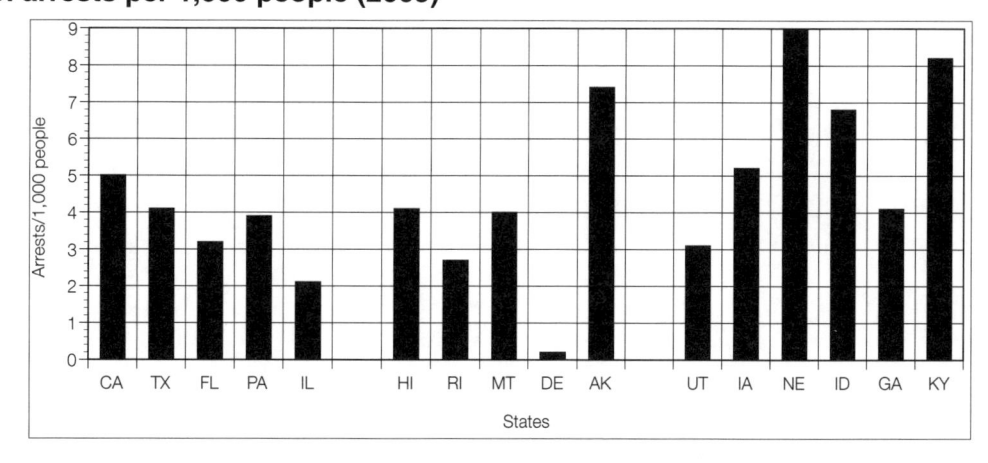

©2008 PRINCIPLE WOODS, INC. Removal of copyright notice and copying are violations of Federal Law.

Unit 9 — *Answer Key — Answer Key — Answer Key*

Use the information in Table 1 and the data in Figures 2 and 3 to circle the letter of the best answer for questions 17–19.

17. Which group has the lowest overall percentage of alcohol-related accidents resulting in death?
    A. Group 1: California, Texas, Florida, Pennsylvania, Illinois
    B. Group 2: Hawaii, Rhode Island, Montana, Delaware, Alaska
    C. Group 3: Utah, Iowa, Nebraska, Idaho, Georgia, Kentucky
    D. Group 4: California, Hawaii, Utah

18. Which group has the highest overall percentage of alcohol-related accidents resulting in death?
    A. Group 1: California, Texas, Florida, Pennsylvania, Illinois
    B. Group 2: Hawaii, Rhode Island, Montana, Delaware, Alaska
    C. Group 3: Utah, Iowa, Nebraska, Idaho, Georgia, Kentucky
    D. Group 4: California, Hawaii, Utah

19. Which group has the highest overall number of DUI arrests per 1,000 people?
    A. Group 1: California, Texas, Florida, Pennsylvania, Illinois
    B. Group 2: Hawaii, Rhode Island, Montana, Delaware, Alaska
    C. Group 3: Utah, Iowa, Nebraska, Idaho, Georgia, Kentucky
    D. Group 4: California, Hawaii, Utah

20. What conclusion might you draw from the data in Figures 2 and 3 regarding the number of people killed in alcohol-related car accidents compared to the number of DUI arrests in those states? Include the data to explain your answer.

ANALYZE EVALUATE EXPLAIN

Student answers could contain facts such as the following:

The group of states with more DUI arrests overall is also the group that has the lowest percentage of deaths overall from alcohol-related accidents. This could mean that the states that enforce DUI laws more strictly are actually saving lives.

Use the short-response rubric to reference the criteria required for an acceptable answer and to determine the points to award.

Answer Key — Answer Key — Answer Key

ABOVE the Influence

Reflect and Respond

21. Assume that you are a police officer. Consider the following questions and then write a few paragraphs explaining whether or not you think celebrities deserve special treatment when they drink and drive. Would you give special treatment to a celebrity who had been drinking and driving? Why or why not? If yes, which famous person (or people) would you give special treatment to? Should you consider the fact that a celebrity's career might be ruined if you were to arrest him or her?

> Answers may vary, but students should address each part of the question. The question is meant to elicit strong classroom conversation about character. Students should be able to decide between right and wrong regardless of the status of the people involved.
>
> Use the character education rubric to reference the criteria and number of points to award.

Unit 9

Answer Key — Answer Key — Answer Key

Reading Instructional Guide for Technical Extension

BEFORE READING

Looking at the Words

Determining How the Word Sounds (Phonics)
Technical texts often necessitate the use of multisyllabic words that are unfamiliar to students. Use the Syllable Guide to help students decode any words they might have trouble reading.

Determining What the Word Means (Vocabulary)

Words to Study	Breaking into Syllables	Short Definition
consumption	con-sump-tion	(n.) the act of eating or drinking
minimum	min-i-mum	(adj.) lowest
minor	mi-nor	(n.) a person under the legal age
possession	pos-ses-sion	(n.) the act of holding
reduce	re-duce	(v.) to bring to a smaller size

Activating Background Knowledge

Graphic Organizer
Either individually or in groups, students may brainstorm about the short- and long-term physical and mental consequences of underage drinking, recalling anything previously learned and any prior experience with the subject. Next, encourage students to see the relationships between their ideas by having them complete a T-chart to demonstrate what they already know about the effects of underage drinking.

Effects of underage drinking

Short-term consequences	Long-term consequences

©2008 PRINCIPLE WOODS, INC. Removal of copyright notice and copying are violations of Federal Law.

Answer Key — Answer Key — Answer Key

ABOVE the Influence

Starter Questions
After completing the Graphic Organizer, generate a group or class discussion to come up with questions about the subject, a prediction about the article, and at least one learning goal. The first question has been provided for you.

Question: Why do you think the minimum legal drinking age in the United States is 21?

Question: _____

Prediction: _____

Goal: _____

DURING READING
Use the Reading Instructional Guide Template found in the front of the book.

AFTER READING
After reading, you may teach reading strategy use by giving students opportunities to do the following:
- Review, paraphrase, and summarize
- Participate in main-idea discussions by describing the information in their own words
- Reflect on concept maps and generate additional discussion starter questions based on the mappings
- Participate in small-group discussions using discussion starter questions

Discussion Starter Questions

The first question has been provided for you.

1. How can we persuade teenagers not to engage in behavior that involves underage drinking?

2. _____

3. _____

©2008 PRINCIPLE WOODS, INC. Removal of copyright notice and copying are violations of Federal Law.

Unit 9

Answer Key — Answer Key — Answer Key

Technical Extension

Underage Drinking: No Minimal Problem

The current minimum legal drinking age in the United States is 21. It was established by the Highway Safety Act in 1984. Then a 1988 law also set 21 as the minimum legal age for purchasing alcohol. The laws were further developed in 1995 when Congress passed the Zero Tolerance Law. This made it illegal for drivers under age 21 to have any amount of alcohol in their bodies.

> A young male with a blood alcohol level of just .02 is five times more likely than a sober male of the same age to be killed in a single-vehicle crash.

There are many reasons for making 21 the minimum legal drinking age (MLDA), but the most important involve driving. When the MLDA laws began to appear in the 1980s, the number of crashes involving alcohol and drivers under 20 years old fell by 59%. These laws are thought to save more than 900 lives a year, mostly from reducing motor vehicle fatalities.

Despite these laws, underage drinking is still a very real problem in the United States. Almost 50% of 8th graders and 75% of 12th graders admit to having used alcohol at least once in the past year. These students are clearly younger than the minimum legal age but continue to drink. The physical effects of this early alcohol use are equally troubling. Medical evidence shows that the brain is not fully developed in most people until age 21. Alcohol use by children under 21 may cause brain damage that cannot be reversed. One study shows that it may even reduce brain performance by as much as 10%.

The long-term effects of heavy alcohol use are too many to name. Some of the more major effects include liver damage and disease and increased risk of cancer and heart disease. There is also the possibility for psychological disturbances. Research shows that drinking at a young age increases the risk of developing alcohol abuse issues later in life. Many young people have difficulty looking into the future. They don't connect their present actions with consequences that may occur 10 or 20 years from now. However, there are plenty of immediate consequences that show the dangers of underage drinking.

Teens ages 12 to 17 who admit to drinking alcohol are twice as likely to report being involved in a school fight than those who do not drink. Underage drinking has been connected to youth crimes, suicides, assaults, and accidental injuries. The most permanent consequence comes when alcohol use causes death.

Even with all the attention, underage drinking remains a problem in this country and in many others. Perhaps teens think they are exempt from the dangerous consequences of drinking alcohol. Whatever the case, young people must realize that their actions today can affect the rest of their lives.

Specific Provisions of MLDA 21 Laws

Possession. All states prohibit minors (people under age 21) from possessing alcoholic beverages.

Consumption. All states prohibit minors from having a positive blood alcohol count. Most states prohibit minors from consuming alcohol (observed drinking).

Purchase. All states prohibit minors from purchasing alcohol.

Selling. All states prohibit selling or furnishing alcohol to minors.

Serving. Most states prohibit minors from serving all types of alcoholic beverages.

Answer Key — Answer Key — Answer Key

ABOVE the Influence

Reading Comprehension

After reading "Underage Drinking: No Minimal Problem," choose the options that best answer questions 1–11.

1. Read this sentence.
   They don't connect their present actions with consequences that may occur 10 or 20 years from now.

   What is the meaning of the word *consequences* as it is used in this sentence?
   A. needs
   B. shows
   C. actions
   D. penalties

2. Read this sentence.
   Perhaps teens think they are exempt from the dangerous consequences of consuming alcohol.

   This sentence means that
   F. teens think they are to blame for the consequences.
   G. teens think they are unaffected by the consequences.
   H. teens think that they can avoid the consequences by not drinking.
   I. teens think they can assist others with learning about the consequences.

3. From the article, the reader can tell that
   A. underage drinking is on the decline.
   B. underage drinking is not a problem in today's society.
   C. underage drinking has many short- and long-term consequences.
   D. teens are becoming more aware of the consequences of underage drinking.

4. What change did Congress make in 1995 to prevent underage drinking?
   F. Congress made it unlawful for drivers 20 years and younger to have traces of alcohol in their system.
   G. Congress passed a law that would financially penalize parents of teens who were caught consuming alcohol.
   H. Congress required all teens that were found guilty of underage drinking to spend time in a rehabilitation center.
   I. Congress approved an education program for schools to teach students about the consequences of underage drinking.

5. The author organizes the article by
   A. comparing and contrasting underage drinking over the years.
   B. describing underage drinking and then presenting the effects of it.
   C. providing examples of teens that have fallen victim to underage drinking.
   D. outlining ways to help someone who has a problem with underage drinking.

6. Which title BEST fits the article?
   F. Rules to Live By
   G. Disastrous Driving
   H. A Costly Mistake for Society
   I. A Dangerous Trend Among Teens

Unit 9

Answer Key — Answer Key — Answer Key

7. According to the passage, underage drinking affects the brain by
   A. impacting learning ability.
   B. causing the brain to swell.
   C. decreasing the brain's function.
   D. causing the brain to hemorrhage.

8. How is the Highway Safety Act of 1984 similar to the Zero Tolerance Law?
   F. Both regulations prohibit underage drinking.
   G. The Highway Safety Act is an amendment to the Zero Tolerance Law.
   H. Both regulations call for strict disciplinary actions for those who are caught drinking underage.
   I. Both regulations encourage parents to get more involved in the prevention of underage drinking.

9. Which fact from the article provides the BEST evidence that drinking has fatal effects?
   A. There is a link between underage drinking and future crime.
   B. Teens that drink a large amount are at risk of having brain damage.
   C. Underage drinking increases the odds of having an alcohol abuse problem in the future.
   D. The risk of a young male being killed in a car accident is increased by 5 times if alcohol is consumed.

10. People who read this article will learn that the effects of underage drinking can cause
    F. difficulty in maintaining a job.
    G. difficulty in getting into college.
    H. mental, behavioral, and physical problems.
    I. a decline in social relationships among friends.

11. Based on the information in the article regarding the effects of underage drinking,
    A. teens who consume alcohol end up learning from and overcoming their mistakes.
    B. teens who engage in underage drinking will most likely grow up leading normal and healthy lives.
    C. teens who engage in underage drinking are more likely to have difficulty in getting along with their peers.
    D. research shows that teenagers who participate in underage drinking do not have a difficult transition to college.

Answer Key — Answer Key — Answer Key

ABOVE the Influence

Technical Writing Prompt

12. As a member of SADD (Students Against Destructive Decisions), your eyes have been opened to the dangers of underage drinking and DUI. You want to use positive peer pressure to encourage your peers to make smart decisions. Create an advertisement to discourage other students from driving while intoxicated and underage drinking. Make the ad convincing by clearly emphasizing facts you have learned about the dangers of drinking and the consequences.

> Student answers may vary.
>
> The student should address the question to the best of his/her ability using the article and personal experience. The question is meant to prepare students to be active citizens who can accurately and effectively use written communication skills.
>
> Use the technical writing rubric to reference the criteria and determine the number of points to award.

Unit 9

Answer Key — Answer Key — Answer Key

Vocational Extension

> **HELP WANTED:**
>
> Sunnyside Rehabilitation is seeking a certified rehabilitation counselor specializing in automobile accident rehabilitation. Applicants must have a degree or comparable work experience in health care, rehabilitation services, or occupational therapy. Interested parties should send a resume and cover letter to Human Resources at hr@sunnyside.org.

The word *rehab* may make you think of celebrity drug and alcohol problems. However, rehabilitation actually includes a broad variety of people with many special needs. Those who serve these needs are called rehabilitation counselors. They make a career of helping others overcome hardship and reach their highest potential. These counselors help people with physical, mental, and social needs become as self-sufficient and whole as possible.

The need for rehabilitation is increasing at a greater rate than ever before. As the need increases, it becomes much more complex as well. As many as 43 million Americans have physical, mental, or psychological disabilities, including addictions to drugs and alcohol. These disabilities sometimes limit their ability be independent. Rehabilitation counselors address more than just addiction issues.

Take a look at the wide variety of problems that benefit from rehabilitation counseling:

- Drug and alcohol abuse and addictions
- Psychiatric disabilities
- Work-related injuries
- Automobile accident injuries
- Hearing and visual disabilities
- Learning disabilities
- Disabilities resulting from stroke or other illness

Most rehab counselors will choose a specific area such as children with learning disabilities. However, all counselors must have knowledge of the general process of rehabilitation. This includes rehabilitation techniques applicable to any special need. Because the goal of rehab is to allow a person to better control his or her life, counselors must use many strategies to work toward this goal.

Rehab counselors must understand areas such as counseling, education, physical rehabilitation, psychology, and basic health care. During high school, one good way to get a head start in the field is to work or volunteer where counselors might work. This could mean volunteering in a nursing home, at an elementary school, or in a hospital. College-level courses in rehabilitation, psychology, human services, or health care are helpful in starting a career as a counselor. To obtain a counseling license further requires a master's or doctoral degree. But a license is not required unless a counselor wants to work in private practice. To become a rehabilitation counselor, it is often necessary to be certified by the Commission on Rehabilitation Counselor Certification. The requirements involve gaining work experience, passing a national exam, and completing 100 hours of continuing education every five years.

Of all the educational and work requirements needed to become a counselor, the most important is a desire to help people achieve their personal best. Being a rehabilitation counselor is a selfless job that requires thinking of others. However, the work is not thankless. It comes with the satisfaction of helping people take control of their lives and giving them the gift of independence.

Unit 9 — **Answer Key — Answer Key — Answer Key**

Looking Forward

13. The goal of a rehabilitation counselor is to help someone who is having difficulty with an aspect of his or her life. Look at the list of problems a rehabilitation counselor can help others with. If you were a rehabilitation counselor, which specialty would you choose? What would you do to ensure that you are properly trained to help others with this problem? Making sure to include personal experience and information from the article, write about why you think you could assist an individual who is having difficulty with this aspect of life.

> Student answers may vary.
>
> The student should address the question to the best of his/her ability using the article and personal experience. The question is meant to encourage students to explore areas of interest for their future and begin to determine how they will prepare for a future career.
>
> Use the extended-response rubric to reference the criteria and determine the number of points to award.

Ethical Dilemma

14. You are a rehab counselor, and most of your clients are recovering from automobile accident injuries. Periodically, you must certify that additional time is needed before clients can return to their jobs. A client asks you to increase the number of injuries reported to the employer so that the return to work is delayed as long as possible. You think that you can get him back to work much faster than he would like. What do you do? If you decide not to do as he asks, how do you respond to him?

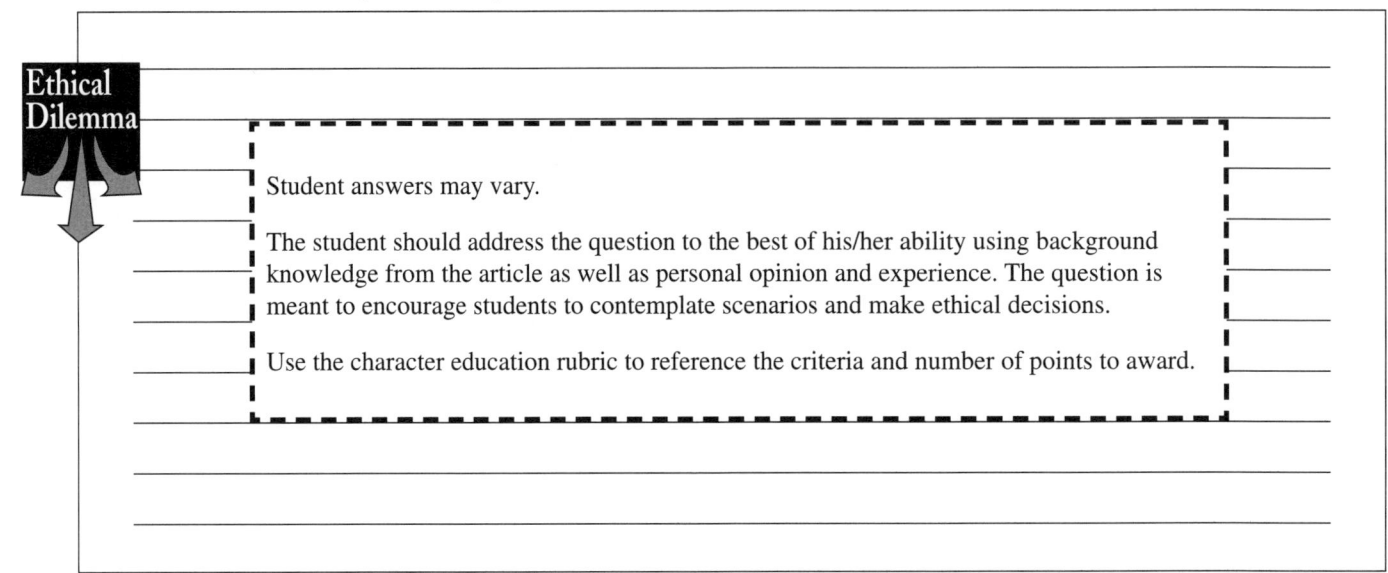

> Student answers may vary.
>
> The student should address the question to the best of his/her ability using background knowledge from the article as well as personal opinion and experience. The question is meant to encourage students to contemplate scenarios and make ethical decisions.
>
> Use the character education rubric to reference the criteria and number of points to award.

208

©2008 PRINCIPLE WOODS, INC. Removal of copyright notice and copying are violations of Federal Law.

Answer Key — Answer Key — Answer Key

ABOVE the Influence

Unit Vocabulary Assessment

Matching
Match each word in Column I to its definition in Column II.

Column I
- **C** 1. apparent
- **A** 2. consumption
- **B** 3. humble
- **D** 4. rehabilitation

Column II
- a. the act of eating or drinking
- b. not proud or boasting
- c. easily seen or understood
- d. the process of restoring health

Multiple Choice
Choose the word that MOST NEARLY replaces the underlined word in each sentence.

5. The team lost possession of the ball when a pass fell incomplete.
   - **A. holding**
   - B. posture
   - C. reputation
   - D. protection

6. He influenced other students to copy him.
   - A. won
   - B. asked
   - C. entertained
   - **D. encouraged**

7. The painting is notable because of its special story.
   - A. new
   - **B. unique**
   - C. named
   - D. not for sale

8. I will reduce your pay if you don't do your job properly.
   - A. redden
   - B. expand
   - **C. decrease**
   - D. clean out

Word Bank
incident
minimum
minor
victim

Fill in the Blank
Choose a word from the word bank to fill in the blank in the sentence below.

9. The **victim** spoke on the witness stand about what she went through.

10. Each individual **incident** is included in her behavior record.

11. The table must have a **minimum** number of people before we will seat you.

12. Because Jane is a **minor**, she is not allowed in that place until she is older.

©2008 PRINCIPLE WOODS, INC. Removal of copyright notice and copying are violations of Federal Law.

Unit 9 — *Answer Key — Answer Key — Answer Key*

Authentic Assessment

Students will create a public service announcement based on the unit "Above the Influence." This activity combines the authentic components of writing, persuasion, and creativity linked to the comprehension of a written text. This assessment will enable students to work cooperatively, brainstorm ideas, create a story, and read to support an opinion. If possible, students will have access to technology such as iMovie, Microsoft Movie Maker, or PowerPoint.

Instructions for Public Service Announcement

1. **Definition.** Explain to students that a public service announcement (PSA) is an advertisement intended to convince the public of something by raising awareness on a particular issue.

2. **Planning.** Assign students to particular groups or allow them to choose their own. Each group will create a PSA on the dangers of driving under the influence. The PSAs should be persuasive. Groups should complete the following questions to begin planning.

    a. What is the purpose of a persuasive PSA?

    b. How will you introduce the issue?

    c. What reasons will you list to back up your viewpoint?

    d. What support will you use for each reason?

3. **Storyboard.** After these questions have been answered, each group will complete a storyboard for the PSA with details of what facts, graphics, etc. will be used for each scene. Groups should decide whether the message will be given by text, voice-over, pictures, or a combination.

4. **Creation and recording.** Next, groups will create and record their PSA on video camera, web cam, or software such as iMovie or PowerPoint. The PSAs will be either shown to the class or performed live, and they will be evaluated for factual accuracy and persuasiveness.

5. **Assessment.** The PSAs will be assessed with the rubric on the following page.

Answer Key — Answer Key — Answer Key

ABOVE the Influence

PSA Rubric

Requirement	8–10 Points	4–7 Points	0–3 Points	Points Earned
Questions	The students answer the questions completely using articles and facts from the unit.	The students answer most questions completely, using some articles and facts from the unit.	The students do not answer the questions completely or do not use articles and facts from the unit.	
Storyboard	The students draw out a storyboard with detail, including any text, graphics, and scripts needed.	The students draw out a storyboard with some detail, but are missing some text, graphics, and scripts.	The students do not draw out a storyboard with detail or do not include text, graphics, and scripts.	
PSA Product	The PSA is well put together, complete, and has a persuasive message.	The PSA is mostly complete, but the message isn't fully persuasive.	The PSA is missing components or is not persuasive.	
Work	Work is neat, legible, and turned in on time.	Work is messy, hard to read, and/or late.	Work is incomplete or not turned in.	

Unit 10

Blood In, Blood Out

Reading Instructional Guide for High-Interest Article

BEFORE READING

Front-Loading Background Knowledge through Read Aloud/Think Aloud

Search the Internet for recent articles on preventing gang involvement and use them to model the effective habits of readers through a Read Aloud /Think Aloud.

Check out articles at the following websites to determine if they would be appropriate for your RATA:
- "Prevent Gang Violence in School." National Youth Violence Prevention Resource Center. http://www.safeyouth.org/scripts/faq/prevgangs.asp.
- "Help Keep Teens Away from Gangs, Violence, and Drugs." The National Youth Anti-Drug Media Campaign. http://theantidrug.com/advice/advice_gangs.asp.

(Please keep in mind that it is the responsibility of the teacher to determine if articles from suggested sites are appropriate. The sites may have changed content since this publication. The publisher takes no responsibility for the current content of the site.)

Looking at the Words

Determining How the Word Sounds (Phonics)
Using the Syllable Guide and the Reading Instructional Guide Template found in the beginning of the book, follow the steps to help students learn how to break a word into manageable parts.

Determining What the Word Means (Vocabulary)

Words to Study	Breaking into Syllables	Short Definition
alternative	al-ter-na-tive	(n.) a choice
graffiti	graf-fi-ti	(n.) markings or drawings drawn or spray-painted on a sidewalk, wall, or building
informant	in-form-ant	(n.) a person who gives information
ritual	rit-u-al	(n.) a ceremony or established pattern of behavior
ruthless	ruth-less	(adj.) without pity or compassion
surreal	sur-re-al	(adj.) seeming like a dream

Activating Background Knowledge

Anticipation Guide
Have students mark each of the following statements True or False:

1. ____ The majority of gang members join a gang when they are in their twenties.
2. ____ Some people join gangs because they have family members who are in gangs.

Answer Key — Answer Key — Answer Key   Blood In, Blood Out

3. ____ Many gangs require their new members to participate in initiation ceremonies prior to becoming official members.
4. ____ Gangs allow their members to freely leave the organizations.
5. ____ MS-13 is an example of a dangerous gang whose members are worldwide.

Starter Questions
After completing the Anticipation Guide, have a group or class discussion with the students using the following questions:

1. Why do gangs like to recruit young members?
2. What are some examples of felonies that gang members commit?
3. Why might a person decide to join a gang?
4. How do television shows influence gangs in real life?
5. What are some after-school activities that have been established to prevent gangs from growing?

Make a prediction about what you think the article will be about.

DURING READING
Use the Reading Instructional Guide Template found in the front of the book.

AFTER READING

Discussion Starter Questions

1. Why do you think gangs require their members to commit a crime prior to leaving?
2. Why do you think young people seem to be more drawn to joining a gang than people who are older?
3. What role do parents need to play in fostering stronger self-esteem in children?
4. What advice would you give a friend or classmate who wanted to leave a gang?
5. How can schools help prevent young children from joining gangs?

Teacher Reflection
Use the Reading Instructional Guide Template found in the front of the book.

Blood In, Blood Out

Visit a city such as Los Angeles, and the signs of the gangs who live and fight there are hard to miss. Graffiti covers buildings, overpasses, walls, and the sides of trucks. Los Angeles is home to more than 100 gangs. As common as gangs may be, they seem surreal and separate from our world.

There are different stories about where gangs come from. Some believe they can be traced back to biblical times. Others say they began during the Revolutionary War. No matter when or how they got here, they exist. Whether it be Al Capone's famous Chicago mafia or one on *CSI: Miami*, gangs are a widespread presence in our society.

But what is it that attracts members to these gangs? If so many know that they're bad, what keeps them going? Why do people do things that they know are against the law?

Most gang members join at a young age. Some join because they find support in gangs. Others are drafted by gangs who are looking for new "soldiers" for their group. Younger is better because it allows the gang to raise that person in the culture of terror. One gang informant recalls being "jumped in" at 8 years old. Gang members beat and kicked him for 13 seconds. Just one year later, he was told to shoot at a rival gang. He closed his eyes to shoot. When he opened them again, he saw one of the rivals on the ground. He doesn't know if he lived. What he does know are feelings of sadness and fear.

Some young people join because a brother, sister, aunt, uncle, or parent has been a member. Often the younger siblings of gang members become the leaders. But there are others who aren't "blessed in" as family members are. They have to perform a task to show the gang that they have what it takes to be a member. This can require the would-be member to commit a crime as small as theft or as large as killing someone. Gangs operate as families—families who raise their children to be ruthless killers.

Don joined a gang at 13. The gang made him do a drive-by shooting to prove that he was worthy. The senior gang members drove him to a rival's house and told him to shoot. He doesn't know if he hit anyone. He didn't read the newspaper or watch TV because he didn't want to know. To this day, Don regrets his decision.

For others, regret may not set in for many years. But the guilt is there. Most gang activity centers around such things as drugs, shoplifting, and car thefts. Every day is a nightmare in which they don't know if they'll get caught. Once they've committed a crime, they can't take it back. For gang members, there's no escape. Once a member, it's very difficult to leave the group. Most gangs require a "blood-out" ritual, where a member commits a murder to leave the gang. One gang called the 18th Street Gang threatens to hurt the family members of those who try to leave.

If all this is true, why do people choose this life? Manuela Venegas was a gang member from the time she was 12 until she was 26. She says that she found support from other female gang members that she did not find at home. Another former gang member, Juan Carlos Ramirez, says that he was having an identity crisis. He felt like he didn't belong, so the only place he felt connected as an immigrant was in his neighborhood.

Most of the time the young kids who join gangs don't have a secure home life. They might like the sense of belonging they receive from gang members. They believe that by joining an exclusive group like a gang, they will be included and have somewhere to go. Others join gangs for status and self-worth. This need to belong explains some members' willingness to break the law. They are so desperate for attention that they are willing to do whatever it takes to gain trust. Still others join gangs because of poverty or media influences. Shows like *CSI: Miami* make gangs seem attractive by showing their tattoos and their ability to fool the cops. But in reality, gangs aren't places of belonging but rings of crime and violence.

For young people who seek a sense of belonging, there are many safe and healthy alternatives to gangs. After-school activities and clubs can offer chances to make friends or learn something new. Positive alternatives include recreational programs, sports, social clubs, youth groups, and support groups. Even a part-time job after school can offer a sense of purpose and commitment. Joining a gang may seem like an opportunity to find acceptance and fill an empty void in life. But going down that path is almost certainly a life sentence to violence and fear.

MS-13: The Birth of an American Gang

Not all gangs began with the purpose of frightening people. One of today's most famous and dangerous gangs, MS-13, was organized by a group of refugees.

Members of Mara Salvatrucha originally came to the United States as they fled the violence of the Salvadoran civil war. When they came to California, they were preyed upon by Mexican gangs. So they formed an organized system of defense. They formed a *mara*, Spanish for "crowd" or "posse," of *salvatruchas*, or street-tough Salvadorans.

What began for protection has become one of the most dangerous gangs in the world. MS-13 has members in 33 American states and five other countries. It has spread with illegal activities such as drug smuggling, selling guns, assassinations, and attempts on police officers' lives. Their violence became so widespread that the U.S. government formed a task force to weaken MS-13. The sad fact is that even once MS-13 is weakened, there will be another gang waiting in the wings to bring about a new reign of terror.

Unit 10

Answer Key — Answer Key — Answer Key

Reading Comprehension

After reading "Blood In, Blood Out," choose the options that best answer questions 1–14.

1. Read this sentence.
   As common as gangs may be, they seem surreal and separate from our world.

   What is the meaning of the word *surreal* as it is used in this sentence?
   A. happy
   B. dreamlike
   C. unorganized
   D. very realistic

2. Read this sentence.
   Whether it be Al Capone's famous Chicago mafia or one on *CSI: Miami*, gangs are a widespread presence in our society.

   What is the meaning of the word *widespread* as it is used in this sentence?
   F. common
   G. organized
   H. widespread
   I. inspirational

3. According to the article, why do many gang members choose to join gangs when they are young?
   A. to find a sense of guidance that they don't find elsewhere
   B. because gangs allow only young people to join their group
   C. to gain necessary life skills before they enter the work force
   D. to enjoy spare time with other gang members prior to high school graduation

4. What is the purpose of a gang initiation ceremony?
   F. to persuade others to join the specific gang
   G. to allow a current member to fully exit the gang
   H. to provide an orientation for prospective members outlining the gang's beliefs and values
   I. to allow potential members to demonstrate their dedication to the gang prior to becoming a member

5. With which statement would the author of the passage most likely agree?
   A. Gangs are no longer a problem in our society.
   B. Gang members are respected by the cities where they started.
   C. Gangs are a dangerous problem, especially for the youth in our society.
   D. Gang members can easily leave a gang when they no longer want to be a member.

6. What method of organization does the author use to present the events of the article?
   F. listing the reasons why a person should not join a gang
   G. sharing the procedure to follow when encouraging a friend to leave a gang
   H. providing background information as to why a person may decide to join a gang
   I. presenting the questions and answers from an interview with a person who recently left a gang

7. Why does the author choose to write about Manuela Venegas and Juan Carlos Ramirez?
   A. to show how gang members can be both male and female
   B. to introduce the reader to two people who enjoy recruiting gang members
   C. to share the story of two people who endured difficulty when trying to leave a gang
   D. to provide examples of young people who looked to gangs to fill a feeling of emptiness in their lives

Answer Key — Answer Key — Answer Key   Blood In, Blood Out

8. If the article were published in a newspaper, which would be the most informative headline?
    F. Gravitating Toward a Gang
    G. Investigating the Gang Culprit
    H. Tackling Society's Gang Numbers
    I. Battling Back from Gang Violence

9. What conflict do many gang members ultimately face?
    A. the need for love versus the desire for money
    B. the need to belong versus feelings of guilt and fear
    C. the need to belong versus the need for money and status
    D. the need to learn violence versus the desire to follow the law

10. Why are after-school activities and/or part-time jobs positive choices for young people?
    F. Both the activities and jobs provide teens with a different way to meet others without looking to gangs.
    G. Both after-school activities and part-time jobs educate teens on how to balance school, life, and other responsibilities.
    H. Jobs and after-school activities assist teens with creating a network of references that can be called upon when looking for a full-time job.
    I. Teens can use their experiences with part-time jobs and after-school activities to assist them with selecting a college upon completing high school.

11. What is a major difference between gangs on television and gangs in real life?
    A. Gangs in real life are friendlier than the gangs on television.
    B. Gangs in real life have younger members than the gangs on television.
    C. Gangs on television appear to participate in more imaginative crimes than gangs in real life do.
    D. Gangs on television are made to look intriguing to the viewer, whereas gangs in real life are full of members who lead fearful and dangerous lives.

12. Which statement provides the BEST evidence that MS-13 has increased its membership since its origination?
    F. A special force has been created to stop the power of MS-13.
    G. MS-13 has become one of the most dangerous gangs in our society.
    H. The original members of MS-13 came to the United States from El Salvador.
    I. There are at least 33 American states and 5 other countries that now have members.

13. People who read this article will learn
    A. the negative aspects of being a part of a gang.
    B. how to prevent gangs from starting in their schools.
    C. the warning signs that someone is a member of a gang.
    D. ways to encourage a family member or friend to leave a gang.

14. Based on the information about both MS-13 and other gangs, which of these conclusions is accurate?
    F. Membership in gangs, especially in MS-13, is on the decline.
    G. MS-13 is a weaker gang that can easily be stopped by authorities.
    H. MS-13 heavily recruits young adults in college to spread their message.
    I. Those who join a gang will be subject to more violence and crime than those who do not join a gang.

Unit 10 — Answer Key — Answer Key — Answer Key

Reading Strategy

Directions: Use information from the article to write facts about gang members on the left side of the chart. Then use your background knowledge and personal experience to fill in the right side of the chart with facts about school bullies.

Too Close to Home

GANG MEMBERS	SCHOOL BULLIES
• Join at young age	• Often have a lack of self-esteem
• Join because siblings or parents are involved	• Often think they have to prove themselves in front of a crowd in order to have status in school
• Have to perform task to prove worthy of becoming gang member	• Bully others to draw attention away from themselves
• Looking for acceptance	• May be victims of abuse themselves (physical or emotional), so only behavior they know
• Seeking status or self-worth	
• Join to feel a sense of belonging	• Violent (physically and emotionally)
• Violent (beatings, shootings)	• Could be victims seeking revenge or retaliation (make connections to Columbine, Virginia Tech)
• Emotionally scarred or drained	• May make connections to the Bluford Series, Give a Boy a Gun, Nineteen Minutes, and other young adult literature

After looking at the facts you wrote, write a sentence here that makes a connection between gang members and school bullies:

Answers may vary. Students might observe that gang members and school bullies may have similar emotional needs.

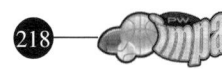

Answer Key — Answer Key — Answer Key   Blood In, Blood Out

Interpreting the Data

Is there a relationship between law enforcement agencies' perception of gang involvement in crimes and the actual crime rates by region across the United States?

It is difficult to determine exactly how many gangs and gang members exist in our country. One problem is that the data relies on the estimates, or best guesses, of law enforcement agencies. Another difficulty is that prosecutors cannot prove that crimes are gang-related when witnesses are too intimidated to testify against the defendants. Also, law enforcement agencies across the country have different definitions of gangs, and denials by law enforcement of gang activity in their communities can make data incomplete.

Nevertheless, the U.S. Department of Justice funded the *2005 National Gang Threat Assessment* to try to measure the threat posed by gangs. They sent questionnaires to law enforcement agencies all over the country asking them to rate gang involvement in crimes in their areas. Table 1 summarizes some of the data gathered. For instance, in Table 1, 21.6% of the agencies who received the questionnaire in the Northeastern region rated gang involvement in felonious assault as "high."

Table 1. Percentage of law enforcement officers by region who believe gangs have a high level of involvement in certain crimes

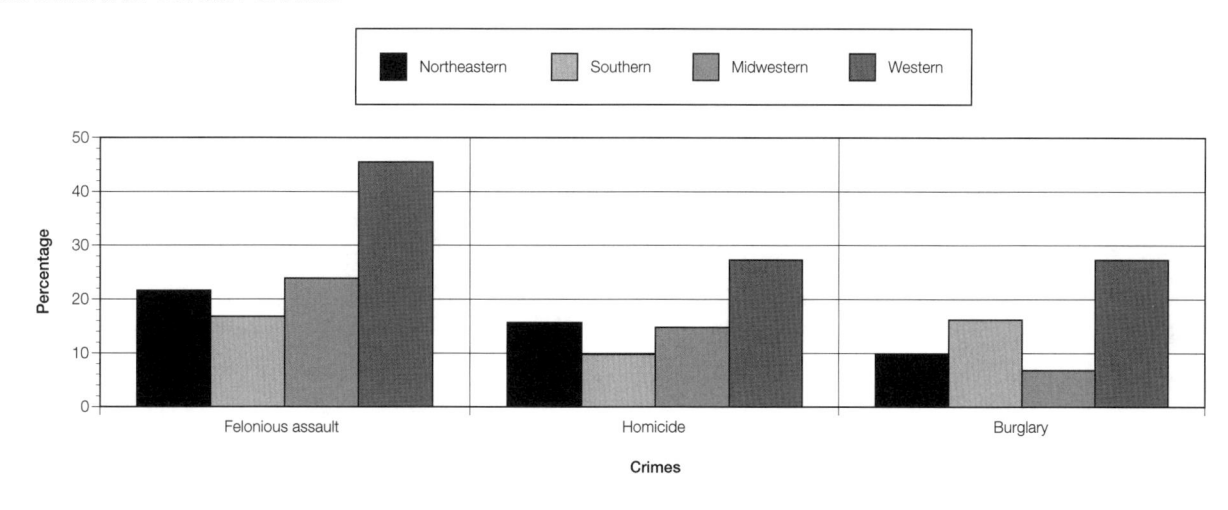

Crime	Northeastern	Southern	Midwestern	Western
Felonious assault	21.6	16.8	23.9	45.5
Homicide	15.7	9.8	14.8	27.3
Burglary	9.8	16.2	6.8	27.3

Use Table 1 to complete the graphs in Figure 1. Then use the graphs to answer questions 15–17.

Figure 1. Percentage of law enforcement officers by region who believe gangs have a high level of involvement in certain crimes

15. In which region did the highest percentage of law enforcement agents believe there was high gang involvement in each of the following crimes?

    Felonious assault: __**Western**__ region

    Homicide: __**Western**__ region

    Burglary: __**Western**__ region

16. In which region did the lowest percentage of law enforcement agents believe there was high gang involvement in each of the following crimes?

    Felonious assault: __**Southern**__ region

    Homicide: __**Southern**__ region

    Burglary: __**Midwestern**__ region

Unit 10 — Answer Key — Answer Key — Answer Key

17. Based on this study, which region appears to have the lowest overall level of gang involvement? Use data to explain your answer.

> **ANALYZE EVALUATE EXPLAIN**
>
> Student answers could include the following:
>
> The Southern region appears to have the lowest overall level of gang involvement based on this study. While law enforcement believed gang involvement in burglary to be high compared to the Northeastern and Midwestern regions, gang activity in the Southern region is ranked lowest in felonious assault and homicides.
>
> Use the short-response rubric to reference the criteria required for an acceptable answer and to determine the points to award.

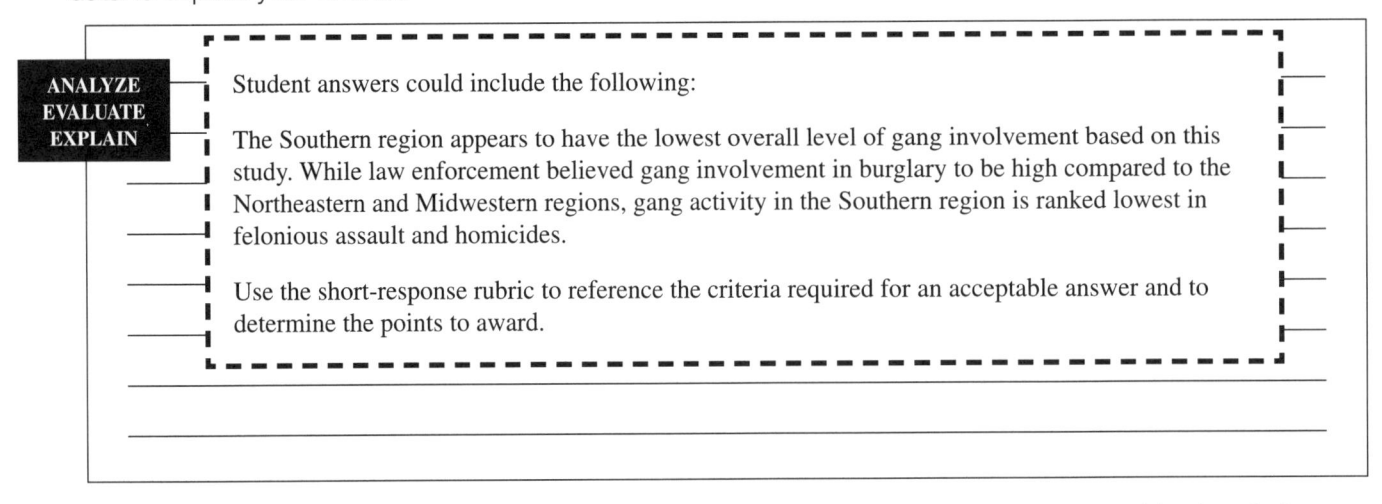

Table 2 lists the actual number of crimes by region in 2005 according to the FBI's database. Use it to help you complete the calculations on this page.

Table 2. Actual number of crimes per region in 2005

	Southern	Northeastern	Midwestern	Western
Population	107,505,413	54,641,895	65,971,974	68,291,122
Murder	7,112	2,403	3,243	3,934
Aggravated assault	381,060	119,868	162,417	199,602
Burglary	965,476	231,973	439,514	517,163

Use the following chart to help you determine how many crimes there were per 100,000 people in each region. The data has already been completed for Murder in all of the regions. See the math instructions to the left of the table.

Steps
1. Divide the number of crimes by the population.
2. Then multiply your answer by 100,000.
3. Round answer to the nearest whole number.

	Southern	Northeastern	Midwestern	Western
Murder	7,112/107,505,413 .0000661 .0000661 X 100,000 =6.61 7 murders per 100,000 people.	2,403/54,641,895 .000439 .0000439 X 100,000 =4.39 4 murders per 100,000 people.	3,243/65,971,974 .0000491 .0000491 X 100,000 =4.91 5 murders per 100,000 people.	3,934/68,291,122 .0000576 .0000576 X 100,000 =5.76 6 murders per 100,000 people.
Aggravated assault	18. 354 aggravated assault per 100,000 people.	19. 219 aggravated assault per 100,000 people.	20. 246 aggravated assault per 100,000 people.	21. 292 aggravated assault per 100,000 people.
Burglary	22. 898 burglaries per 100,000 people.	23. 425 burglaries per 100,000 people.	24. 666 burglaries per 100,000 people.	25. 757 burglaries per 100,000 people.

©2008 PRINCIPLE WOODS, INC. Removal of copyright notice and copying are violations of Federal Law.

Answer Key — Answer Key — Answer Key   Blood In, Blood Out

Rewrite your answers in Table 3.

Table 3. Number of crimes per 100,000 people per region in 2005

	Southern	Northeastern	Midwestern	Western
Murder	7	4	5	6
Aggravated assault	18. 354	19. 219	20. 246	21. 292
Burglary	22. 898	23. 425	24. 666	25. 757

26. Use all tables and graphs from this unit to compare the *2005 National Gang Threat Assessment* data per region with the actual number of crimes per region according to the 2005 report. Then rank the regions from lowest to highest for both the perceived gang threat and the actual number of crimes. (A rank of 1 is considered the lowest perceived gang threat or actual number of crimes, and a rank of 4 is the highest.)

Write the rankings in Table 4.

Table 4. Regional rankings of perceived gang threat and number of crimes committed

	Southern	Northeastern	Midwestern	Western
2005 National Gang Threat Assessment	1	3	2	4
Number of crimes committed	4	1	2	3

27. Is there a strong relationship between the rankings based on the threat assessment report and the rankings based on the number of crimes in 2005 per region? What conclusions can you draw from this data?

ANALYZE EVALUATE EXPLAIN

Student answers could contain facts such as the following.

A comparison of the threat assessment rankings and the actual crime rankings shows no proven strong relationship between law enforcement estimates of gang involvement and the actual number of crimes in particular regions. For example, in looking at the gang threat assessment rankings, the Southern region has the lowest ranking compared with other regions, but it has the highest actual crime rates in murder, aggravated assault, and burglary. Also, the Northeastern region ranks second highest in gang threat assessment, but it ranks lowest overall in actual crimes.

There are several possible explanations. This data could show inaccuracies in law enforcement estimates about gang activity. Or it may be that areas reporting high gang involvement keep actual crime numbers down due to heightened awareness of gangs. The lack of proven relationship between perceived gang activity and actual crime rates could also simply indicate that many crimes are committed by individuals who are not gang members. In any case, the comparison shows the difficulty in getting solid data on gangs.

Use the extended-response rubric to reference the criteria required for an acceptable answer and to determine the points to award.

Unit 10 — Answer Key — Answer Key — Answer Key

Reflect and Respond

28. Young people often join gangs because they are looking for companionship or they lack self-esteem. Describe the value of at least two present opportunities at your school that could develop self-esteem or a sense of belonging. Come up with a creative idea for something new that would help students develop their self-esteem and sense of belonging. Explain how it would help and what you would need to do to implement it. Try to "think outside the box" to come up with a new idea that does not already exist (something other than clubs, sports teams, etc.).

> Answers may vary, but students should address each part of the question. The question is meant to elicit strong classroom conversation about character. Students should be able to make connections based on the situations illustrated in this unit. They should then be able to use those connections to be creative and think of ideas that could be implemented in order to have alternatives to the gang lifestyle.
>
> Use the character education rubric to reference the criteria and number of points to award.

©2008 PRINCIPLE WOODS, INC. Removal of copyright notice and copying are violations of Federal Law.

Answer Key — Answer Key — Answer Key   Blood In, Blood Out

Reading Instructional Guide for Technical Extension

BEFORE READING

Looking at the Words

Determining How the Word Sounds (Phonics)
Technical texts often necessitate the use of multisyllabic words that are unfamiliar to students. Use the Syllable Guide to help students decode any words they might have trouble reading.

Determining What the Word Means (Vocabulary)

Words to Study	Breaking into Syllables	Short Definition
caricature	car-i-ca-ture	(n.) a picture that exaggerates or emphasizes a person's features
entwine	en-twine	(v.) to twist together
intimidate	in-tim-i-date	(v.) to fill with fear
misdemeanor	mis-de-mean-or	(n.) a criminal offense or breaking of a law
regulation	reg-u-la-tion	(n.) a law or rule created by authority
tolerate	tol-er-ate	(v.) to allow

Activating Background Knowledge

Graphic Organizer
Either individually or in groups, students may brainstorm about the graffiti of taggers and street gangs, recalling anything previously learned and any prior experience with the subject. Next, encourage students to see the relationships between their ideas by having them complete a Venn diagram to demonstrate what they already know about the similarities and differences between the graffiti of taggers and the graffiti of street gangs.

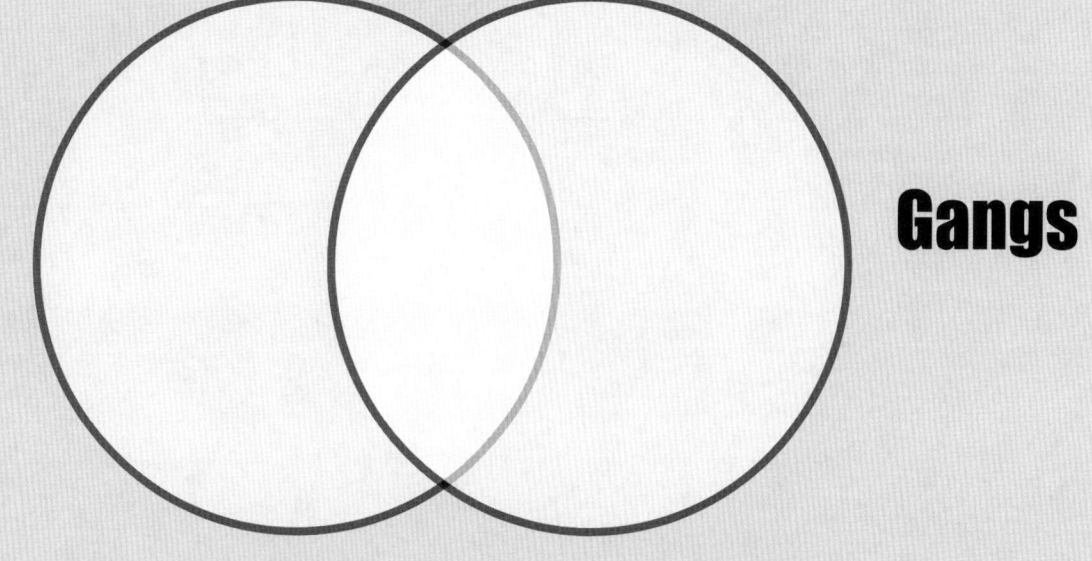

Taggers ⬭⬭ **Gangs**

Answer Key — Answer Key — Answer Key

Unit 10

Starter Questions

After completing the Graphic Organizer, generate a group or class discussion to come up with questions about the subject, a prediction about the article, and at least one learning goal. The first question has been provided for you.

Question: What is graffiti?

Question: _____

Prediction: _____

Goal: _____

DURING READING

Use the Reading Instructional Guide Template found in the front of the book.

AFTER READING

After reading, you may teach reading strategy use by giving students opportunities to do the following:

- Review, paraphrase, and summarize
- Participate in main-idea discussions by describing the information in their own words
- Reflect on concept maps and generate additional discussion starter questions based on the mappings
- Participate in small-group discussions using discussion starter questions

Discussion Starter Questions

The first question has been provided for you.

1. In addition to the ideas mentioned in the article, how do you think we can prevent gangs from vandalizing our communities with graffiti?

2. _____

3. _____

©2008 PRINCIPLE WOODS, INC. Removal of copyright notice and copying are violations of Federal Law.

Technical Extension

The Writing on the Wall

We all have seen the huge writing on overpasses and walls of buildings as we travel through our cities and towns. These markings, called graffiti, are used to send messages and to express artistic talent. So, what's up with these symbols? Do they really mean anything? Or are they the result of kids with too much time on their hands?

Graffiti is sometimes communication between and among gang members. This type of graffiti is also called "the newspaper of the streets." Graffiti is also done as an art form called "tagging." But how are we supposed to know the difference? And does it matter which type it is when it appears in our own neighborhoods?

Graffiti produced by "taggers" is usually more complex and more "artistic." Bubble letters that are entwined or turned sideways or upside down are usually examples of tagging. Several colors may be used. Caricatures, or cartoon-like pictures, are popular with taggers.

There is a world-wide network that connects taggers and their work. There are even contests in which they try to outdo one another with the difficulty of their "tags." Taggers sometimes put themselves at risk when their work is done in dangerous locations. They might climb multiple-story buildings, water towers, billboards, or the sides of railroad or subway cars. Those who participate in this "art" form call this "tagging the heavens."

Taggers like to put their names, or "tags," in as many places as possible. One way they accomplish this is to write their signature on as many name tags as they can and then stick them on every flat surface they see. In general, taggers are not gang members.

Gang graffiti is a method of communication between members of a gang as well as a way of threatening rival gangs. These markings boast about a gang's power and status. They mark the territory controlled by the gang. Gang graffiti is also a way of trying to scare the residents of a neighborhood. The gang hopes that people will not call the police when the markings appear or trouble breaks out. This type of graffiti is one of the first signs that violent gangs are active in a community.

Graffiti placed by gangs usually includes the gang name in some form and sometimes the marks of some of the members. The design might also include a threat targeting a rival gang or member. Sometimes numbers are used that correspond to police codes for various crimes, such as a number that means murder or armed robbery.

Gangs usually develop their own codes for their graffiti. One example is to replace numbers for letters of the alphabet. Generally, a gang's name or a person's name with an "X" marked through it or written upside down is a form of disrespect to that gang or person. It is a "put down," and gang members write this way to "dis" rival gangs. Threats of rival gangs are taken seriously and will not be forgotten. The results are often gang wars. Another code is the substitution of dollar signs for the letter "S" in a message. This means that the gang is selling drugs. Codes are usually unique to each gang. They have to be broken by police based on community characteristics and information.

Unfortunately, there is a high price to pay among gang members for not knowing or understanding their own local code. Many gangs have books of rules, regulations, and history that all members must memorize. This includes what their graffiti means. Members are required to recite their "book" at the whim of the gang leaders, with strict consequences if they make mistakes.

Unit 10

Answer Key — Answer Key — Answer Key

The 4 R's of Graffiti

Read it	Gang graffiti can be dangerous! It can contain an outright threat.
Record it	Graffiti should be photographed for future use.
Report it	Graffiti should be reported to local law enforcement.
Remove it	Graffiti should be removed as soon as possible.

Whether graffiti is a result of gangs or tagging, both forms are illegal. Most cities and other urban areas have laws against it. Regardless of the content of the message or the artistic skill of the creator of the messages, it's not allowed. Graffiti is considered a misdemeanor or a felony depending on the amount of damage done to the structure. The consequences may include a fine, jail time, or both.

If graffiti is a problem in your town or neighborhood, officials recommend removing it as quickly as possible. In some cities, community groups such as the YMCA or the Scouts will remove graffiti upon request. This alerts the gangs and taggers that the markings and their messages will not be tolerated in the area. The groups will move on to another area and try to set up shop there. However, a word of caution from those who know: Never confront or challenge someone who is painting graffiti. They may be dangerous.

Tagging or gang graffiti may serve a particular need for those who participate in it. But it's important to remember that danger for all of us lurks beneath the symbols. We must decide if we want to live in communities governed by fear.

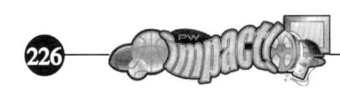

Answer Key — Answer Key — Answer Key   Blood In, Blood Out

Reading Comprehension

After reading "The Writing on the Wall," choose the options that best answer questions 1–11.

1. Read this sentence.
   Gang graffiti is a method of communication between members of a gang as well as a way of threatening rival gangs.

   What is the meaning of the word *rival* as it is used in this sentence?
   - A. new
   - B. violent
   - C. harmless
   - **D. competing**

2. Read this sentence.
   Members are required to recite their "book" at the whim of the gang leaders, with strict consequences if they make mistakes.

   What is the meaning of the word *whim* as it is used in this sentence?
   - F. need
   - **G. impulse**
   - H. demand
   - I. whimper

3. According to the article, what is the general purpose of gang graffiti?
   - A. to list members' names
   - B. to demonstrate their power
   - C. to show off a member's artistic ability
   - **D. to communicate with their own members as well as with rival gangs**

4. According to the article, which of the following is true?
   - F. Tagging is legal.
   - G. Gang graffiti is harmless.
   - **H. Both forms of graffiti are illegal.**
   - I. Tagging is an art form that is appreciated by cities.

5. What method of organization does the author use to present the information in this article?
   - A. giving testimonials
   - **B. comparing tagging and gang graffiti**
   - C. telling stories of gangs who use graffiti
   - D. using stories of taggers who turned to gang membership

6. What is the main idea of this article?
   - F. Tagging is a legal form of graffiti.
   - G. Both gang graffiti and tagging lead to gang warfare.
   - **H. Any kind of graffiti can signal danger for a community.**
   - I. Graffiti is a harmless pastime for young people who are bored.

7. Why is it recommended that graffiti be removed as quickly as possible?
   - A. It erodes buildings.
   - B. It causes younger children to join gangs.
   - C. Police will patrol neighborhoods more frequently.
   - **D. It alerts gangs and taggers that their activities won't be tolerated.**

Answer Key — Answer Key — Answer Key
Unit 10

8. What is one difference between tagging and gang graffiti?
   - F. Gang graffiti is primarily art.
   - **G. Tagging is usually more elaborate.**
   - H. Gangs have world-wide contests to break their codes.
   - I. Tagging never identifies the artist who creates the work.

9. Which statement about graffiti is LEAST accurate?
   - **A. Graffiti is meaningless.**
   - B. Gangs interpret their graffiti using a local code.
   - C. Tagging is primarily an artistic form of expression.
   - D. Gang members must memorize their gang's code and are dealt with severely if they make mistakes.

10. People who read this article will learn
    - F. to draw a moniker.
    - G. to crack a local gang's code.
    - **H. the difference between tagging and gang graffiti.**
    - I. the best way to remove graffiti in their own community.

11. By using the information in the article and the text box, the reader will understand
    - **A. the importance of removing graffiti.**
    - B. the numbering system used in gang graffiti.
    - C. that "tagging the heavens" is a harmless practice.
    - D. that "dissing" rival gang members is usually ignored by the rival gang.

Answer Key — Answer Key — Answer Key   Blood In, Blood Out

Technical Writing Prompt

12. You have moved from a large city with visible gang activity to a smaller city. As you walk into your new office building one morning, you see graffiti on the wall. Your co-workers are unfamiliar with graffiti and what it means. Write a clear and concise memo to educate your co-workers about whether the graffiti appears to be gang-related activity or just a form of self-expression. Use facts to support your conclusion and include the steps you recommend taking to have the graffiti removed.

Student answers may vary.

The student should address the question to the best of his/her ability using the article and personal experience. The question is meant to prepare students to be active citizens who can accurately and effectively use written communication skills.

Use the technical writing rubric to reference the criteria and determine the number of points to award.

Unit 10

Answer Key — Answer Key — Answer Key

Vocational Extension

HELP WANTED:

Local television station is looking for interns who want to move up in the world of broadcasting. Position will last a minimum of three months, with intern performing tasks such as editing tape and shooting video in the field. Intern will then move into writing articles and reporting the news on camera. Upon completion of internship, paid positions will be offered to energetic team players. Send resume to Jim Kraft, Station Manager, at jkraft@wksl.com.

Do you have a story you want to tell? Do you like being in the middle of the action? Then you might want to think about a career in news. Reporters for newspapers, television, and radio go out with pen and notebook to talk to all kinds of people. Their job is to gather information about what's going on. Then they report it to the rest of the community.

Reporters chase "breaking news" stories and gather the facts from the scenes of the action. From these facts, they write their "copy." An editor then approves it or sends it back for corrections. Some reporters focus only on a particular type of story, such as sports, politics, fashion, or money.

A good understanding of English is a requirement because all kinds of people read the news. The writing must be clear. News people can't put their own opinions in their reporting. They must report the facts accurately. Therefore, they focus on the 5 Ws in writing their stories for the public. These are: who, what, when, where, and why? This makes sure that a story covers everything that a reader wants to know. The importance of the events is often pointed out as well.

The best way to prepare for a news career is to start early. Most high schools have a newspaper, so that would be one way to get started. It's also necessary to have a four-year college degree. Media outlets now require a degree when they hire new employees. Degree choices include English, journalism, communications, or public relations.

A good way to get started is to work for free as an intern for a newspaper or television station. This gives future reporters a chance to try out the career. It will also give them on-the-job experience that might be useful later. The employer may offer interns a job at the end of the internship period if things go well.

A news reporter's "typical day" is actually not typical at all! Most reporters get to work very early to receive their assignments or to decide on their next articles. They make phone calls to people to get facts. Some sources might be interviewed in their homes or offices. Then the article is written and must be approved by the editor. Sometimes a workday might be very long. Today's story will be old news tomorrow, so reporters stay until their work is done.

The pay for this job can vary. Average earnings for reporters are between $31,000 and $38,000 per year. Experienced reporters can move into positions as news analysts, and their salaries may be much higher.

So, if this sounds like it fits your need to be "in the thick" of the action, grab a pen and notebook. There's a story out there waiting for you!

Unit 10 — Answer Key — Answer Key — Answer Key

Looking Forward

13. Imagine that you are interviewing for a job as a news reporter with your local newspaper. The interviewer asks you what personal qualities you think are important for a news reporter to have and whether those qualities describe you. Use personal experience and information from the article to write your honest answer to this question.

> Student answers may vary.
>
> The student should address the question to the best of his/her ability using the article and personal experience. The question is meant to encourage students to explore areas of interest for their future and begin to determine how they will prepare for a future career.
>
> Use the extended-response rubric to reference the criteria and determine the number of points to award.

Ethical Dilemma

14. You have an hour before the deadline for your article about ethical violations in City Council. Earlier in the day, you interviewed a source at City Hall who asked that she not be quoted directly for fear of losing her job. She provided good information, but you need a second source to verify it. Your editor is anxious to get the article for review, but you can't find another source. Should you violate your promise to the City Hall informant and quote her in order to meet your deadline? What are the possible consequences for both the source and for you in the future if you do so?

> Student answers may vary.
>
> The student should address the question to the best of his/her ability using background knowledge from the article as well as personal opinion and experience. The question is meant to encourage students to contemplate scenarios and make ethical decisions.
>
> Use the character education rubric to reference the criteria and number of points to award.

Answer Key — Answer Key — Answer Key   Blood In, Blood Out

Unit Vocabulary Assessment

Matching
Match each word in Column I to its definition in Column II.

Column I
- **C** 1. misdemeanor
- **D** 2. intimidate
- **A** 3. regulation
- **B** 4. surreal

Column II
- a. a law or rule
- b. seeming like a dream
- c. a criminal offense or breaking of a law
- d. to fill with fear

Multiple Choice
Choose the word that MOST NEARLY replaces the underlined word in each sentence.

5. Most gang rituals are dangerous, and many are illegal.
   - A. hangouts
   - **B. ceremonies**
   - C. competitions
   - D. requirements

6. His treatment of the young man was ruthless.
   - A. dangerous
   - B. reasonable
   - **C. without pity**
   - D. without respect

7. The rope was entwined through the huge oak tree's branches.
   - A. hung
   - B. entered
   - **C. twisted**
   - D. formed

8. Students have many alternatives other than joining a gang.
   - **A. choices**
   - B. methods
   - C. members
   - D. ways to choose

Word Bank
caricature
graffiti
informant
tolerate

Fill in the Blank
Choose a word from the word bank to fill in the blank in the sentence below.

9. The **graffiti** on the wall showed the gang's moniker.

10. Shara is an **informant** for the police and gives them information on a regular basis.

11. The **caricature** of our family exaggerated the size of our noses!

12. There is no reason to **tolerate** unacceptable or dangerous behavior.

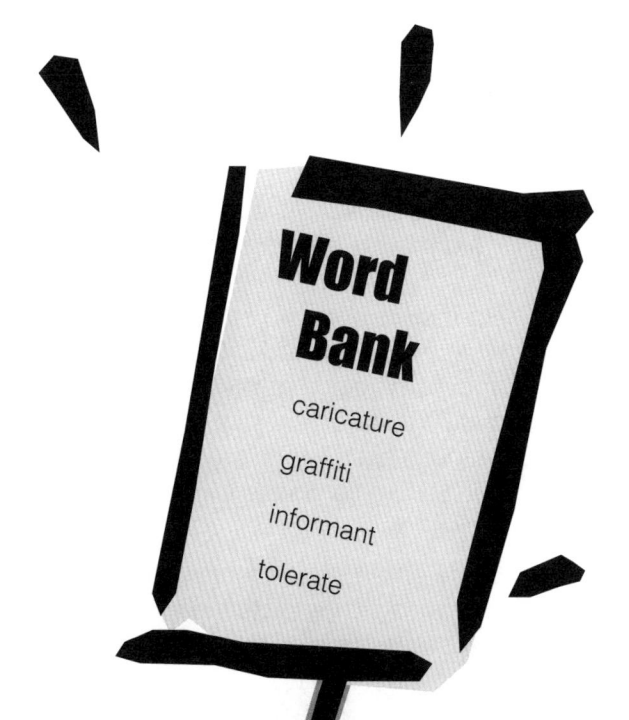

Unit 10 — Answer Key — Answer Key — Answer Key

Authentic Assessment

Students will create two unique story endings based on the unit "Blood In, Blood Out." This activity combines the authentic components of creative thinking and writing linked to the comprehension of a written text. The teacher should provide basic guidance on elements of a story as well as guidelines for requirements of students' writing.

Instructions for Story Ending Project

1. **Story beginning.** Have students read the following story beginning and then discuss as a class what is going on in the story:

    Derek is a 14-year-old young man with a troubled history. His father left his home at a young age. His mother and four brothers have struggled day to day just to have food and shelter. His mother is stressed and overworked, with little time for family life. One of his older brothers has recently joined a well-known street gang. Derek's brother tells him that gang life is just what he needs—people to look out for him, a family to belong to, and acceptance for who he is. Derek knows the dangers of gang life, but at the same time longs to be accepted and to be approved by his brother. He tells his brother…

2. **Brainstorming and sequencing.** After students are familiar with what has happened in the story so far, they should brainstorm about where they think the events in the story will go next. They should think of two different scenarios: one in which Derek's situation ends with his joining a gang, and one in which it does not. Before beginning to write, students should create two sequencing charts of the events that will complete their stories.

3. **Story endings.** Students should use information from the unit on gangs to complete their two story endings according to the guidelines set forth by the teacher. To do this, they might think about the following:

    a. The dangers of gang life

    b. Rituals one must complete to join/leave a gang

    c. What it is like to be in a gang

    d. Alternatives to joining a gang

4. **Discussion.** After students have written their story endings, they should compare them with those of their peers, either in small groups or as a class. Each person should then identify the one element that is the most important reason not to get involved in a gang and discuss with the small group or the class why it is the most important element.

5. **Assessment.** The story endings will be assessed using the rubric on the following page.

Answer Key — Answer Key — Answer Key   Blood In, Blood Out

Story Ending Rubric

Requirement	8–10 Points	4–7 Points	0–3 Points	Points Earned
Sequencing Charts	The student creates two complete sequencing charts after brainstorming endings.	The student creates only one sequencing chart or two incomplete charts after brainstorming endings.	The student does not create sequencing charts or demonstrates no effort to make the charts complete.	
Guidelines	The student writes two distinct and complete endings, following teacher guidelines.	The student writes one complete ending or two partially complete endings, following teacher guidelines.	The student demonstrates no effort to write two endings or does not follow teacher guidelines.	
Elements	The student's writing considers various elements of gang life.	The student's writing partially considers limited elements of gang life.	The student's writing does not consider elements of gang life.	
Conclusion	The student participates in a discussion about the story endings and makes a statement that is based on what he or she learned from the unit.	The student partially participates in a discussion about the story endings and makes a statement that may not be based on what he or she learned from the unit.	The student does not participate in a discussion about the story endings and/or does not make a statement.	

Answer Key — Answer Key — Answer Key

Rubrics

Reading Short-Response Rubric
Created for ᴾᵂImpact!

2 points	The student fully understands what is being asked for. The student's answer is correct, complete, and addresses all aspects of the assigned task. The student provides detail and support from the text in order to support his/her answer. Any additional information provided by the student is related to the assigned task and acts as support for his/her response.
1 point	The student partially understands what is being asked for. The student's answer is correct; however, it is generalized and not specific enough. The student is missing any specific details and support from the text that would prove his/her full understanding of the text and the assigned task.
0 points	The answer is completely incorrect, has nothing to do with the assigned task, or no answer is provided.

Reading Extended-Response Rubric
Created for ᴾᵂImpact!

4 points	The student fully understands what is being asked for. The student's answer is correct, complete, and addresses all aspects of the assigned task. The student provides detail and support from the text in order to support his/her answer. Any additional information provided by the student is related to the assigned task and acts as support for his/her response.
3 points	The student understands what is being asked for. The student's answer is correct and addresses all aspects of the assigned task. The student provides detail and support, but it is not fully complete or directly from the text.
2 points	The student partially understands what is being asked for. The student's answer is correct; however, it is generalized and not specific enough. The student is missing any specific details and support from the text that would prove his/her full understanding of the text and the assigned task.
1 point	The student has very little understanding of what is being asked for in the task. The answer is not complete, has many things wrong with it, or addresses very little of what has been asked for.
0 points	The answer is completely incorrect, has nothing to do with the assigned task, or no answer is provided.

Answer Key — Answer Key — Answer Key

Interpreting the Data Short-Response Rubric
Created for ᴾᵂImpact!

2 points	The student fully understands what is being asked for. The work is completed correctly and efficiently. There is a full demonstration of the know-how necessary to accurately answer the problem provided. If applicable, the explanations and interpretations are clear, complete, and concise. Any small mistakes do not take away from the overall display of understanding.
1 point	The student seems to understand what is being asked for, but the answer is only partially correct. The answer may be correct, but it is apparent that there is a lack of full awareness in the know-how necessary to complete the problem. Or there is a full awareness of the know-how necessary to complete the problem, but the answer is incorrect.
0 points	No answer is provided, the answer is completely incorrect, or there is absolutely no demonstration of the know-how necessary to complete the problem (even if the answer provided is correct).

Interpreting the Data Extended-Response Rubric
Created for ᴾᵂImpact!

4 points	The student fully understands what is being asked for. The work is completed correctly and efficiently. There is a full demonstration of the know-how necessary to accurately answer the problem provided or others like it. If applicable, the explanations and interpretations are clear, complete, and concise. Any small mistakes do not take away from the overall display of understanding.
3 points	The student understands what is being asked for. The answer is essentially correct, but the demonstration of the know-how necessary to explain how the student came to the answer is slightly flawed. The answer contains some minor errors that could be due to lack of attention to detail in the demonstration of the know-how necessary to answer the problem or others like it.
2 points	The student seems to understand what is being asked for, but the answer is only partially correct. The answer may be correct, but it is apparent that there is a lack of full awareness in the know-how necessary to complete the problem or others like it. Or there is a full awareness of the know-how necessary to complete the problem, but the answer provided is incorrect.
1 point	There is a very limited understanding of what is being asked for. The answer is incomplete and has errors. There is some demonstration of the know-how necessary to answer the problem or others like it, but the answer is incomplete, totally incorrect, or inadequate.
0 points	No answer is provided, the answer is completely incorrect, or there is absolutely no demonstration of the know-how necessary to complete the problem (even if the answer provided is correct).

Answer Key — Answer Key — Answer Key

Character Education Rubric
Created for PWImpact!

4 points	The student uses information from the reading selection and his/her life and formulates a strong answer that demonstrates what conclusions about character he/she has drawn from the article.
3 points	The student gives examples from either only his/her life or only the reading selection and formulates a strong answer that demonstrates what conclusions about character he/she has drawn from the article.
2 points	The student gives few examples from his/her life or the reading selection, but formulates an answer that demonstrates what conclusions about character he/she has drawn from the article.
1 point	The student does not use examples from his/her life or from the reading selection. It is difficult to determine whether the student has drawn any conclusions about character from the article.
0 points	The student has provided no response or a completely incorrect response. The student does not demonstrate that he/she has drawn any conclusions about character from the article.

Technical Writing Rubric
Created for PWImpact!

4 points	The student clearly and concisely conveys specialized information in a way that shows a keen understanding of the specific audience/purpose and supports general statements with an abundance of relevant facts.
3 points	The student communicates specialized information in a way that shows a general understanding of the specific audience/purpose and supports statements with a sufficient number of relevant facts.
2 points	The student communicates information in a way that is unclear, shows limited understanding of the audience/purpose, and/or uses few relevant facts.
1 point	The student communicates information in a way that is unclear, shows minimal understanding of the audience/purpose, and/or uses very few facts.
0 points	The student either does not answer the question at all or shows no understanding of the assigned writing task.

©2007 PRINCIPLE WOODS, INC. Removal of copyright notice and copying are violations of Federal Law.

Answer Key — Answer Key — Answer Key

Notes

Unit 1: Ready or Not?
High-Interest Article

Since then, almost...: Christensen, Martin K.I., "Worldwide Guide to Women in Leadership," http://www.guide2womenleaders.com/index.html (accessed January 25, 2008).

Some political analysts...: Cohen, Sharon, Associated Press, "Does Obama's Win Show U.S. Is Colorblind?" *AOL News*, January 5, 2008, http://news.aol.com/story/_a/does-obamas-win-show-us-is-colorblind/n20080105125709990005.

One survey showed...: Cohen.

Another survey resulted...: Newsweek Poll conducted by Princeton Survey Research Associates International, July 2–3, 2007, http://www.pollingreport.com/politics.htm.

Controversial radio host...: *Associated Press*, "Clinton, Obama, Fuel Race, Gender Debate," *MSNBC.com*, January 14, 2008, http://www.msnbc.msn.com/id/22653232/.

Even former president...: Givhan, Robin, "On the Subject of Race, Words Get in the Way," *Washington Post*, January 20, 2008, www.washingtonpost.com/wp-dyn/content/article/2008/01/18/AR2008011800890_pf.html.

Interpreting the Data

Table 1: Data from Barney, Chuck, "A Black or Woman for President? TV and Film Have Been There, Done That," *Contra Costa Times*, April 21, 2008, http://www.contracostatimes.com/ci_8999330.

Technical Extension

Each state gets...: "United States Electoral College," *Wikipedia*, http://en.widipedia.org/w/indes/php?title=United_States_Electoral_College&printable=yes.

Many people in...: "The Electoral College," Social Studies for Kids, 2002–2008, http://www.socialstudiesforkids.com/articles/government/theelectoralcollege.htm.

Electoral College Box (text box)...: Table copied from U.S. Electoral College, Office of the Federal Register, http://www.archives.gov/federal-register/electoral-college/scores2.html#2000.

Vocational Extension

An interesting fact...: "Hourly Rate Survey Report for Job: Administrative Assistant," PayScale, 2000-2008, http://www.payscale.com/research/US/Job=Administrative_Assistant/Hourly_Rate.

Unit 2: Batman vs. Iron Man
Interpreting the Data

Figure 1 and Table 1: Data from The Numbers, http://www.the-numbers.com/, and Box Office Mojo, http://boxofficemojo.com/.

Technical Extension

Detective Comics, now...: Daniels, Les, *DC Comics: A Celebration of the World's Favorite Comic Book Heroes*, Billboard Books, New York, 2003, p.14.

Then, in May...: Daniels, p.32.

Marvel comics introduced...: "Iron Man (Anthony Stark)," Marvel Universe, 2007, http://www.marvel.com/universe/Iron_Man.

Older readers (the...: Daniels, p.13.

The most important...: Albert, Aaron, "Finding Comic Book Values," About.com: Comic Books, 2007, http://comicbooks.about.com/od/collectingcomics/p.value3.htm.

Some people have...: Malloy, Alex G., *Comics Values, Annual 2005*, KP Books, Iola, Wisconsin, p.38

In 2006 a...:"Heritage Comic Signature Auction Brings $2.19 Million+!" Press Release, Heritage Auctions, Inc., September 13, 2006, www.ha.com/common/info/press/default.php?ReleaseID=1218.

Action Comics # 1...: "Excerpt from *The Rough Guide to Superheroes*," *USA Today*, November 23, 2004, http://content.usatoday.com/community/utils/idmap/12614954.story.

Collectors who collect...: Malloy, p.11.

Some collectors look...: Malloy, p.11.

Vocational Extension

Graffiti artists, known...: Whakaahua, Kaipeita, "Mural Artists: Tasks and specializations," CareerServices, http://www.careers.govt.nz/default.aspx?id0=10103&id1-J80215.

Successful artists must...: "Welcome to Job Guide," Australian Government: Department of Education, Employment, and Workplace Relations, http://jobguide.thegoodguides.com/au.

Some work alone...: "Artist," U.S. Department of Labor, Bureau of Labor Statistics, http://www.bls.gov/K12/music03.htm.

Experienced art directors...: "Artist."

Average salaries range...:"Artist."

Unit 3: Image: Unattainable
High-Interest Article

In fact, research...: Hellmich, Nanci, "Do Thin Models Warp Girls' Body Image?" *USA Today*, September 26, 2006, http://www.usatoday.com/news/health/2006-09-25-thin-models_x.htm.

Trying to control...: Bryant, John, "Body Image Produces a Distorted Picture," Copyright 1999, Times Newspapers Ltd., http://www.caringonline.com/eatdis/misc/bryantslife.htm.

They won't allow...: Yeoman, Fran, Carolyn Asome, and Graham Keeley, "Skinniest Models Are Banned from Catwalk," *The Times*, September 9, 2006, http://www.timesonline.co.uk/article...349467,00.html.

One day, just...: Kay, Karen, "Are Size 0 Models Too Thin for the Catwalk?" *Daily Mail*, September 18, 2006, http://www.dailymail.co.uk/pages/live/femail/article.html?in_article_id=405600&in_page_id=1879.

Large strides have...: Kay.

"The promotion of..." (text box): Hellmich.

Interpreting the Data

Table 1: "Age-Adjusted Percent Distributions of Body Mass Index (BMI) Among Persons 18 Years of age and Over by Selected Characteristics: 2004," Table 199, 2008 *Statistical Abstract of the United States*, U.S. Census Bureau, http://www.census.gov/compendia/statab/cats/health_nutrition/health_risk_factors.html.
(Some footnotes and categories have been deleted to make the table easier for secondary students to read.)

©2007 PRINCIPLE WOODS, INC. Removal of copyright notice and copying are violations of Federal Law.

Answer Key — Answer Key — Answer Key

Figures 1 and 2: Data from "U.S. Obesity Trends 1985–2006," Centers for Disease Control and Prevention, Department of Health and Human Services, http://www.cdc.gov/nccdphp/dnpa/obesity/trend/maps/index.htm.

Figure 3: Data from "Per Capita Consumption of Selected Beverages by Type: 1980 to 2005," Table 203, 2008 *Statistical Abstract of the United States*, U.S. Census Bureau, http://www.census.gov/compendia/statab/cats/health_nutrition.html.

Technical Extension

Body mass index…: "Body Mass Index," Nemours Foundation: TeensHealth, http://www.kidshealth.org/PageManager.jsp?dn=KidsHealth&lic=1&ps=307&cat_id=201.

Two best friends…: "What's the Right Weight for My Height?" Nemours Foundation: TeensHealth, July 2007, http://www.kidshealth.org/PageManager.jsp?dn=KidsHealth&lic=1&ps=307&cat_id=205.

You might walk…: "Healthy Weight for Teen," WebMD: Public Information from the U.S. Department of Health and Human Services, April 2006, http://www.webmd.com/parenting/healthy-teen-weight.

Or they may…: "Anorexia Nervosa," National Women's Health Information Center, September 2006, http://www.4woman.gov/faq/easyread/anorexia-etr.htm.

So customers may…: Earnest, Leslie, "What's With Women's Clothing Sizes?" *LA Times*, May 1, 2005, http://community.discovery.com/eve/forums/a/ptc/f/7521920016/m/705109916/xsl/print_t.

Anorexia affects your (text box)…: Reproduced from "Anorexia Nervosa," Office on Women's Health, U.S. Department of Health and Human Services, women'shealth.gov, http://www.4woman.gov/faq/easyread/anorexia-etr.htm.

Vocational Extension

Trainers must be…: "A Personal Trainer Salary Depends on You and What You Can Offer," Health and Fitness Solutions, http://www.englandcoach.com/become%20a%20pt.html.

One drawback of…: "2005 Salary Survey Results," http://www.acefitness.org/salary.

Unit 4: Circle of Friends
High-Interest Article

Dunn has praised…: "Michael Vick to Judge: 'I Am Not the Beast'," *CNN.com*, December 14, 2007, http://www.cnn.com/2007/US/law/12/14/vick.letters/index.html.

Hank Aaron, Major…: "Michael Vick to Judge: 'I Am Not the Beast'."

Wynn felt that…: Merrill, Elizabeth, "In Life, and in Death, Taylor Was a Natural Mystery," *ESPN.com*, December 2, 2007, http://sports.espn.go.com/nfl/news/story?id=3135111.

Taylor said, "I'm"…: "Sean Taylor's Death Leaves Redskins in Mourning," USA Today, November 27, 2007, www.usatoday.com/sports/football/nfl/2007-11-27-taylor-obit_N.htm.

After his transformation…: Merrill.

Interpreting the Data

Federal indictment (summarized excerpts): United States District Court for the Eastern District of Virginia, Richmond Division, July 17, 2007, http://alt.cimedia.com/ajc/pdf/vick0717.pdf.

Figure 1: Data from the Official Site of the National Football League, http://www.nfl.com.

Technical Extension

Engaging in violent…: "Player Policies," NFL Players Association, 2007, http://www.nflplayers.com/user/template.aspx?fmid=181&lmid=336&pid=0&type=n.

These are the…: Bell, Jarrett, "NFL Will Confront Discipline Issue, Unveil New Policy within Days," *USA Today*, http://www.usatoday.com/sports/football/nfl/2007-04-09-conduct-policy_N.htm/.

Integrity is defined…: *American Heritage Dictionary of the English Language*, Barleby.com, http://www.bartleby.com/61/70/I0177000.html/.

"Players got to…: Hotard, Scott, "Jim Kelly: Goodell's Conduct Policy 'About Time'," *Naples Daily News*, naplesnews.com, April 14, 2007, http://www.naplesnews.com/news/2007/apr/14/jim_kelly_goodells_conduct_policy_about_time/.

Fines and other…: Bell, Jarrett.

On the other…: Schrotenboer, Brent, "NFL Crime and Punishment/Part One: Cars, Booze, and Race," SignOnSanDiego.com, April 22, 2007, http://www.signonsandiego.com/sports/nfl/20070422-9999-lz1s22arrest.html/.

"You want your…: Hotard, Scott.

Former player Deion…: Bell, Jarrett.

National Football League (text box)…: "Player Policies," NFL Players Association, http://www.nflplayers.com/user/template.aspx?fmid=181&lmid=336&pid=0&type=c.

Vocational Extension

College studies that…: McKay, Dawn Rosenberg, "Athletic Coach: Career Information," About.com: Career Planning, 2007, http://careerplanning.about.com/cs/occupations/p/sports_coach.htm?p=1.

A day at…: McKay.

In 2004 the…: McKay.

They also offer…: Upton, Jodi, and Wieberg, Steve, "Contracts for College Coaches Cover More Than Salaries," *USA Today*, Nov. 16, 2006, http://www.usatoday.com/sports/college/football/2006-11-16-coaches-salaries-cover_x.htm.

Several coaches at…: "Big 12 Coaches Salaries," The Lubbock Avalanche-Journal's Red Raiders.com, December 12, 1997, www.redraiders.com/news/97/12/12/.

Unit 5: Riding Dubs
High-Interest Article

To celebrate the…: del Mundo, Lyle, "With a Hit Album Chicago's Own Maintains a High Profile in his H2," *Car Audio and Electronics*, 2007, http://www.caraudiomag.com/features/0407cae_twista/index.html.

He is Puerto…: "Owner Profile: Will Castro," Unique Autosports, http://www.uniqueautosport.com/ucrew.html.

At each stop…: "Galleries: 2007 Custom Auto Show and Concert Tour," *DUB Magazine*, http://www.dubmagazine.com/dubshow/galleries.html.

Answer Key — Answer Key — Answer Key

Interpreting the Data

Table 2 (Combined miles per gallon): "Find and Compare Cars," United States Department of Energy Efficiency and Renewable Energy/United States Environmental Protection Agency, http://www.fueleconomy.gov/.

Table 2 (MSRP): Ford Showroom, Ford Motor Company, 2007, http://www.showroom.fordvehicles.com/Showroom.jsp.

Table 3: Data from "U.S. Finished Motor Gasoline Product Supplied," Energy Information Administration, updated December 21, 2007, http://tonto.eia.doe.gov/dnav/pet/hist/mgfupus2a.htm.

Figure 2: Data from "U.S. Retail Gasoline Prices," Energy Information Administration, http://www.eia.doe.gov/oil_gas/petroleum/data_publications/wrgp/mogas_home_page.html. (CPI adjusted using http://www.measuringworth.com/uscompare/.)

Technical Extension

They will give...: Ostroff, Jeff, "The Top 10 Car Dealer Scams, 2006," CarBuyingTips.com, http://www.carbuyingtips.com/scams.htm.

Did you know...: "Auto Loan Criteria a Consumer Should Know," Moto Auto Cars, uniTEC, http://www.motoautocars.com/buyerguide/factors.

Unit 6: The Right to Support Them
High-Interest Article

In real life...: "Bruce Willis Sings for the Troops: Actor Tours Iraq with His Band, The Accelerators," *CBS News*, September 26, 2003, http://www.cbsnews.com/stories/2003/09/26/entertainment/main575209.shtml.

Matt Damon joins...: Sheppard, Noel, "Matt Damon Insults Military, Thinks Bush Twins Should Be in Iraq," *NewsBusters*, December 16, 2006, http://newsbusters.org/node/9690.

Unlike many celebrities...: Kasindorf, Martin, and Steve Komorow, "USO Cheers Troops, but Iraq Gigs Tough to Book," *USA Today*, December 22, 2005, http://www.usatoday.com/news/world/iraq/2005-12-22-uso-cover_x.htm.

Though these celebrities...: Josar, David, "Troops Outside Secure Compounds Bemoan Lack of USO Entertainment," *Stars and Stripes*, European edition, February 24, 2004, http://www.estripes.com/article.asp?section=104&article=19883&archive=true.

Newton says that...: Kasindorf and Komarow.

Others, such as...: Kasindorf and Komarow.

Comedian Al Franken...: "Why Aren't More Celebrities Going to Iraq?"(video), *ABC News*, January 1, 2006, http://abcnews.go.com/Video/playerIndex?id=1528960.

Stallone reportedly answered...: Dominus, Susan, "Not Bob Hope's USO," *New York Times*, November 13, 2005, www.nytimes.com/2005/11/13/movies/13uso.html?pagewanted=print.

On the first...: Adaso, Henry, "50 Cent Rattled by Death Threat in Iraq," About.com: Rap / Hip-Hop, November 28, 2006, http://rap.about.com/b/a/257972.htm.

Interpreting the Data

Figure 1: This graph summarizes data released by two separate polls.
Washington Post-ABC News Poll, *Washington Post*, 2005, http://www.washingtonpost.com/wp dyn/content/graphic/2005/06/08/GR2005060800301.html.
USA Today/Gallup Poll, *USA Today*, July 2007, http://www.usatoday.com/news/washington/2007-07-09-bush-pollresults_N.htm?loc=interstitialskip.

Table 1: Data is taken from the following analysis:
Carroll, Joseph, "Opinions of Iraq War Show Little Movement," Gallup.com, November 9, 2007, http://www.gallup.com/poll/102655/Opinions-Iraq-War-Show-Little-Movement.aspx#3.

Technical Extension

About 9.7 million...: "Daily Newspapers in the United States," Infoplease, December 2007, http://print.infoplease,com/toptens/usnewspapers,html.

Today about 72%...: "Most Get News from Broadcasters," *United Press International*, Feb. 25, 2006, http://www.upi.com/NewsTrack/Business/2006/02/25/most_get_news_from_broadcasters/4.

While 39% of...: "Blogs Reach 50 Million Americans," socaltech.com,
August 9, 2005, http://www.socaltech.com/blogs_reach__million_americans/s-0002250.html.

Percentage of Americans (text box)...: Pew Internet & American Life Project Tracking surveys, March 2000–March 2007, http://pewinternet.org/trends.asp.

Unit 7: A Moment to Lose
High-Interest Article

In a statement...: "Miss Nevada Katie Rees Fired Over Raunchy Photos," *Fox News*, December 22, 2006, http://www.foxnews.com/story/0,2933,237897,00.html.

The coach pointed...: "Leinart's Party Photos Disappoint Cardinals' Coach," *Los Angeles Times*, April 3, 2008, http://www.latimes.com/sports/printedition/la-sp-leinart3apr03,1,153314.story.

In fact, one...: Verardi, Nicole, "MySpace in College Admission," National Association for College Admission Counseling Newsletter, April 2006, http://www.nacacnet.org/MemberPortal/News/StepsNewsletter/myspace_students.htm.

Many sites will...: "Preventing Cyber-slander," *Rachael Ray*, aired on April 17, 2008, http://www.rachaelrayshow.com/show/segments/view/preventing-cyber-slander/.

Just keep in...: Verardi.

It Could Happen (text box)...: Verardi.

Interpreting the Data

Figure 1: Data from

Rainie, Lee, and Paul Hitlin, "The Internet at School," Pew/ Internet: Pew Internet & American Life Project: Reports: Education, August 2, 2005, http://www.pewinternet.org/PPF/r/163/report_display.asp.

Lenhart, Madden, Macgill, Smith, "Teens and Social Media: The use of social media gains a greater foothold in teen life as they embrace the conversational nature of interactive online media." Pew/ Internet: Pew Internet & American Life Project, December 19, 2007, http://www.pewinternet.org/.

Figure 2: "Teens and Social Media."

Figure 3: "Teens and Social Media."

Figure 4: "Teens and Social Media."

Figure 5: "Teens and Social Media."

©2007 PRINCIPLE WOODS, INC. Removal of copyright notice and copying are violations of Federal Law.

Answer Key — Answer Key — Answer Key

Technical Extension

The First Amendment…: Rose, Carol V., "The Constitutional Right to Privacy," January 2001, http://www.mass.gov/mgis/mgic/01_01/rose/sld004.htm.

However, who we…: The Free Dictionary, 2008, http://encyclopedia2.thefreedictionary.com/right+to+privacy.

Most countries have…: Hoisen, Gus, "Privacy and Cyberspace: Questioning the Need for Harmonisation," June 2005, http://www.itu.int/osg/spu/cybersecurity/docs/Hosein_Privacy_and_Cyberspace.pdf

Teens online (text box)…: Lenhart, Amanda and Mary Madden, "Teens, Privacy & Online Social Networks;" Pew/Internet, Pew Internet & American Life Project, April 18, 2007, http://www.pewinternet.org/pdfs/PIP_Teens_Privacy_SNS_Report_Final.pdf.

Vocational Extension

Educational requirements for…: Kane, Sally, "Career Profile: Lawyer," About.com: Legal Careers, 2007, http://legalcareers.about.com/od/careerprofies/p.Lawyer.htm?p=1.

Most of these…: Kuther, Tara, "What type of jobs can you get with a law degree?" About.com: Graduate School, 2007, http://gradschool.about.com/od/lawschool/f.lawjobs.htm?p=1.

Starting salaries for…: "Prosecuting Attorneys," Harvard Law School, October 24, 2007, www.law.harvard.edu/students/opia/planning/areas/prosecution.php.
Jones, Leigh, "Lawyers' Salaries Projected to Rise 5.4 Percent," *The National Law Journal*, December 11, 2007, www.law.com/jsp/article.p?id=1197281076304.

In 2004 the…: "Kane, Sally, "Career Profile: Lawyer," About.com: Legal Careers, http://legalcareers.about.com/od/careerprofiles/p/Lawyer.htm.

Unit 8: Journey of the Tiger
High-Interest Article

He also used…: "Tiger Woods Biography," NetKushi.com, http://www.netkushi.com/hollywood/tiger_woods.php.

Because of his…: "Tiger 1997: The Buzz That Rocked the Cradle," Golf.com, April 1, 2007, http://www.golf.com/golf/tours_news/article/0,28136,1594277,00.html.

It is estimated…: "What We Do: Empowering Youth, Tiger Woods Foundation, http://www.tigerwoodsfoundation.org/.

Tigers have a (text box)…: "Tiger Culture: Why Use the Chinese Tiger as the Emblem?" Save China's Tigers, http://english.savechinastigers.org/node/316.

Technical Extension

Athletes must practice…: Scott, Jennifer, "Train Your Inner Mind to Lower Your Golf Score," Own the Zone Golf, Feb. 11, 2008, http://www.ownthezonegolf.com/lower/shtml.

You might hear…: Beilock, Sian, "Why Do We Choke Under Pressure? Skilled Golfers Putt More Poorly When Self-Conscious," APA Online, December, 16, 2001, http://www.apa.org/releases/choke.html.

According to Sean…: Cochran, Sean, "How to Correctly Weight Train for Golf Like Tiger, Vijay, and Phil," Deep Fitness, 2004-2008, http://deepfitness.com/3275/How-to-Correctly-Weight-Train-for-Golf-Like-Tiger-Vijay-and-Phil.aspx.

Golfers train in…: Hill, Susan, "How Do the Golf Pros Train?" About Golf and More, 2004, http://www.golf4u.co.cc/article.cfm/id/6020.

Quinn Early, former…: Hallender, Jane, "Tai Chi Catching on with NFL," Kung Fu Fighting Arts Community at the Dragons List, http://www.golf4u.co.cc/article.cfm/id/6020.

Extreme sports athletes…: Cunningham, Christine, "Training the Sports Enthusiast," Life Fitness, 2005, http://us.commercial.lifefitness.com/content.cfm/trainingtheextremesportsenthusiast?ppf=1.

This means a…: Stein, Alan, "Keeping Your Basketball Players on the Court," CoachLikeaPro.com, 2007, http://www.coachlikeapro.com/injury-prevention.html.

Exercise Vocabulary (text box)…: http://www.alphadictionary.com/index.shtml.

Vocational Extension

Caddies are an…: "How to Become a Professional Caddy," eHow: How to Do Just About Everything, http://www.ehow.com/how_2084728_become-professional-caddy.html.

A good way…: "How to Become a Professional Caddy."

There are usually…: "How Can I Become a Tour Caddy?" TourCaddies.com, http://www.tourcaddies.com/faqs.htm.

The course is…: "Caddie Apprenticeship Program," PCA Worldwide.com, http://www.pcaworldwide.com/school.htm.

The final part…: "Caddie Apprenticeship Program."

The caddy's job…: "How Can I Become a Tour Caddy?"

Tour caddies have…: "How Can I Become a Tour Caddy?"

He made about…: Woolsey, Matt, "Top-Earning Caddies," Forbes.com, June 11, 2007, http://www.forbes.com/2007/06/08/caddy-golf-pro-forbeslife-cx_mw_0611caddy.html.

Unit 9: Above the Influence
High-Interest Article

In fact, one…: "Celebrity News: Celebrity DUI Spotlight," TotalDUI.com, Total DUI, Inc., 2007, http://www.totaldui.com/celebrity_dui_spotlight.htm.

After this incident…: Cohen, Sandy, "Lohan Gets 1 day in Jail on DUI Plea," *ABC News.com*, August 23, 2007, http://abcnews.go.com/Entertainment/wireStory?id=3517140.

Nicole Richie was…: "Celebrity News: Celebrity DUI Spotlight."

This simple mistake…: "Celebrity News: Celebrity DUI Spotlight."

Possible DUI Penalties (text box)…: "DUI Penalties: Know the Risks of a DUI Conviction," TotalDUI.com, Total DUI, Inc., 2007, http://www.totaldui.com/dui_penalties.htm.

Interpreting the Data

Figure 1: Data from Alcohol Alert Website, KeRo Corporation World Headquarters, Scottsdale, Arizona, 2007, http://www.alcoholalert.com/drunk-driving-statistics-2004.html.

Table 1: Data from Alcohol Alert Website.

Figure 2: Data from Alcohol Alert Website.

Figure 3: Data from "Arrests by State," Table 69, *Crime in the United States 2005*, Federal Bureau of Investigation website, http://www.fbi.gov/ucr/05cius/arrests/index.html.

Technical Extension

Answer Key — Answer Key — Answer Key

When the MLDA…: "Transportation Research Circular E-C123," Traffic Safety and Alcohol Regulation: A Symposium, Transportation Research Board, November 2007, http://onlinepubs.trb.org/onlinepubs/circulars/ec123.pdf.

Almost 50% of…: "Transportation Research Circular E-C123."

One study shows…: "Transportation Research Circular E-C123."

Teens ages 12…: "Transportation Research Circular E-C123."

A young male (text box)…: "Transportation Research Circular E-C123."

Specific Provisions of (text box)…: "Transportation Research Circular E-C123."

Vocational Extension

As many as…: "The Growing Profession of Rehabilitation Counseling," Langston University (citing a National Council on Rehabilitation Education Inc. brochure), http://www.lunet.edu/rehab/profession.htm (accessed January 8, 2008).

Take a look…: "Counselors," *Occupational Outlook Handbook*, 2008-09 Edition, Bureau of Labor Statistics, U.S. Department of Labor, http://www.bls.gov/oco/ocos067.htm.

Unit 10: Blood In, Blood Out
High-Interest Article

Some believe they…: Walker, Robert, Gangs OR Us: Gang Identification Training and Expert Witness, http://www.gangsorus.com/ganghistory.html.

One gang informant…: Ling, Lisa, *Explorer Blog*: "World's Most Dangerous Gang," National Geographic Channel, January 31, 2006, http://blogs.nationalgeographic.com/channel/blog/2006/01/explorer_gangs.html.

Some young people…: Focus Adolescent Services, "Gang Awareness, Prevention, and Intervention: Why Do Young People Join Gangs?" http://www.focusas.com/Gangs.html.

But there are…: Carlie, Michael K., *Into the Abyss: A Personal Journey into the World of Street Gangs*, http://faculty.missouristate.edu/m/MichaelCarlie/what_I_learned_about/GANGS/join_a_gang.htm.

Interpreting the Data

One problem…: *2005 National Gang Threat Assessment*, National Alliance of Gang Investigators Association, http://www.ojp.usdoj.gov/BJA/what/2005_threat_assesment.pdf.

Another difficulty…: Jackson, Alan, "Prosecuting Gang Cases: What Local Prosecutors Need to Know," Bureau of Justice Assistance, April 2004, http://www.ndaa.org/pdf/gang_cases.pdf.

Also, law enforcement…: *2005 National Gang Threat Assessment*.

Table 1: Data from the *2005 National Gang Threat Assessment*, Tables 9, 13, 17, 21.

Table 2: Data from *Crime in the United States 2005*, Table 5, U.S. Department of Justice, Federal Bureau of Investigation, http://www.fbi.gov/ucr/05cius/data/table_05.html.

Technical Extension

There is a….: "Graffiti: That Writing on the Wall," http://www.slsheriff.org/html/org/metrogang/graffiti.html.

Those who participate…: "Graffiti: That Writing on the Wall."

These markings boast…: "Graffiti: The Newspaper of the Street," http://www.gripe4kids.org/graffiti.html.

Sometimes numbers are…: "Graffiti: The Newspaper of the Street."

Another code is…: "Graffiti: The Newspaper of the Street."

Members are required…: "Street Gang Dynamics," The Nawojczyk Group, Inc., 1997, http://www.gangwar.com/dynamics.htm.

Graffiti is considered…: "Information on Gangs and Graffiti," San Antonio Police Department, 1998-2005, http://www.sanantonio.gov/saPD/YouthGangs.htm.

If graffiti is…: "Graffiti: That Writing on the Wall."

The 4 R's of Graffiti (text box)…: "Graffiti: The Newspaper of the Street."

Vocational Extension

Some reporters focus…: "Newspaper Reporters," Labor Market Information, State of California, Employment Development Department, 1998, http://www.calmis.cahwnet.gov/file/occguide/NEWSREP.HTM.

The importance of…: "Newspaper Reporters."

It's also necessary…: "Newspaper Reporters."

The employer may…: "How to Get a Job in TV News," FabJob.com, 1999-2008, http://www.fabjob.com/tvsample.html.

Average earnings for…: "News Analysts, Reporters, and Correspondents," U.S. Department of Labor, Dec. 18, 2007, http://stats.bls.gov/oco/ocos088.htm#earnings.

Answer Key — Answer Key — Answer Key

Lexile Measures

High-Interest Article	Lexile	Technical Extension	Lexile	Vocational Extension	Lexile
Ready or Not? The Changing Face of American Leadership	970	The Election of an American President	1020	Administrative Assistant	860
Batman vs. Iron Man	930	The Case for Comics	820	Artist	810
Image: Unattainable	940	Whose Body Is It?	910	Personal Trainer	1010
Circle of Friends	870	Integrity On and Off the Field	950	Athletic Coach	910
Riding Dubs	970	Car Buying 101	970	Mechanic	860
The Right to Support Them	970	The Information Highway	890	Political Analyst	1000
A Lifetime to Build, a Moment to Lose	930	Big Brother and the Right to Privacy	1020	Attorney	870
Journey of the Tiger	930	Training to Perfection	850	Caddy	1040
Above the Influence	800	Underage Drinking: No Minimal Problem	900	Rehabilitation Counselor	940
Blood In, Blood Out	880	The Writing on the Wall	1010	Reporter	890

244

©2007 PRINCIPLE WOODS, INC. Removal of copyright notice and copying are violations of Federal Law.